THE BOSS OF
NEW ORLEANS

THE BOSS OF
NEW ORLEANS

MARTIN BEHRMAN
AND MACHINE POLITICS
IN THE CRESCENT CITY

RALPH ERIC CRISS

Louisiana State University Press
Baton Rouge

Published by Louisiana State University Press
lsupress.org

DESIGNER: Mandy McDonald Scallan
TYPEFACES: Sentinel, text; S&S Baldwins Serif, display

JACKET PHOTO: Martin Behrman at his desk in the mayor's office, New Orleans City Hall. The Historic New Orleans Collection, Gift of Mrs. Jeanne Rabig, acc. no. 1994.115.16.

Portions of this text first appeared, in different form, in "Unplugging the Machine: Martin Behrman, the New Orleans Navy Yard, and the Louisiana Elections of 1920," *Louisiana History* 61, no. 2 (Spring 2020): 133–61.

Library of Congress Cataloging-in-Publication Data
Names: Criss, Ralph Eric, author.
Title: The boss of New Orleans : Martin Behrman and machine politics in the Crescent City / Ralph Eric Criss.
Description: Baton Rouge : Louisiana State University Press, [2024] | Includes bibliographical references and index.
Identifiers: LCCN 2023020129 (print) | LCCN 2023020130 (ebook) | ISBN 978-0-8071-8029-7 (cloth) | ISBN 978-0-8071-8122-5 (pdf) | ISBN 978-0-8071-8121-8 (epub)
Subjects: LCSH: Behrman, Martin, 1864–1926. | Mayors—Louisiana—New Orleans—History—20th century. | Machine politics—Louisiana—New Orleans—History—20th century. | New Orleans (La.)—Politics and Government—20th century. | New Orleans (La.)—History—20th century.
Classification: LCC F379.N557 C75 2024 (print) | LCC F379.N557 (ebook) | DDC 976.3/3506092 [B]—dc23
LC record available at https://lccn.loc.gov/2023020129
LC ebook record available at https://lccn.loc.gov/2023020130

for Kelli, Elizabeth, and Nathanael

You can't enforce a really unpopular law.

—Martin Behrman

CONTENTS

ACKNOWLEDGMENTS

Many scholars laid the foundation for this book, and I am indebted to each of them. The sheer volume of their research and writing is amazing to me. To have the privilege of distilling their efforts into a single page, paragraph, or even a footnote, is humbling. My earnest hope is that I have respectfully and appropriately acknowledged their work while accurately reflecting their views—even where I may disagree with them. Any errors or omissions are my own, and I take full responsibility for the contents herein.

In particular, I would like to thank Dr. Neil Jumonville. It was Neil who first encouraged me to pursue a PhD in history and to publish a book, even though I was already in the later stages of my career and raising a family. Neil is not only a brilliant intellectual historian, but an all-around amazing human being. He is one of the better teachers I've known. During my many interactions with Neil, I never saw him lose patience with a class or an individual student. He came close only once that I remember—and rightly so—when a small group of us went off on a tangent about "cycles of history," taking for granted that such "cycles" actually exist. With a slight edge of frustration in his voice, Neil asked, "Why cycles? Why does history have to come in cycles?" For Neil, I think it wasn't so much that he agreed or disagreed with the concept, but that we all agreed so readily and uncritically with the idea. He encouraged us to think through our assumptions more carefully, as we should have. In addition to working with Neil, I benefited from the encouragement and wisdom of historians Michael Creswell, Nathan Stoltzfus, and Ed Gray in researching and writing this book.

The archivists and librarians in Washington, DC, New Orleans, and Baton Rouge are too numerous to recognize individually, but this book would not have been possible without them. It always amazed me to drop a random email to someone like Sarah Waits, an archivist at the Archdiocese of New Orleans, and receive a response within hours—usually with the exact information I needed. And many a day I walked hopefully but anxiously into the massive archives of the Library of Congress or the collections at Tulane, only to receive a musty folder containing one-hundred-year-old correspondence from the Navy secretary or letters from a nurse during one of New Orleans's many yellow fever epidemics.

Among the many people at LSU Press who made this book possible, I am grateful for the patience and understanding of Rand Dotson, editor in chief, and Catherine Kadair, managing editor. Rand helped me push and pull and twist the narrative structure and content into an end product that I hope readers will find enlightening. Catherine's assistance in polishing the final product was indispensable. Thank you as well to the peer reviewers who painstakingly helped to shape the outcome of my writing and research. I am grateful to all.

Finally, I would like to thank my family for their patience, understanding, and encouragement. My in-house editors and proofreaders from early stages to book were my wife, Dr. Kelli Criss, and her mother, Dr. Sandra Mobley. My kids, Lizzie and Nate, continue to inspire me. My mother, Shelby Criss, and my brothers and sisters shaped my life and the perspective I bring to this book. Thank you all.

THE BOSS OF
NEW ORLEANS

INTRODUCTION

Before Huey Pierce Long—the self-proclaimed "Kingfish" of Louisiana—there was "Papa," Martin Behrman of New Orleans. The Crescent City's leader was arguably the most powerful man in Louisiana. But on a cold January night in 1920, thousands of anti-machine reformers gathered in Lafayette Square to plot his exit from political life. The crowd was celebrating John Parker's victory in the campaign for governor, hoping it would lead to Behrman's defeat in the coming mayoral election. Nighttime torches glowed while a raucous band played "There'll Be a Hot Time in the Old Town Tonight" and "Hail, Hail, the Gang's All Here."[1] Some people carried brooms representing a "clean sweep" of their ward for Parker. Others carried signs that read, "They can't whip us into line." Behrman was now a lame duck, or so they hoped.[2] Some dared him to run for reelection with slogans such as "Martin You Are Doomed."

For many anti-machine reformers, Parker's victory was long awaited. The patronage and resources that accompanied the governor's mansion in Baton Rouge gave them a genuine opportunity to defeat the sixteen-year incumbent and machine leader, Mayor Behrman, in New Orleans's municipal elections later that year.[3] Indeed, despite winning four straight city elections, Behrman and his New Orleans machine were in trouble.

Behrman's supposed lame-duck status exhilarated the throng. The September municipal election would be a "duck hunt," shouted a group from the Third Ward as they streamed past City Hall. One man carried a box symbolizing City Hall. It was creatively decorated with a duck on top representing "Old Marty Behrman." In the city famous for its culinary prowess, another denizen foisted a sign proclaiming, "We want Duck Soup."[4] As the throng whooped and cheered, rally speakers exclaimed that defeating the "Ring" in the coming municipal election was key to finishing off the hated political machine forever.[5]

The rally drew anti-machine reformers from all over Louisiana to hear the newly elected Governor Parker bash Behrman and "bossism."[6] Hours before the event began, the crowd swelled to three thousand. Women in narrow-brimmed cloche hats and men sporting slim-fitting "jazz suits" clogged the streets around the square. When speakers launched into their tirades against the machine, late arrivals could not squeeze within half a block of the stage. Their optimism was not wasted. Parker and the anti-machine reformers ousted Behrman in the fall of 1920, after sixteen years in office.

✦   ✦   ✦

Huey Long observed the gubernatorial and mayoral campaigns of 1920 with great interest. In them, he saw a template for his own future success, later adapting Parker's dogged attacks on the machine for his gubernatorial campaigns in 1924 and 1928. In this manner, the anti-machine attacks of 1920 not only led to Behrman's defeat but also contributed to the rise of the Kingfish— one of the most recognizable figures in American political history.[7]

Martin Behrman and Huey Long crossed paths at crucial moments in Louisiana's political history. Their careers and personalities shed light on each other. Both were political prodigies with distinct strengths, weaknesses, and styles. Huey was confrontational and uncompromising, while Behrman was an affable dealmaker. The two men were arguably the most influential figures in twentieth-century Louisiana politics. But unlike Huey, whose volatile career and temperament made him infamous, Behrman remains relatively unknown.

In 1908, Huey was barely in his teens and volunteering in Winn Parish politics, while Behrman was already beginning his second term as mayor of New Orleans. By the 1920s, however, the two men were actively working against each other. In 1924, Behrman led the fight to defeat Huey in his bid for governor. The next year, Huey struggled to stop Behrman's comeback attempt in the New Orleans mayoral campaign.

Huey was bitter about his defeat in the 1924 gubernatorial election and maintained his dream of becoming governor. With the sting of Behrman's political skills and influence fresh in his mind, Huey began to develop his strategy for 1928. But first he wanted to find a candidate to defeat Behrman and the machine in the 1925 New Orleans municipal campaign, the same way Parker and the anti-machine reformers had done in 1920. Huey feared a resurgent Behrman and Regular machine. If Behrman and his crowd recaptured the power and patronage of the mayor's office, they could cut a deal based on raw power politics and join forces with a different candidate to ensure Huey would never get the votes out of New Orleans that he needed to become governor. Unfortunately for Huey, Behrman faced weak opposition in the 1925 election—Francis Williams and Andrew McShane. Williams initially had the support of John Sullivan's "New Regular" faction, which had previously split off from Behrman's machine, and McShane was the incumbent mayor who defeated Behrman in the reform wave of 1920.

By themselves, Williams and the New Regulars were not strong enough to pose a serious threat to Behrman. They drew only middling support from anti-machine reformers, whose power and popularity waned significantly from their high-water mark of 1920. Mayor McShane's political organization, called the Orleans Democratic Association, was obsolete and unhelpful.[8] Four years after defeating Behrman and the Regulars on John Parker's coattails, it was now McShane who was viewed as the lame duck. And "Old Marty Behrman" was about to go on a "duck hunt" of his own.

When the Regular machine leaders caucused to select their standard bearer, City Commissioner Paul Maloney challenged Behrman for the nomination. Maloney had been the machine's lone victorious city council candidate in its disastrous campaign of 1920, but Behrman had run the machine for decades. Behrman prevailed in a bitter internal fight, securing the nomination as a reward for his loyalty during the out years between 1920 and 1925. The strife within the organization proved costly, however, when Maloney and his followers defected and ran their own campaign.

From Huey Long's perspective, Maloney's decision to launch a bid for mayor and split the Regulars seemed a golden opportunity. Huey worked feverishly against Behrman, successfully urging Williams to withdraw from the campaign and throw his support behind Maloney.[9] Huey met with John Sullivan, head of the New Regular faction, who soon announced the organization's support for Maloney. He also met with Colonel Robert Ewing, publisher of the *New Orleans States,* who soon thereafter announced his support for Maloney.[10] Huey thus orchestrated Behrman's only serious opposition in 1925. The final field in the election consisted of City Commissioner Maloney, Mayor McShane, and Behrman.

The campaign unfolded quickly. Behrman and the Regulars constantly reminded voters of their opposition's broken promises. They emphasized unmet expectations for civil service reform and the pretense and hypocrisy of anti-machine reformers like former governor John Parker and Mayor McShane. Behrman even accused Sullivan of defecting to join Governor Parker during the 1920 campaign because he refused to do favors for Sullivan's brewery clients.

It helped Behrman's cause that Huey Long was on the rise and was perceived by many anti-machine reformers and newspaper editors as a radical demagogue—the commander of an army of peasants with pitchforks, ready to descend upon New Orleans. This perception led many former foes to support Behrman in 1925. He and the Regulars had the muscle, or so it was believed, to stop Huey. T. Harry Williams noted that "the New Orleans press was torn between a desire to oppose the machine and a compulsion to destroy Huey."[11] Newspaper editors and voters alike reconsidered Behrman's usefulness. Perhaps he was not the "vulture" they had portrayed him to be just four short years prior.[12]

During the campaign, Behrman was tagged with the nostalgic nickname "Papa." He enjoyed the support of many longtime friends and even some former enemies. In the process Behrman succeeded, at least to some extent, in redefining his legacy. These efforts, combined with a broader shift in the political atmosphere, helped him defeat Maloney. The race was close, however, with Behrman winning 35,911 votes and Maloney tallying 33,471.[13] Huey's candidate lost, but his coalition made a respectable showing and Huey himself built important relationships during the campaign—including the influential political operative John Sullivan and powerful newspaper publisher Robert Ewing.[14]

❖   ❖   ❖

On November 12, 1959, T. Harry Williams, president of the Southern Historical Association, delivered his address at the organization's annual meeting. His topic was "The Gentleman from Louisiana: Demagogue or Democrat." The occasion was a full decade before Williams released his acclaimed biography of Huey Long. The people of Louisiana, Williams began, were not strictly interested in "the whir of slot machines, the pounding of horses' hoofs at the Fair Grounds, and the clink of ice in a Sazerac cocktail."[15] He further rejected the stereotype that Louisiana was some kind of "banana republic." Williams conceded, however, that Louisianans' view of corruption was unique and one that made politics in the Pelican State "undeniably different." They tended to be less "sanctimonious," and furthermore, "there is even a tendency to admire a 'deal' if it is executed with skill and a flourish and, above all, with a jest."[16]

Williams's speech foreshadowed a sympathetic view of Long's corruption that later drew criticism. He asserted that "corruption, which as defined by purists often means only the compromises that are required to keep the machinery of democracy running, has appeared in all states where it has been worth-while and at all levels of government and has been practiced by all classes."[17]

The "purist" view of corruption cannot be casually brushed aside, however. Opposition to corruption in the Long organization and other machines contributed to civil service reform, campaign finance reform, and other laws that brought an end to the machine era of American politics. Historians rightly pushed back against Williams's laid-back characterization of Huey Long's political corruption. But Huey was not alone in straying into legal gray areas, or in disregarding the law altogether to achieve his goals. Far from it. George Washington Plunkitt of Tammany Hall described the logic underpinning Huey's corruption and much of the machine politics of his day:

> Everybody is talkin' these days about Tammany men growin' rich on graft, but nobody thinks of drawin' the distinction between honest graft and dishonest graft. There's all the difference in the world between the two. Yes, many of our men have grown rich in politics. I have myself. I've made a big fortune out of the game, and I'm gettin' richer every day, but I've not gone in for dishonest graft—blackmailin' gamblers, saloonkeepers, disorderly people, etc.—and neither has any of the men who have made big fortunes in politics. There's an honest graft, and I'm an example of how it works. I might sum up the whole thing by sayin': "I seen my opportunities and I took 'em."[18]

Behrman ran a turn-of-the-century political machine that differed in many ways from Plunkitt's Tammany Hall in New York and Huey's statewide machine in Louisiana. In this sense, Behrman is an interesting study. He is one of several exceptions to both the factual and fictional historical portrayals of the urban political machine. And while remnants of such machines exist even today, the classic city and state organizations of the nineteenth and early twentieth centuries never again reached the heights of power they attained under leaders like Behrman. Indeed, the narrative surrounding Behrman and other machine leaders has been at least partially rewritten.

In 2017, Terry Golway asserted that emphasis on criminal acts of Tammany leaders ignores the important role of the machine in American politics. Golway wrote that Tammany Hall was not only a defender of otherwise powerless immigrants but also a forerunner of progressive policymaking that lifted an underserved class of Americans out of poverty.[19] Other historians claim that city machines provided crucial services to new immigrants—a place to collect their mail, find a job, and even help with language translation.

Another thread of the machine narrative argues that Franklin Roosevelt's New Deal programs transformed patronage between state and local machines, hirelings, and loyal voters. Using broad social programs to support large swaths of the American population, these programs essentially bureaucratized the traditional functions of the machine. The Works Progress Administration, for example, made the federal government the largest employer in the United States and dealt a devastating blow to city machines like the Regulars. Other strategies, such as civil service reform, sped the decline of the political machine. The literature on the machine's demise is not unanimous, however. For instance, some scholars assert that political machines in Pittsburgh and Kansas City, rather than being crushed by FDR's New Deal, were rejuvenated by the local distribution of federal largesse.[20]

The earliest studies of machines are mostly unhelpful. They rely on discarded stereotypes perpetuated by muckraking newspapers and magazines, often promoting racist and nativist viewpoints. Bitterly biased and partisan, they condemned the machine almost universally as a danger to American democracy. Those who claimed to "study" the machine, such as James Bryce, asserted that urban government in America was a failed experiment thanks to the machine. According to one scholar, "it was Bryce who helped to put such terms as 'boss' and 'ring' into the vocabulary of urban political history."[21]

Lincoln Steffens agreed with Bryce, first in a series of articles and then in his book *Shame of the Cities*. Steffens was, however, somewhat less nativist in his approach, arguing that the fault for flourishing machines could be placed at the feet of voters and politicians rather than the "foreign element." Nonetheless, immigrants and Catholics were most often identified as the parties responsible for graft and patronage—the twin evils upon which the machine was constructed, according to these early accounts. One exception to the early analyses of the machine is Moisei Ostrogorski's *Democracy and the Organization of Political Parties*, volume 2, a comparative study of machines in multiple cities across the United States. Ostrogorski concluded there was far more to the American political machine than had been previously asserted, including services to the poor and imposition of order on chaotic urban communities.[22]

Over time, studies of the machine became more sophisticated and the body of scholarship grew more voluminous. In 1935, J. T. Salter published *Boss Rule: Portraits in City Politics*, in which he considers the prevalence of political machines, their operation, and the reasons voters support them. Salter believed the strongest party organizations, regardless of location or party label, used the same methods to "woo" voters.[23] He placed voters in two broad categories: those who don't vote because they don't feel their vote matters and those who do vote because they do believe their vote matters. Among those who bother to vote, said Salter, there are generally two distinct groups: "the pro- and anti-organization voters" (meaning pro-machine and anti-machine).[24] Regardless of which party controls the machine, or who votes and why, argued Salter, "the individualistic formula of laissez faire has been abandoned . . . and their growth in expenditures indicates, in a measure, their increase in municipal functions, in new services to the people."[25]

A year later, in 1936, George M. Reynolds published *Machine Politics in New Orleans, 1897–1926*, a study I found helpful in writing this book. Reynolds's book was significant for its mostly neutral observations of the New Orleans machine and because it was perhaps the first major study dedicated solely to the study of a machine in the South. Reynolds offered detailed explanations of the New Orleans machine's Get-Out-the-Vote efforts and concluded that Tammany Hall in New York and the Choctaw Club in New Orleans were substantially similar from an organizational standpoint, with the exception of Martin Behrman's unique dual role as mayor and boss of the machine. This, Reynolds said, "sharpened the interest of the Machine in the welfare and efficiency of city government."[26]

Machine scholarship continued to evolve as the power of the machine itself waned further. In the 1950s, Robert K. Merton identified social services to the poor and social mobility as important functions of the machine. His study *Social Theory and Social Structure* emphasized the "latent functions" of the machine—a theory historians Richard Hofstadter and Oscar Handlin relied upon for their subsequent works, *The Age of Reform* and *The Uprooted*, respectively. Merton considered the machine's role in propagating vice, observing that "just as the political machine performs service for 'legitimate' businesses, so it operates to perform not dissimilar services for 'illegitimate business: vice, crime and rackets.'" He urged analysts to put aside their own morals and give practical consideration to the needs of the "actual workings of the organization." Describing "vice, crime and the rackets" as "big business," Merton compared the 500,000 prostitutes operating in the United States in 1950 to only 200,000 physicians.[27]

In the 1960s and 1970s, machine scholarship began to recognize that anti-machine "reformers" often adopted the practices of the machine—creating organizations that were difficult to distinguish from the old-guard machine itself. According to David Colburn and George Pozzetta, many reformers, including Fiorello LaGuardia of New York, "established organizations which were very similar to the machines they overthrew."[28] The reverse was also found to be true. In a scenario that harkens back to the reforms of the Behrman era, Joseph Huthmacher described how the machine worked with immigrant lower classes to become key drivers of reform: "the urban lower class provided an active, numerically strong, and politically necessary force for reform. . . . this class was perhaps as important in determining the course of American liberalism as the urban middle class, about which so much has been written."[29]

By the 1980s, critics of the midcentury scholars became more vocal. In "The Politics of Urban History versus the History of Urban Politics," Terrence McDonald criticized Hofstadter's overreliance on the "easygoing and pragmatic boss" who "understood the immigrant's desire for concrete personal gains from political participation." Similarly, McDonald wrote that Handlin viewed the boss as effective because he so often came from the ranks of the immigrants and remained their "champion." The problem with this interpretation, said McDonald, was that these authors perpetuated a myth of the political machine's "omnipotence." In so doing, they erroneously argued that the political machine caused municipal government to succeed. In reality, asserted McDonald, "there is abundant evidence that the all-powerful urban boss rarely, if ever, existed. In fact, urban politics was simply too contested, urban policymaking simply too complicated, and urban policymakers—believe it or not—too responsible to support the image of the all-powerful urban boss."[30]

McDonald's theory illustrates how the debate surrounding machines like the Regulars in New Orleans became more complex over time. It supports the idea that Behrman was extremely powerful but not all-powerful. Instead, Behrman was the leader of a complex urban political organization whose longevity is attributable to balancing the demands of anti-machine reformers with the practical policy imperatives of the city and the concerns of the rank-and-file voters.

Scholarly debates aside, some historical facts are undeniable. City machines often confounded anti-machine reformers with their success at the ballot box, skillful use of patronage, and close ties to the community.[31] Precinct captains and ward leaders lived and worked in the same neighborhoods for decades, placing a premium on their proximity to voters. Eighteen out of twenty of Behrman's peers across the nation—those who also ran city machines—became active in local politics at an early age.[32] Behrman did the same by taking the U.S. Census in his hometown of Algiers on the West Bank of the Mississippi River (opposite New Orleans and today part of the city) and by volunteering with the local fire department in Algiers and for various political campaigns. Like many machine leaders, Behrman came from a family of modest means and enjoyed little formal education.[33] He proved, as did other machine leaders, that starting early, staying close to constituents, and delivering on promises to voters isn't a bad formula for success in politics.

After forming the Choctaw Club in 1897, Behrman and the Regulars rapidly accomplished their mission of regaining control of local government. During the first two decades of the twentieth century, their hegemony in city politics was unparalleled except in New York. Even in the Empire State, Tammany leader George Olvany described Behrman as a "strong organization Democrat and a loyal friend," and New York City mayor James Walker called Behrman a "constant source of inspiration" and "a class A soldier" for the Democratic Party.[34]

Behrman was elected to lead the municipality five times, and his remarkable life reflects the political and social tensions of early twentieth-century America. Those who claimed the mantle of reform often despised him, and his role as chief of the political machine raised many traditional concerns about bossism. In their eyes, Behrman stood for the old way of doing things: undemocratic and corrupt "machine" politics that spread vice across the city.

Anti-machine reformers often exaggerated these allegations for their own political benefit, but they were not entirely unfounded. Use of municipal funds to advance the political interests of incumbent political parties was commonplace in American cities such as New York, Chicago, and New Orleans. Taxpayer money was often used, directly or indirectly, to support machine candidates. Government employees, for example, were often expected to work as "volunteers" for campaigns. Prior to the implementation of many civil service reforms, these were legally permissible political activities and hallmarks of politics in the machine age.

Aside from these usual machine activities, Behrman was not the typical "boss." He served both as mayor of New Orleans and as leader of the Regular machine. In most cities, these were two distinct roles. The Tammany leader in New York, for example, did not also serve as mayor. Behrman filled the traditional role of machine leader by acting as a "connecting link between his party and the city government and between organizations, businesses, and interests which gave support to his faction."[35] And he did so while also acting as the top executive of city government. Anti-machine reformers labeled this hybrid configuration of politics and policy "Behrmanism." Although intended as a pejorative, Behrmanism was driven by reform and federalism. It represented the future and became one of the prominent characteristics of the American body politic. In their official roles, presidents such as Roosevelt, Truman, Eisenhower, and even Reagan became rulers of a sprawling administrative state and commanders of vast political parties collecting and disbursing enormous amounts of money from both the government and their respective party organizations. In this sense, they served in dual roles much like Behrman.

As mayor and machine leader, Behrman followed a course of civic reform in education, infrastructure development, and government operations that many other cash-starved southern states were slow to implement. Scholar Robert Williams framed Behrman's influence this way: "The story of this man, Martin Behrman, is the story of municipal politics in New Orleans for most of the first quarter of the twentieth century."[36] Nevertheless, no significant study of Behrman has been published since 1977. There are only two published books singularly focused on Behrman: *Martin Behrman of New Orleans: Memoirs of a City Boss,* edited by John Kemp and published in 1977, and *Machine Politics in New Orleans, 1897–1926,* by George M. Reynolds, published in 1936. As curator of the Louisiana Historical Center, Kemp distilled a series of Behrman's autobiographical articles published in the *New Orleans Item* in his book. Reynolds's project was an outgrowth of his PhD dissertation written at Columbia University. Behrman and the Regulars also appeared in Charles Van Devander's *The Big Bosses,* published in 1944. In addition, Matthew J. Schott published several articles on Behrman and the Regulars, including "The New Orleans Machine and Progressivism," published in *Louisiana History* in 1983. In 1988, Edward F. Haas penned *Political Leadership in a Southern City,* one of the more insightful and detailed books discussing Behrman, the city machine, and New Orleans politics in the late nineteenth and early twentieth centuries. In contrast, the expansive literature on Tammany Hall and William Tweed dwarfs the two books dedicated to Behrman. Out of a dozen widely published books on Tweed and Tammany Hall, two of the more recent works include *Boss Tweed: The Rise and Fall of the Corrupt Pol Who Conceived the Soul of Modern New York,* by Kenneth D. Ackerman, and *Machine Made: Tammany Hall and the Creation of Modern American Politics,* by Terry Golway.

Martin Behrman and the Regulars merit the same scrutiny as Boss Tweed and Tammany Hall because their story offers a unique lens for the study of early twentieth-century American politics. Few politicians blended consensus building with the exercise of raw power as effectively as Behrman. He is, without a doubt, among the most consequential and least understood of America's big-city mayors.

Late in life, Behrman confessed, "I often wonder what will become of my own memory long after I am dead." He noted that "future writers of history" would use the speeches, articles, and other historical records of his day to construct his legacy. After he left office, the *Item,* which had opposed Behrman in 1920, began warming toward the former mayor. By 1922, it took on the task of publishing his memoirs.[37] These autobiographical pieces appeared regularly in 1922 and 1923 and became a sort of front-page digest of Behrman's life and career, where he wrote of his advocacy for education reform and emphasized efforts to stamp out disease and revitalize New Orleans.

Behrman also attempted to justify resisting civil service reform, defending Storyville, and leading efforts to constitutionally disenfranchise Black voters. Legacies can be complicated things.

Here, the Huey Long comparison is again helpful. With books and movies dedicated to his tumultuous rule, Huey is remembered by some as a controversial figure who did a lot of good in Louisiana.[38] This is an assertion many modern scholars dispute. Glen Jeansonne, for example, argues that Huey's vaunted education spending is exaggerated—even with respect to his prized Louisiana State University. In 1931, the university spent only $837.57 on its law school but $14,345.65 on the marching band—at Huey's behest. Huey spent virtually nothing on other universities in the state, and his record with elementary and secondary schools is no better. Teacher salaries declined every year Huey was in office.[39] Meanwhile, Behrman remains a footnote to the machine era, and to the extent he is remembered, it is often incorrectly.

Ironically, Behrman's and Huey's roles were flipped in the imagination of early historians. Through a combination of legend, self-promotion, and misguided scholarship, Huey became the reformer who did a lot of good and some bad while Behrman was portrayed as the anti-progressive, undemocratic boss of New Orleans. Behrman, of course, had his flaws. He was complicit in the shameful act of suppressing the Black vote, as were the anti-machine reformers. In the absence of civil service laws, he used patronage to influence policy outcomes and elections, and he held local reformers at bay over closing the Storyville vice district. Nevertheless, Behrman was not the stereotypical machine politician—immoral, corrupt, and lazy, growing fat on the backs of ward heelers and taxpayers.

The political attacks he endured, dating as far back as 1904, were distortions of the man and his public service; rather, his fatherly moniker, "Papa," is apropos. It exceeds mere sentimentality. Behrman was a reformer who won plaudits for his work in areas such as education, transportation, and water and sewer infrastructure. He earned a reputation as a hardworking, detail-oriented manager of city and machine affairs. As mayor, Behrman successfully managed the last epidemic of yellow fever in New Orleans and built new schools and infrastructure that moved the city along the path of modernity. Behrman also advocated, albeit unsuccessfully, for free textbooks for children in both public and private schools—and he did so more than two decades before Huey Long accomplished the feat.

Near the end of his career, "Papa" Behrman was rather incredibly viewed as the same man of high character that he was in the beginning. By all accounts, Behrman was a dedicated family man who did not patronize the prostitutes of the vice district. There are no stories, or even whispers, of mistresses or sordid affairs. He governed as a husband, father, and loyal ally to many friends. His career reflects an amazing consistency between these public and private roles. One might even call this his secret to success. Yet, as with every political leader, there were times when these roles conflicted.

Today, Martin and Julia Behrman's modest one-story home still stands on Pelican Avenue in Algiers. Its tall green shutters, wide front porch, and ornate woodwork reflect the popularity of the Queen Anne style of architecture in the late nineteenth and early twentieth centuries. The couple raised their oldest child, Stanley, and daughter, Mary Helen, there and, for a brief period, their precious Isabella, who died at the age of two. Upon Behrman's death, his nemesis, the *New Orleans Times-Picayune,* accurately insisted that "the late mayor possessed a gift for inspiring loyalty and warm affection which must have been in a large measure responsible for his remarkable success."[40] Many voters could scarcely recall anyone other than Behrman sitting in the mayor's parlor in Gallier Hall. During his lifetime, Behrman came to be viewed as an institution unto himself, and the father of New Orleans in the early twentieth century—an astonishing accomplishment for an orphan of immigrant parents.

✦ ✦ ✦

As Behrman gained power and influence, major American cities absorbed immigrants and rural job hunters in massive numbers. In 1907, the peak year of immigration during this period, approximately 1.3 million immigrants moved to the United States and 13.3 million total foreign-born individuals resided in the country.[41]

New Orleans and other cities became enormous, multilinguistic urban spaces where English, Irish, German, Polish, Italian, and other immigrants resided. Many of these urban areas developed red-light districts where prostitution, gambling, and alcohol formed a perfect storm of political corruption, disease, and human devastation. Immigration and vice therefore became linked by a fiction produced in certain corners of the progressive movement.[42] Historian Richard Hofstadter and others pounced on this as evidence of the nativist and racist tendencies of progressives, but later scholars recognized the movement as far too broad to accommodate such labels. In New Orleans, neither the Regular Democrat reformers (machine) nor the anti-machine reformers can be neatly categorized as racist or nativist. Terrence Fitzmorris asserts, for example, "It would be a mistake, however, to assume—and a close reading of the historical record does not suggest—that social prejudice, class distinctions, moral considerations, and anti-democratic sentiment formed the basis of progressive municipal reform in New Orleans."[43]

Nonetheless, at the turn of the century, most large American cities contained a widely recognized red-light district where prostitution thrived.[44] In New Orleans, the district known as "Storyville" was shuttered on November 12, 1917, under threat from the United States to move its navy yard elsewhere. Behrman wielded his considerable influence in Washington, DC, to resist closing the vice district but eventually succumbed to federal pressure. In 1920, that support cost Behrman and the Regulars the election. The *Times-Picayune* compared Behrman to a vulture who "hampered" and "held down" the city.[45] A trip Behrman previously made to Washington, DC, to appeal to the military brass to leave the vice district open was portrayed as a "secret mission," and the mayor was alleged to have acted on the orders of Tom Anderson, vice lord, legislator, and chief pimp of the red-light district. The real story is far more complex.

With the exception of his fight to preserve Storyville, Behrman had an instinct for public opinion and tended toward caution on controversial matters. In this regard, Behrman usually sought the middle ground in politics, employing a strategy of triangulation comparable to the one used by President Bill Clinton in the 1990s. In so doing, Behrman placed himself equidistant from the outer edges of public opinion on the most controversial issues of a turbulent period in American history.[46] Behrman, for example, supported women's suffrage after first opposing it, much as President Clinton twice vetoed welfare reform before ultimately signing the legislation. Commenting on his own political philosophy, Behrman stated that, in politics, "You must impress a wide circle of friends and acquaintances with the idea that you are practical, that you can do things and get them done and that you will not loaf on the job when they expect something from you."[47]

The welfare reform analogy, though, contains one important flaw. Bill

Clinton didn't want to sign the welfare reform bill. Rather, he was forced to sign the popular legislation in the face of sagging poll numbers and the looming midterm election. Behrman, on the other hand, embraced reform. He believed it was both good policy and good politics. Unlike the anti-machine reformers of his day, however, Behrman prioritized transportation and infrastructure over tighter regulation of prostitution and alcohol.[48] This wasn't acceptable to anti-machine reformers who viewed prostitution and alcohol as severely corrosive of the fabric of society—an attack on the nation's morals and democracy. To the extent that urban political machines enabled or even profited from such immoral activity, they had to be eliminated.

❖　❖　❖

Some clarification of frequently used terminology is necessary. First, Behrman was chief of the Regular Democratic Organization. The group was loosely referred to as "the Regulars," "the Old Regulars," and "the Choctaw Club"—all nicknames used interchangeably by scholars and newspaper reporters. The substantive difference between them is that the Choctaw Club was not organized until 1897. Prior to this date, only the terms "Regulars," "Regular Democratic Organization" (RDO), and "Ring" were commonly used. While their memberships overlapped, the Choctaws were the social branch of the machine and the Regulars were the political arm, organized by ward and precinct. Each of these terms became part of the vocabulary of Louisiana politics.

Second, the terms "progressivism" and "reform" are used throughout this text. During the Behrman era, there was no consensus about what constituted "reform" or "progressivism." Moreover, the progressive movement was hardly a "movement" at all in the sense that it was highly factionalized—more so than today. Differences among progressives fell along regional, gender-based, issue-based, class, and even religious lines. In the early twentieth century, for example, some of the most fervent "progressives" were rural Christian evangelicals and urban Catholics. Yet they often split on issues such as national Prohibition and women's suffrage. Progressivism was not a monolithic movement, either in the nation as a whole or in New Orleans.

This book uses the terms "reformer" and "progressive reformer" to describe Behrman and the Regulars, with the caveat that their brand of reform was sometimes condoned by other progressives and other times not. To describe John Parker and other civic and commercial elite reformers in New Orleans, this book uses the term "anti-machine reformers." While there were many political factions in Louisiana during the Behrman era, the pro-machine and anti-machine reformers dominated the state's political landscape. It's worth noting, however, that even these two groups were sometimes internally fragmented.

Perhaps ambiguous terminology and divisive politics are prominent features of the Behrman era, at least in part because the meaning of "reform" was so often in the eye of the beholder. For example, as archaic as it may seem today, in the late nineteenth century, the disenfranchisement of Black voters was considered "reform" among many southern progressives—a key to the restoration of social order and respectability. For the purposes of this study, "reform" is simply a change in public policy that, at one time and in one place, was thought to lead to an improvement in the general condition of society. Readers can decide for themselves whether a given public policy resulted in positive change.

Finally, "populism" is another important term. Broadly speaking, the populist ideology is similar to progressivism. Both stake claim to the people, or the common man, and both claim to prioritize public policy that lifts up the forgotten and downtrodden, moving society forward while emphasizing its shared values and humanity. Populism became influential in the late 1800s with the formation of the Farmers' Alliance and other farmers' groups that successfully lobbied for passage of the Interstate Commerce Act and the Sherman Anti-Trust Act, and fought for other economic reforms in the midst of difficult economic challenges. In its early stages, populism was predominantly an agricultural movement, but it grew to include many regions of the nation, both rural and urban.[49]

The scholar Wilfred E. Binkley described populism as a renewed attempt at "social revolt" by groups that were socially and politically disempowered after Reconstruction.[50] According to Binkley, populists posed such a dire threat to southern Democrats that they were denied the right to vote. Election boards simply chose to count them or not, depending on the circumstances. In addition, Binkley asserts, Black votes were often manipulated to offset the populist vote and to preserve the power of Democrats. Later, this would help Democrats portray the disenfranchisement of Black voters as a type of election "reform."[51] In keeping with this pattern, populists in Louisiana charged the Democratic "Ring" with stuffing ballot boxes with fraudulent Black votes to win elections.[52]

Into this political fray of the 1890s entered the young Martin Behrman. Shortly thereafter, the Louisiana Constitution of 1898 effectively suppressed the Black vote. Some scholars argue the new constitution also repressed the populist movement in Louisiana for nearly thirty years, until the emergence of Huey Long. This portrayal of populist history in Louisiana is a fallacy—and an important one. It lays the groundwork for the argument that little "progress" was made in the state and in the city of New Orleans under Behrman's leadership. Historian Henry Dethloff notes that the theory of repressed populism "ignores" the social and political shakeup caused by the Constitution of 1898 and Black disenfranchisement. Furthermore, it falsely portrays populists and Long supporters as lower-class "rednecks." And finally, it "totally ignores or discounts any progressive reforms in Louisiana between 1900 and 1924."[53] In reality, with the singular (and deeply troubling) exception of the disenfranchisement of Black voters, Martin Behrman led an era of reform in New Orleans—one that kept pace with the broader movement in the United States. And it was a quick pace indeed.

The U.S. Constitution was amended four times in the ten-year span between 1909 and 1919. These amendments addressed weighty issues, including the income tax, election of U.S. senators by popular vote, national Prohibition, and women's suffrage. In comparison, the Constitution has not been amended a single time in the last decade, and only twice in the last five decades. These more recent changes were relatively minor tweaks relating to congressional pay-raise implementation and lowering the voting age. Observing the momentous changes of his time, Behrman said, rather famously, "You cannot enforce a really unpopular law."[54] The quotation risks misinterpretation because Behrman was not the lawless type. Instead, Behrman had in mind the controversial new laws of his age, many of which found their way to the U.S. Supreme Court. In other words, Behrman spoke to his time and place in history, and to his long experience as the executive of a major American city.

Indeed, during Behrman's day, sittings of the U.S. Supreme Court regularly produced outcomes of historic importance. In *Muller v. Oregon*, for example, the court limited work hours. It was a crucial victory for the labor movement and a blow to business owners, who objected to the move as an interference with their freedom of contract. The linchpin of *Muller* was the famed Brandeis brief supporting the new law. Louis Brandeis, who was later nominated to the U.S. Supreme Court by President Woodrow Wilson, wrote that women's health was particularly vulnerable to longer workdays, potentially affecting their ability to bear children. Brandeis argued that such an outcome might have a negative impact on the nation as whole given the centrality of healthy, growing families to America's future. Such reasoning, though later rejected by feminists, was nonetheless effective in its day.[55] Protection of "hearth and home" was not a new political theme. It served as an on-ramp for women into politics, revived a stalled temperance movement in the nineteenth century, and propelled the Prohibition and suffrage movements to victory in the twentieth century. Politicians who misread this thread of the reform movement did so at great risk to their careers.

I.
A DIFFICULT JOURNEY

1

PASSAGES
Surviving New Orleans

Antebellum New Orleans was an unruly, violent, disease-ridden place.[1] The city's pervasive threats included getting shot, stabbed, beaten to death, and contracting yellow fever.[2] Historian Jo Ann Carrigan noted that New Orleans's frequent yellow fever epidemics earned the city "an unenviable reputation as one of the nation's worst centers of pestilence."[3] Carrigan vividly described how the "black vomit" that often accompanied yellow fever killed at least a few people almost every year. And during the nineteenth century, it resulted in a much larger death toll several times each decade. As one of the foremost ports in North America, New Orleans often imported the disease from warmer climates.[4] The danger of lynching was an added concern for Black city dwellers and some immigrants.[5]

In spite of its problems, New Orleans was nevertheless a thriving urban center. Before the Civil War began, it had a diverse population of 170,000, including one of the largest concentrations of free people of color.[6] Almost one million enslaved people were moved into the Deep South, more than 100,000 of whom passed through New Orleans—a $185 million per year business.[7] In addition to the slave trade, New Orleans possessed a thriving financial sector, major port, boatyards, manufacturers, and more.[8] For those who could withstand its dangers, the South's largest city promised opportunity. But the same slave trade that contributed so much to the city's economy would also bring it to its knees during a long occupation by Union soldiers.

In New York City, thirteen hundred miles away from the deprivation of occupied New Orleans, Henry and Frederica Behrman witnessed the birth of their first and only child on October 14, 1864. His name was Martin. Eighteen short months later, soon after the war ended, Martin's mother and father departed New York for the French Quarter in New Orleans, where they settled into a second-floor apartment at Bourbon and St. Peter Streets. Henry planned to take advantage of postwar opportunities in the city's cigar trade, but he died shortly after the move.[9] Martin was fatherless at the age of two. He survived the tumult of nineteenth-century New Orleans because he was a fighter—not in the traditional sense, with his fists, but with his heart, mind, and grit. It is not an exaggeration to say that, after surviving his youth, Behrman was prepared to tackle just about any challenge the twentieth century could throw his way.

Henry Behrman was one of millions of Jews who emigrated from Russia in the early 1860s. In 1863, Henry was listed in a New York City directory as a "Segar Mkr," or cigar maker, at 45 Canal Street.[10] This coincides with the first wave of Russian immigration into the United States—a turbulent period of Russian history when Emperor Alexander II issued the Emancipation Manifesto freeing the serfs and many minorities, peasants, and urban poor who sought to escape tsarist oppression.

This timeline puts Henry in New York City well before Ellis Island opened in 1892. Instead, he likely would have been processed through Castle Garden, America's first official immigration center. The site, known today as Castle Clinton National Monument in Battery Park, operated between 1855 and 1890 and processed the entry of millions of Irish, German, and other immigrants.[11] Henry remains an obscure figure because he was seldom mentioned by Martin Behrman. Given that Behrman never really knew his father, this comes as no surprise.

Martin Behrman spoke more frequently, and quite fondly, of his mother. The details of Frederica's movements may be surmised from the history of European emigration to the United States, likely resulting from the German Wars of Unification between 1848 and 1871. Many troubles among the German-speaking states led to the wars, including conflict over political consolidation; social and economic instability; and a wave of industrialization putting craftsman, laborers, and farmers out of work. America therefore became an attractive destination for desperate Germans, about six million of whom emigrated to the United States from the middle of the nineteenth century through the early twentieth century. Frederica likely emigrated in the major wave of the 1850s, when over one million Germans joined with Polish and Russian émigrés, hurrying along the streets of busy seaports such as Bremerhaven, where mothers, fathers, and children boarded ships bound for America.[12]

Most immigrants traveled as steerage passengers, the cheapest way to make the journey. It was a difficult and unpleasant voyage. Typically, a traveler slept on a thin straw mat covering the hard boards of a bunk bed. The quarters were dark, unsanitary, without toilets, and often smelled of vomit due to rough waves. The 45 to 100 days at sea bred diseases such as cholera and typhoid, occasionally resulting in death.[13] A higher rate of deaths was attributable to a group of "typhus fevers," also known as "ship fever," caused by bacteria spread to humans by fleas, lice, and chiggers. One report described the voyage in 1879:

> Imagine a wooden cell some 36 feet or so in length, 12 feet wide at one end, but narrowing to about 5 feet at the further extremity; instead of a ceiling, a hatchway opening on to the main deck; two dirty ladders, placed almost perpendicularly, forming a staircase.
>
> On two sides, running the length of the den, a wooden partition had been constructed of bare boards, reaching to within 10 inches of the top. At intervals in this boarding were eight doors, numbered, showing that behind these were our sleeping berths. The boards had once upon a time—evidently a very remote time—been painted.... The floor was strewn with sawdust.... The stench, combined with the heat, was simply intolerable. I scrambled up the nearest ladder on to the main deck—not the upper deck be it understood—and there, close to the hatchway, which of course was the entry into the steerage, stood three barrels, each of them half filled with kitchen refuse. These were standing directly under the rays of the sun the temperature being over 99 degrees in the shade. And there where foul stuff remained during the whole of our voyage to Liverpool, receiving daily additions from the kitchen and scullery.[14]

Like the voyage across the Atlantic, surviving Henry's death in postwar New Orleans was no small accomplishment for Frederica—or for Martin. Children react differently to the loss of a parent based on their age, gender, and personality, but scholarly literature suggests Behrman was probably highly stressed by the loss of his father.[15] Financially and emotionally drained, the mother-son pair made the best of a bad situation.[16]

As a child, Behrman absorbed the ambiance of an international city that grew up on the river—one that reached the four corners of the globe. From the family's home in the French Quarter, Martin could walk south from Bourbon Street to find his mother selling dry goods at the French Market. By the time of Henry's death, New Orleans had grown to become the second largest port in the nation, ranking only behind New York City. One of Behrman's favorite childhood memories was watching the arrival of large loads of bananas and other fruits from major international shippers. He waited patiently as dockworkers unloaded cargo from the United Fruit Company, Cuyamel Fruit Company, and Bluefields Fruit and Steamship Company. Occasionally, a sailor dropped a piece of fruit into his hands, drawing a big smile and "thank you" from the polite little boy.

The United Fruit Company alone transported over fifteen million stems of bananas to New Orleans annually by the time Behrman was an adult.[17] Fruit of all kinds arrived daily by refrigerated and passenger steamships from Honduras, Mexico, Jamaica, Costa Rica, Guatemala, and Panama, after which it was loaded onto railcars and distributed throughout the United States and Canada. New Orleans saw its population increase dramatically during this period. Between 1870 and 1900, the city's population grew from 191,418 to 287,104, or 67 percent in just three decades. It is likely that up to a third of the city's population at this time was Black.[18] Being of German descent, Frederica Behrman shared a common heritage with many other immigrants in the city. Between 1847 and 1849 alone, approximately 30,000 Germans arrived in New Orleans. While 10,000 of these immigrants continued up the Mississippi River to St. Louis and other cities, a sizable German population remained in New Orleans, affecting the city socially, culturally, and politically.[19]

Many members of the German American community found jobs in the beer industry, ranging from production to sales and transportation.[20] Between 1850 and 1900, New Orleans developed a thriving beer industry that included approximately thirty breweries.[21] Unfortunately, the population boom that did so much for beer drinkers also put significant stress on the city's schools. With buildings often overcrowded and understaffed, some students were called upon to help teach their young immigrant peers, including "Italians, Slavs, Greeks, Bohemians, and a few Austrians." This was a task Behrman himself performed as a young student. He attended the private German American school and the St. Philip School, but his education was interrupted when Frederica passed away in 1876, only a decade after Henry died.[22]

Struck by the death of both parents in the span of a decade, Martin was now an orphan at twelve years old and well acquainted with bereavement. It is difficult to overstate the impact of his loss on Behrman's psyche. As a small child, Behrman may have believed his father would someday return.[23] Losing his mother as a preteen, Behrman would have been acquainted with the concept of death and likely pondered Frederica's feelings about dying. Most children at this age are mature enough to feel deep compassion and, in all likelihood, Martin felt concern for any physical pain his mother may have experienced.[24] All of these feelings were compounded by an obvious concern for what the future held. Behrman lost the only parent, the only caregiver and protector, he ever truly knew. In astonishing fashion, Behrman did more than endure the stress of losing both parents at an early age. He excelled in life, even as a young boy.[25]

Behrman worked to support himself with a grocery-store job and paid tuition fees out of his own pocket to continue his schooling. Out of the fifteen dollars he earned each month at Samuel's Dollar Store, Behrman paid two to attend Dolbear's school at night.[26] While there is no record of Behrman having been enrolled in an orphanage, it is worth noting that he and other orphans faced significant challenges in the eighteenth and nineteenth centuries—a time when child labor was used extensively throughout the economy.[27] According to one source, 32 percent of institutionalized orphans worked as indentured servants. Many of the children in homes still had at least one living parent who could not care for them for one reason or another.[28]

By 1850, there were nearly eight thousand orphanages across the United States.[29] The first was reportedly established in 1729, less than two hundred miles from New Orleans, in Natchez, Mississippi. The institution was created to care for white children whose parents were killed in a conflict with Native Americans. In New Orleans itself, orphanages founded in the nineteenth century were created to support children that came to them as a result of frequent epidemics or immigration.[30] The Poydras Home for female orphans, for example, was organized in reaction to the many children orphaned by yellow fever. Throughout the South, there was virtually no public assistance available to orphans, making such institutions critical to their care. Between 1817 and 1914, approximately three-fifths of the children in New Orleans orphanages were between the ages of six and eleven and the average age was seven years old. At this time, the proportion of immigrant children in orphanages was always greater than it was in the city at large. And prior to the widespread availability of public schools, most orphanages provided education to the children.[31]

Black children were not admitted to most of the larger and better-known orphanages.[32] Nevertheless, Margaret Haughery, the most celebrated "Friend of Orphans" in New Orleans, is said to have provided for children regardless of their race or religion. She was also known as the "Bread Woman," "Mother of Orphans," and "Angel of the Delta." Haughery was an entrepreneur who started a dairy and bakery that made her wealthy. Upon her death, her considerable estate was divided among the children's charities across New Orleans. Haughery was only the second woman in the United States to have a statue constructed to honor her life and service. It was commissioned after her death in 1882 and completed in 1884 in the Lower Garden District at the intersection of Prytania and Clio Streets. It remains there today.[33]

Behrman apparently did not spend time in any of New Orleans's orphanages. Instead, one historian has indicated that, soon after his mother's death, Behrman was taken in by a "kinsman living in Algiers, where he operated a retail grocery." It is not clear in what sense the term "kinsman" was used. It could have been a blood relative or merely someone of the same nationality or ethnic group. Behrman himself asserted that he "had no relatives" after his mother died.[34] The "kinsman" was likely Mike Gallagher, but it may have been the proprietor of Samuel's Dollar Store or James Lawton. Regardless, by 1880, according to the U.S. Census, the fifteen-year-old Behrman was a "boarder" and "store clerk" with Mike Gallagher, his wife Ellen, and their children on Patterson Street in Algiers.[35] Though he moved on from the Gallagher residence, it was there at the end of the Texas cattle trail where Behrman started his family and political career. He lived the rest of his life among German, Irish, and other immigrant families of Algiers.[36]

Behrman believed that his mother would have seen to it that he went to college if she had lived. He wrote, "A later impression, that has remained always with me, was her repeated advice that I should get an education. . . . I am quite certain that if she had lived and kept good health, I would have had the best school training New Orleans then afforded and if she had had the money she would have sent me to college."[37] Behrman twice emphasized this point in the *New Orleans Item*. Such palpable regret manifested itself in concrete policy proposals. Behrman lobbied for free textbooks for all students and predicted the "time is not so far off when every detail of a common school education will be free."[38] Behrman had succeeded through grit and determination—indeed, Behrman's childhood experiences gave him a unique perspective on life. He wanted other children to have the opportunities he had not enjoyed after losing his parents.

✦ ✦ ✦

In addition to losing both parents at an early age, Behrman experienced the violence of post–Civil War New Orleans, much of it driven by racial political competition. He witnessed "the fight against the Metropolitan police and the carpet baggers" when "a negro policeman came running out St. Peter street, tearing off his Metropolitan buttons as he ran." The Black policeman threw his rifle under a department store display. Behrman retrieved the Winchester, complete with bayonet, and kept it for himself "as spoils of war."[39]

Black residents created social and political clubs to engage in the democratic process. Organized by ward, these Black centers of political activism included the Colfax Defenders and Grant Invincibles. Frustrated white Democrats grew fearful of a permanent shift in power to Republicans and Black voters. White political clubs were formed and grew in membership up to fifteen thousand people. These clubs included the Workingmen's Club and the Innocents, the latter being the most feared. The Innocents were composed chiefly of Sicilians who paraded in red shirts and caps and carried banners sometimes portraying violent acts against Black citizens of the city.[40]

White voters maintained a numerical advantage over Black voters, causing Republicans to lose control of Louisiana by 1866. To increase their numbers and restore themselves to power in Baton Rouge, Republicans sought a new state constitutional convention giving Black citizens the right to vote. This effort resulted in the riots of July 30, 1866, in which over two hundred people died, most of them Black.[41] The violence was encouraged by police. In total, approximately fifteen hundred whites first attacked Black veterans in the streets and then surged inside the Mechanics' Institute, where the convention was planned. Inside, a former governor was badly beaten and others were killed. The high-profile attack brought new awareness to conditions in the South, especially in the nation's capital. Congress quickly initiated military rule across the South while new policies stripped former Confederates of power and prestige, promoting the political participation of Black voters and increasing the influence of Republicans. These actions plus further changes to the Louisiana Constitution resulted in the election of a Republican governor, Henry Clay Warmoth, in 1868.

The presidential election of 1868 pitted Republicans Ulysses S. Grant and Schuyler Colfax against Democrats Horatio Seymour and Frank Blair. Black voters in Louisiana hoped the election of Grant, a famous Union general, would guarantee the recent victories they won with the rewrite of the Louisiana Constitution. White Democrats were counting on Seymour and Blair to reverse the gains made by Black voters. On September 22, 1868, gunfire broke out at a restaurant and saloon called Dumontiel's Confectionary. Black rioters threw lighted lamps through the saloon's windows in pursuit of whites who had allegedly taunted them with cheers for Seymour and Blair. One Black man died, and others were injured in the violence that ensued. Just two weeks earlier, Pinckney Benton Stewart Pinchback, a Union Army soldier and one of the most influential Black men in Louisiana politics, warned, "The next outrage of the kind which they [the white Democrats] commit will be the signal for the dawn of retribution." He warned, "this city will be reduced to ashes."[42]

On Saturday, October 24, Democrats of the Workingmen's Club marched to express support for their candidates. Such political parades were commonplace in New Orleans during this era, and when the Democrats encountered a Republican parade, both sides cheered for their candidates without incident. The separate parades continued until a small group of gun-toting Democrats emerged from some trees in the middle of Canal Street. They shot and killed seven Black Republicans. The youngest victim was ten-year-old Joseph Antoine, who was seemingly trampled to death during the chaotic gunplay.

Republican retribution was swift. The streets of New Orleans filled with violence and bloodshed, and at least twenty innocent citizens died—Black and white, Republican and Democrat. The bloodshed and property damage did not subside until October 28.[43] Such violence and political turmoil led to a tightly knit, temporary coalition that included powerful Democratic ward organizations and laid the foundation of machine politics in New Orleans for decades to come. Ten years later, the white Democratic coalition split in the municipal election of 1878.[44] The rupture became a lasting feature of New Orleans's political landscape with the "Regulars," or pro-machine reformers, on one side and the anti-machine reformers on the other. Both groups staked their claim to "reform," but the anti-machine reformers were often more successful in this endeavor.

2

THE ARENA
Marriage and Politics

After working for Mike Gallagher at Samuel's Dollar Store, Behrman accepted a salesclerk position at James Lawton's grocery store. In his memoir, Behrman described the place as a "big country store with a bakery and a steamboat for deliveries."[1] On that fateful day when he left Gallagher's grocery store for greener pastures, Behrman could not have conceived of the many positive consequences of his decision. Almost immediately, this new path led to Julia Collins. The Irish Catholic beauty happened to be visiting family in the home next door to Lawton.[2] Martin and Julia fell in love and planned to be married in Sts. Peter and Paul Catholic Church—but only after Behrman converted to Catholicism. Behrman's choices were beginning to shape his destiny.

Although both of his parents had been Jewish, becoming a Catholic may not have been a big leap for Behrman. He lived and worked with Irish Catholics such as Gallagher and Lawton, and New Orleans itself was a bastion of Catholicism where those who practiced the faith were mostly insulated from the type of discrimination they experienced in other parts of the United States in the late nineteenth and early twentieth centuries. New Orleans's Catholic foundation was simply too strong, dating back to French colonization and the formation of the Archdiocese of New Orleans in 1793. Originally known as the Diocese of Louisiana and the Floridas, the Archdiocese of New Orleans evolved with both French and Spanish influence. This early joint venture between the king of Spain and the pope was strengthened by Catholic immigration.

An influx of Germans in the 1750s, Irish in the 1830s, and then Italians and Sicilians in the 1890s and early 1900s strengthened the Catholic Church in New Orleans. These immigrants often found comfort in their Catholic faith during an otherwise difficult transition from their homeland, as they "were able to weave their traditions into the extant Catholic community."[3] To the extent that these populations faced discrimination, and they often did, it had more to do with ethnicity than religion.[4] For example, the city's ethnic populations often practiced a distinct variety of Catholicism with liturgies and devotional practices unique to their own traditions. Conflict and bias among these subcultures was common. The French Creole laity and clergy of New Orleans frequently ridiculed ethnic Catholics, including the Irish.[5]

It is of no small consequence that Catholics in New Orleans did not struggle against the evident prejudice they experienced in places such as New York City. It distinguished the tone and direction of political debate in New Orleans from those of other cities. The *Times-Picayune* and the *Item* did not share the propensity of the New York press to link Martin Behrman and the Regulars to the Catholic Church. For example, when John Kelly, boss of Tammany Hall, married the niece of the archbishop of New York, newspapers and cartoonists there jumped at the opportunity to sensationalize the fact. An editorial in the magazine *Puck* charged that Kelly's attempts to lower the salaries of New York City's public school teachers was an attempt to fund private Catholic schools rather than balance the city's budget.[6]

In New Orleans, by contrast, many Catholic leaders and organizations were held in high esteem in the press for their active outreach across the city. In the nineteenth century, when the city was ravaged by frequent epidemics of yellow fever and other diseases, and when poverty and slavery were hallmarks of the human experience for the less fortunate and unlucky, the women of the Catholic Church provided solace to the forlorn members of society. For example, in April 1869, the Sisters of Mercy began visiting inmates incarcerated in the New Orleans city prison. During regular visits, they provided the inmates with books, catechisms, beads, medals, and small favors. They also gave instruction in the Catholic faith to those who were so inclined.[7] Other Catholic religious groups contributed to New Orleans's social safety net. These included the Daughters of Charity, Sisters of Mount Carmel, School Sisters of Notre Dame, Sisters of St. Joseph, Sisters of the Good Shepherd, and the Dominicans. All were an integral part of daily life.[8]

Later, many parish organizations supported New Orleans's immigrants and contributed to the web of support for those in need. The Holy Name Society, for example, was organized in Sts. Peter and Paul Church, where Martin and Julia Behrman were married. The group raised money for, among other things, the installation of a ceiling in the school hall. Others included the

Catholic Athletic Association, the Catholic Ladies Benevolent Association, and the Ladies Auxiliary of the Society of St. Vincent de Paul.[9]

* + +

By the fall of 1887, Behrman sat nervously in the church parlor at 2317 Burgundy Street, waiting to speak with Father Robert Moise and arrange for his marriage to Julia. He was so anxious, in fact, that he requested something to read to get his mind off the enormity of the moment. Behrman was promptly handed an old city directory, which he perused column by column until Father Moise appeared and they could discuss details of the big day.

Behrman learned that he and Julia would need witnesses and a marriage license, and the ceremony would cost twenty-three-year-old Martin and twenty-two-year-old Julia ten dollars—no small sum for a young man in the 1880s. The marriage would be performed by Father Moise himself.[10] When the big day came on October 13, 1887, the happy couple was joined by Behrman's business partner, Peter Lawton, and his wife, Isabella ("Bella"). Julia's sister, Margaret Collins, and other guests were present at the small ceremony. Father Moise battled his own nerves, this being the first wedding he had ever performed. Recalling the joyous occasion, Behrman remarked that the priest "was fully as nervous as I myself."[11]

With the drama of the ceremony behind them, Martin and Julia made Algiers their home. They soon settled into their long-term residence on Pelican Avenue. While at this time Algiers could be reached only by boat, it was a busy port. Approximately 85 percent of the cargo passing from the East Coast to the West Coast went through Algiers. And the Southern Pacific Railroad employed four thousand people in Algiers alone. Many of these workers were involved in unloading cargo and transferring it to boxcars for destinations such as San Francisco and Seattle.[12]

Through his association with the Lawton family, Behrman had not only met Julia but also found a business partner in James Lawton's son, Peter. Together they opened a grocery store in Algiers.[13] Behrman and Lawton increased foot traffic in their retail space by accepting mail for residents, a move that increased Behrman's exposure to the citizens of Algiers. Later, he worked extensively in wholesale grocery sales of one kind or another. He sold produce for Wallace and Van Horn, and dairy products for F. O. Trepagnier and Edward C. Bres. One of his last grocery industry jobs before entering politics was wholesale sales for C. Doyle and Company, offering general grocery and whiskey. Behrman's education thus consisted of both formal schooling and work experience in grocery sales. He sharpened these skills when he entered politics as a volunteer in his early twenties—a time when divisions were beginning to appear among Democrats in Louisiana and across the South.

✦　✦　✦

After the Civil War, Democrats across the South were mostly united by the goal of defeating Black candidates and other Republicans. This short-term coalition quickly dissipated after Reconstruction ended in 1877 and federal troops departed. Local white control was no longer the top priority for Democrats. Historian Joy Jackson notes that, "Slowly, painfully, since the removal of Federal troops from Louisiana in 1877, the city had been groping its way out of the miasma of Reconstruction violence and corruption."[14]

The Democratic Party subsequently splintered into factions that often aligned against the Democratic machine in New Orleans. The names of these anti-machine splinter groups changed from election to election. They included labels such as the People's Democratic Association in 1880, the Independent Party in 1882, and the Young Men's Democratic Association in 1888. Such factions emerged as growing numbers of Democrats came to believe "the party's highly effective electoral mechanism was only a weapon of expediency in the battle against the Republicans and their Black allies."[15] These reformers called for abandoning the ward organization and political machinery they claimed resulted in widespread fraud and corruption. In so doing, they framed the issue of reform to suit their political ambitions, an effort that met with mixed degrees of success. Many of these reformers advocated for change fitting squarely into the progressive agenda of the late nineteenth and early twentieth centuries, including direct primaries, the commission-council form of government, and municipally owned mass transit and public utilities. They viewed disfranchisement and cracking down on vice as keys to ending political corruption.[16] In Louisiana, no two men embodied the battle to define reform more than John Parker and Martin Behrman.

Parker and Behrman entered politics in New Orleans as this wave of reform swept across the United States—Behrman, who rose through the Regular machine, and Parker, who founded the most successful of the early anti-machine reform groups in New Orleans, the Young Men's Democratic Association. The group consisted of "merchants, businessmen and lawyers," drawn from the city's professional classes.[17] Over the years, Parker and his comrades fought against the lottery and supported policies such as the commission form of municipal government, civil service reform, the secret ballot, and much more.[18] Battles between Behrman and Parker mirrored the broader national debate over progressive reform and sometimes spilled into that larger arena.

In 1888, Parker and Behrman were both involved in successful political campaigns. Parker led the Young Men's Democratic Association to victory in the New Orleans mayoral race, and Behrman served as secretary of the Fifteenth Ward in Algiers for winning gubernatorial candidate Francis T. Nicholls. Parker and his allies guarded polling places with shotguns, propelling Joseph Shakespeare to a win against machine candidate Robert C. Davey in the New Orleans mayoral contest, 23,313 votes to 15,635. Although Nicholls's victory over the Republican Henry Clay Warmoth was never really in doubt, Behrman's wide network of relationships in Algiers was an asset to Nicholls during the primary. Nicholls ultimately defeated Warmoth 136,746 votes to 51,993, and the 1888 campaign set the stage for a political competition between Behrman and Parker that would last for more than thirty years.[19]

Behrman was rewarded for his good work on the Nicholls campaign with an offer to become the deputy assessor of Algiers. The position paid $150 per month and required less travel than Behrman's duties at C. Doyle and Company. This was a welcome opportunity with the birth of his son, Stanley. After consulting with Julia, Behrman quickly accepted the offer. While serving as deputy assessor, Behrman applied for and was granted employment with the Algiers Water Works and Electric Light Company. He was paid a salary of $100 per month.[20] This decision to work for a private company over which he held direct or indirect taxing authority would become a major issue in his 1904 campaign for mayor of New Orleans.

In addition to working in the assessor's office and with the electric utility, Behrman took the 1890 census—a job he accepted in order to gain a detailed knowledge of Algiers as much as a paycheck. Noting this fact, Behrman once asserted that he had likely met "every man, woman and child in Algiers."[21] At different points in his career, Behrman also served on the school board and worked as a clerk on the city council.[22] During these early years of his political life, the state lottery became an important issue for the anti-machine reformers.[23]

Lotteries offered the same attraction in the nineteenth century as they do today. A quarter bought dreams of life on easy street. Tickets sold for as much as $40 in hundreds of lottery shops throughout New Orleans, and drawings for winning numbers brought crowds of excited citizens hoping to win as much as $600,000.

The controversial Louisiana Lottery Company was created in 1868. It operated with a twenty-five-year charter, and many people viewed it as a corrupt enterprise. Founder Charles T. Howard allegedly used the company's profits to gain favor with elected officials, including the Regulars in New Orleans. Most Regular politicians supported the lottery and pointed to its contributions to Charity Hospital and the French Opera House.[24]

In 1892, Behrman supported the machine candidate for mayor, John Fitzpatrick, who emerged victorious after a bitter campaign against reformers. Behrman was rewarded with the post of clerk of the city council budget committee—a position that placed him squarely in the middle of the city's biggest challenges, including fire protection. It was the age of great urban fires, and fire protection was therefore of the utmost importance in New Orleans and other major cities. During this period Chicago, Baltimore, San Francisco, and New York all suffered devastating fires. The cost was enormous. For example, in 1866, $57 million in property burned in the United States, and by 1880, the figure increased to nearly $75 million. Then, by 1900, the loss had increased to $160 million—nearly tripling the figure from just thirty-four years prior.[25]

Behrman's experience with such disasters was not limited to emergency planning. Around midnight on October 25, 1895, a blaze began to burn in a small fruit store in the "Old Rookery" at Bermuda and Morgan Streets in Algiers.[26] Three steam engines and a fire truck were brought to the scene almost immediately. However, there was no pump infrastructure in Algiers at the time. Water was drawn from wells, which soon ran dry. The fire then spread rapidly, eventually consuming nine and a half blocks. An estimated two hundred homes and businesses were destroyed, including the courthouse at Duverje Plantation.[27]

As a volunteer fireman, Behrman helped to battle the inferno. He believed the hero of the entire affair was Jim Reynolds, who rescued an elderly woman overcome by smoke. Reynolds rushed into the burning building, climbed to the second story, and emerged several minutes later carrying the unconscious woman in his arms. There were other selfless acts, like that of Charles Featherling, an engineer who started the pump at a mill where he worked and used its water to prevent the fire from spreading. When word arrived at the mill that his own home was in danger, Featherling refused to leave the pump. While other residents hustled their most valuable possessions to safety, he fought the fire. Everything he owned was lost.

Behrman noted that "He [Featherling] had his choice between saving a great deal of other people's property and had a chance of getting some of his own saved and he chose to work for the majority."[28] Organized emergency relief of the type needed in Algiers did not exist in the 1890s. Behrman therefore helped organize an emergency relief fund and acted as secretary. The group raised thousands of dollars for the estimated twelve hundred citizens left homeless by the fire.[29] Behrman's leadership during and after the big fire in Algiers enhanced his stature in the community.

✦ ✦ ✦

The fire in Algiers capped off a run of bad luck and controversy for Mayor Fitzpatrick and the Regulars. A combination of corrupt practices among city council members and lingering resentment from the 1892 municipal campaign throttled the machine's political ambitions. No charges were made against Behrman, but the city council was attacked in the newspapers and labeled the "Boodle Council" by opponents. The optics were some of the worst ever for the New Orleans machine.[30] Ultimately, a mix of perceived and actual corruption led to a series of libel suits and jail terms for some city officials. Fitzpatrick himself was exonerated of any criminal activity, but much damage was done to the Regulars' reputation. The "Ring" epithet reformers stuck on the city machine seemed more appropriate than ever.

Due to the "Boodle Council" controversies, Mayor Fitzpatrick chose not to run for reelection in 1896. The Regulars nominated Charles F. Buck, a loyal Regular who confidently espoused the group's principles. Buck could not overcome voter distrust of the Regulars in the wake of the Fitzpatrick controversies, however. He lost 23,345 to 17,295 to reform candidate Walter

Flowers of the Citizens' League.[31] The Regulars thus relinquished their hold on the mayor's office in 1896, and reformers took control.[32] Forced to reassess virtually every aspect of their strategy, the Regulars met in early 1897 and formed the Choctaw Club.

Attendance estimates for the inaugural meeting of the Choctaw Club range between forty and seventy-five people.[33] One attendee, Martin Behrman, continued to accumulate power and knowledge of the city while remaining quietly in the background throughout the contentious 1890s. In March of 1897 the charter of the Choctaw Club was approved by its members and the first board of governors was chosen. The Choctaws took up residence in a creole-style building with wrought-iron balconies only a block from city hall.[34] The caricature of the club was that its members "were not the fashionable elite from uptown or the Garden District. Instead, they were a rougher crowd, mostly heavy-set, cigar-smoking men who, if necessary, could use their fists to settle their frequent arguments."[35]

Officially, the Choctaw Club's mission was to preserve democracy, but the unofficial mission was more sophisticated and consequential. In recalling this purpose decades later, Behrman noted that the Choctaw Club was organized "the year after the negro vote elected the Citizen's League ticket in New Orleans and came very near to electing the Republicans in the state."[36] Moreover, he said, "the Convention that put the negroes out of politics came the next year, in 1898."[37] This second statement gets more to the point of the Choctaw Club's mission—to preserve *white* democracy by disenfranchising Black voters and ensuring that others, including illiterate white and ethnic voters, would remain valuable supporters of the Choctaw Club and the Regulars. New Orleans mayor John Fitzpatrick and other Regulars "urged Democrats in the Third Ward to register to vote so that suffrage could be withheld from a 'certain worthless class.'"[38] Behrman, Fitzpatrick, and other Regulars were "the vanguard of those who advocated disenfranchising Black voters."[39]

The convention to which Behrman referred was the February 8, 1898, Constitutional Convention at Tulane Hall in New Orleans. Former governor Francis T. Nicholls opened the proceedings. The one-armed, one-legged, one-eyed Civil War veteran now served as Louisiana Supreme Court chief justice. Next, the attendees elected Ernest Kruttschnitt president of the convention. In his acceptance speech, Kruttschnitt noted that the convention had a single purpose: "This convention has been called together by the people of the state to eliminate from the electorate the mass of corrupt and illiterate voters who have degraded our politics during the last quarter century."[40] The convention proceeded along this line of reasoning, immediately disenfranchising Black voters.

Literacy tests, which had been the most common method of denying Black citizens the opportunity to participate in elections, became less useful when applied to other minorities and to illiterate whites who leaned toward machine candidates. Immigrants, including the large population of Italians in New Orleans, could vote in elections—even if they were not yet official American citizens. They merely had to express an intent to become citizens to vote. Because of their loyalty to the Regulars, getting Italians to the polls on election day was a high priority for ward leaders.[41] Unfortunately for the Regulars, many Italians could not meet the literacy requirements used to disenfranchise Black voters. The question then became how to suppress the Black vote while encouraging the Italian vote. The answer was a simple exemption for immigrants naturalized prior to passage of the new Constitution. This left the great majority of Italians eligible to vote and disenfranchised Black citizens.[42]

Exempting only naturalized citizens from literacy requirements created yet another problem: how to enable illiterate whites to vote without permitting Black citizens to do the same. The two methods debated were the understanding clause and the grandfather clause. The understanding clause was used elsewhere in the South, including Mississippi. It permitted a voter registrar to read part of the state constitution to a potential voter, who, if he could appropriately interpret what had been read to him, would be allowed to vote.

The grandfather clause eliminated property and literacy requirements only for those individuals who had been allowed to vote prior to Reconstruction. This rule permitted illiterate whites to continue voting while disenfranchising illiterate and non-property-owning Black citizens who were not permitted to vote until after the Civil War. At the 1898 convention, Louisiana chose the grandfather method to keep Black people from exercising their voting rights, but when that device was later declared unconstitutional by the U.S. Supreme Court, Louisiana switched to the "understanding" subterfuge.[43]

Reflecting on his role at the convention, Behrman openly confessed what he saw as the hazards of allowing Black citizens to vote and asserted that he "had a hand in putting the negroes out of politics." This, he said, "was the best thing done for Louisiana in my time."[44] Fear that Republicans would use the "negro vote" to win elections, combined with the desire for order and social status, led to widespread, institutionalized discrimination. The strategy endured throughout the "Solid" Democrat South until the civil rights movement in the 1960s.[45]

The 1898 Constitutional Convention was a significant event in Behrman's career. To secure his place at the convention, Behrman worked harder than ever to win 647 out of 865 votes cast. "I called on every white voter I could get to," proclaimed Behrman.[46] He hoped to serve on the suffrage committee of the convention, but this privilege was reserved almost exclusively for lawyers who crafted language disenfranchising Black voters—without explicitly violating the U.S. Constitution. Instead, Behrman served on the education, taxation, and city of New Orleans committees.[47]

Behrman sponsored an ordinance that required compensation for landowners in New Orleans whose property was taken by the government to build levees.[48] At a time when public education still carried the shame of carpetbagger reforms, Behrman sponsored an ordinance to provide free textbooks for all Louisiana schoolchildren. In the face of opposition, Behrman was forced to add a provision requiring proof that a family could not afford to purchase a child's books without financial assistance from the state. It was not until Huey Long pushed the idea through the legislature in 1928 that all Louisiana students received free textbooks for their education, whether in public school or private school, rich or poor.[49]

Behrman "long believed that the school authorities should have some degree of autonomy from the city council."[50] Prior to 1898, New Orleans's public schools relied solely on the whims of council members for their funding. Behrman therefore introduced an amendment that "the city of New Orleans shall make such appropriation for the support, maintenance and repair of the public schools of said city as it may deem proper but not less than eight-tenths (.08) of one mill for any year: and said school shall also continue to receive from the Board of Liquidation of the City Debt the amounts to which they are now entitled under the constitutional amendment adopted in the year 1892."[51] For the first time ever, New Orleans's children relied on a guaranteed annual appropriation from the city council.

✦ ✦ ✦

Throughout the 1890s, the anti-machine reformers continued fighting the lottery and corruption in government while concern for victims of sex crimes increased. Prostitution was big business in New Orleans—which, according to one scholar, was "estimated to be second in dollar value only to the Crescent City's port itself."[52] The first significant attempt to regulate and license prostitution in the United States was enacted in 1857 by the New Orleans City Council. Entitled "An Ordinance Concerning Lewd and Abandoned Women," it was mostly ineffective.[53] There had been little effort to restrict prostitution in the antebellum period and the immediate wake of the Civil War; however, by the 1890s, the Reverend Alfred E. Clay and the Society for the Prevention of Cruelty to Children began high-profile rescues of teenage girls from brothels in New Orleans.[54] Newspapers such as the *Mascot* began to call for European-style regulation of vice with defined boundaries around a prostitution district, as well as the registration and medical examination of prostitutes. Finally, the proliferation of brothels in the Garden District and French Quarter swayed business owners and reformers into creating a fixed geographic area to contain the problem.[55]

Early in 1897, Alderman Sidney Story presented and the council passed an ordinance limiting prostitution to a defined area. The ordinance was carefully written to limit prostitution while surviving potential legal challenges. By not legalizing prostitution within the district but rather outlawing prostitution outside of fixed geographic boundaries, the city prevailed in the face of legal challenges, including the U.S. Supreme Court case *L'Hote v. New Orleans*.[56] A bitter controversy erupted over Storyville, lasting for the next quarter century. This local prostitution debate was further federalized by American soldiers' patronage of prostitutes along the Mexican border and passage of the Mann Act prohibiting the transportation of women and girls "for immoral purposes."[57]

3

ASCENT
Don't Let Them Make You Do It

When the twentieth century commenced, Martin Behrman was thirty-six years old. He and Julia enjoyed a family of their own and a home across the Mississippi River in Algiers. The couple had welcomed Mary Helen, their eldest child, into the world on May 12, 1888. She became "Nellie" to friends. Julia gave birth to their son, Stanley, on June 12, 1891.[1] In total, the couple had five children, but as was typical in the nineteenth century, only three of them survived childbirth. Mary Helen and William Stanley grew to adulthood. A third child, Isabella, likely named after Isabella Lawton, died at the age of two years.[2] The children who did survive, Nellie and William (who preferred his middle name, Stanley), led productive and happy lives.

As a little boy, Stanley attended McDonogh No. 4, a grammar school for boys—one of the many funded by Algiers resident John McDonogh. Stanley's was an idyllic childhood in most ways, one exception being the rattan cane the principal used on the hands of misbehaving boys. Miss Liz, as she was known, employed her cane to dole out discipline, but the boys were little thwarted by the short-term pain she inflicted. Instead, they ran wild in the undeveloped areas of Algiers, playing sandlot baseball and constructing their own playgrounds. One of their "rides" they called the "valdador"—a crude merry-go-round made from a tall post with a rope tied to the top, and a burlap sack for the seat. The boys pushed and pulled each other around and around until the contraption became unstable and everyone scrambled to avoid having their skulls crushed by the falling post. Most injuries were minor, and good times were had by all.

Generally, the valdador boys of Algiers did not continue their education after grammar school, which in those days typically extended to eighth grade, or about the age of fourteen. Instead of continuing school, such boys often took apprentice jobs that paid around 75 cents per day, usually in the machine shops of the Southern Pacific Railroad. Stanley was an exception. He took a ferry to New Orleans daily to attend the Boys School, a three-year high school program. Stanley graduated from high school in 1909 with a ceremony in the French Opera House.

Stanley and Nellie grew up immersed in politics. Torchlight parades were staples of their youth. Stanley learned how to build crowds, demonstrating public support for his father and the candidates he supported. Sometimes the parade of dignitaries at his home on Pelican Avenue seemed as busy as the torchlight parades in the Twelfth, Thirteenth, and Fourteenth Wards.[3] The two children maintained a close relationship throughout their lives.

At the dawn of World War I, Stanley was commissioned a first lieutenant in the U.S. Army at Fort Logan H. Root in Little Rock, Arkansas. He was promoted to captain soon before he left for France. At twenty-eight years of age, Nellie Behrman became Nellie Bond when she married Louisiana state representative Nathaniel "Nat" W. Bond, a graduate of Tulane Law School. Bond served as New Orleans city attorney, secretary to Congressman Garland Dupré, and later as a justice on the Louisiana Supreme Court. Sadly, Nellie passed away in 1929, leaving Judge Bond a widower. After Nellie's death, Stanley maintained the relationship with his brother-in-law. In 1940, Stanley married Alva Bond Ehrhart in Judge Bond's home on Carondelet Street with W. W. Holmes officiating the small ceremony. Stanley lived a quiet life and enjoyed a successful career in business. He never ran for public office but maintained a critical eye on politics in Louisiana for the rest of his life. Stanley fondly recalled the sandlot baseball and torchlight parades of his youth until the time of his death in 1978.[4]

❖ ❖ ❖

Closing out the 1890s, Behrman continued his methodical climb, diligently organizing for the Regulars. As the recognized leader of the Fifteenth Ward, Martin Behrman felt "settled and confident of the future."[5] By 1904, he was recruited to run for state auditor against incumbent auditor W. S. Frazee and Louisiana treasurer LeDoux E. Smith. Unintimidated by recent changes to election laws designed to limit the power of the Regulars, Behrman accepted the challenge. He visited almost every parish in Louisiana and gave his first big speech in Morgan City. With plenty of barbecue and a big crowd—really big, one of the largest Behrman would ever see outside of New Orleans—it was a grand scene. There were train rides and "low rate excursions on the Atchafalaya River and Bayou Teche."[6] The highlight of the day was the debate between two men who sought to be governor, Newton Blanchard and General Leon Jastremski.

Politics in Louisiana could be rough—even deadly. As the two men stood on the debate platform, insults were exchanged, then physical blows, and soon revolvers waved around the stage in Ponchatoula like an old western movie set.[7] Behrman found himself in the vicinity of the eruption between Blanchard and Jastremski and spent "most of about two minutes changing positions so that if Chairman Davidson decided to pull the trigger the bullet would not hit me."[8] Once again, Behrman's steady nature had served him well in the Wild West culture of the day. The event was long remembered, however, and when John Parker challenged Ruffin Pleasant to a debate in the race for governor twelve years later, Pleasant declined, citing the dangerous situation that arose in Ponchatoula.[9]

After the gunplay, Behrman waited his turn to speak. He was one of the last on stage to address the crowd and, although his "feet wouldn't stay put" and he "didn't know what to do with his hands," he acquitted himself well. As an orator, he was unimpressive, but unlike most politicians, Behrman knew when to shut up. After an unsteady start, the candidate announced he was campaigning for the position of auditor, an office that did not require fancy speech, and furthermore, that if it did, he would not be a candidate for such an office. He "did not have that qualification." Then Behrman sat down. In the heat of the Louisiana summer, his concise speech and self-deprecating approach pleased the crowd.[10]

Behrman was a cagey candidate who accounted for his own limitations and, where possible, turned them to his advantage. Because his Morgan City tactic succeeded, and because his opponent, Auditor Frazee, was a good speaker, whenever Behrman knew they would appear together on the dais, he called ahead to event organizers and suggested that Frazee speak first. On the day of the event, after Frazee spoke, Behrman consistently delivered a lean speech, suggesting the work of auditor required few words.

On election day, Behrman won the Democratic primary without a majority. This was, of course, the only election that mattered in the one-party state of Louisiana. But prior to the election, anti-machine reformers and influential newspapers in Louisiana, including the *New Orleans Times-Democrat,* had successfully advocated for direct primaries in statewide elections. They hoped to loosen the Regulars' grip on power.[11] Because Behrman came up six hundred votes short of an outright majority, the new rules required a runoff election. Fortunately for Behrman, the second-place candidate bowed out of the race, leaving Behrman the winner. His tireless campaigning, combined with an unusual grasp of his own limitations as a candidate, helped Behrman succeed.[12]

As state auditor, Behrman discovered irregularities in some state accounts and earned a reputation for honesty—a sought-after credential and one not possessed by your average machine politician.[13] Later that summer, Behrman was called to a meeting of influential leaders at the offices of the *Daily Picayune*. Those present included U.S. senator and former governor Murphy J. Foster, state senator T. H. Thorpe, future congressman Samuel Gilmore, manager of the *Daily Picayune* Thomas Rapier, and others. They asked Behrman to run for mayor. Returning home to discuss the matter with Julia, he was not surprised by her response. In a tone familiar to many candidates and their spouses, Julia implored her husband, "Don't let them make you do it."[14]

Behrman initially sought other candidates to run, including Charles Janvier, an influential city leader and founder of the Citizens' League of 1896. Behrman's family had only recently moved from New Orleans to Baton Rouge. The idea of turning right around and moving back to New Orleans was naturally unappealing, not to mention the prospect of another campaign so soon after finishing a statewide race for auditor. Furthermore, the mayor's job was tougher in many ways than the state auditor's post. It also paid less. Finally, Behrman, having already been elected to statewide office, may have reasonably coveted the governor's mansion rather than city hall. For all of these reasons, his resistance to running for mayor was probably sincere. Janvier, however, declined to run for mayor "for business reasons," and other recruitment efforts stalled. Behrman accepted the nomination and announced his campaign for mayor on August 24, 1904.[15]

New Orleans newspapers immediately staked out their positions. The *Times-Democrat* framed the race as a battle to keep New Orleans out of "the hands of the Ring" and called Behrman unqualified for the office of mayor. While conceding that he was "a man of pleasant personality and popularity," the paper suggested that Behrman embodied "the very elements that would assure misgovernment of the city."[16] The city's business community and economy would surely suffer because of his election, the newspaper concluded. Regular leader Robert Ewing ensured the *States* had nice things to say about Behrman, while the *Daily Picayune* described him as "industrious and trustworthy" but also perhaps not experienced enough for the job.[17]

Much to the chagrin of the *Times-Democrat*, the Regular machine was in a strong position to push the likeable and popular Behrman over the finish line. In the municipal election of 1900, the Regulars had recaptured control of city patronage with the mayoral victory of Paul Capdevielle.[18] They also gained control of state patronage inside the city beginning with the election of Governor Murphy Foster in 1896 and later with Governor William Heard's successful campaign in 1900. Then, in 1904, Governor Newton C. Blanchard agreed to cooperate with the Regulars and place state patronage in the city under their control. In addition, the Regulars controlled, or at least heavily influenced, the Parish Democratic Committee, and they completely owned the candidate nominating process at the convention (there was no primary election at this time for the nomination of city candidates).[19]

By 1904, Black citizens were completely disenfranchised and the Republican Party was decimated by the loss of 95,000 Black voters.[20] The Democrats' absolute control contributed to internal divisions, and a faction known as the "Home Rulers" emerged. The source of conflict was bitterness over Governor Blanchard's endorsement of Porter Parker for district attorney in New Orleans. After lurid stories of backroom dealmaking and betrayal in the local papers, a mass meeting of five thousand people was held on September 24 at the Liberty Monument on Canal Street. The group announced that it intended to appoint an executive committee and field a slate of candidates in opposition to Governor Blanchard, Behrman, and the Regulars.[21] Notably, Behrman and the Regulars had not even supported Blanchard's candidate for district attorney. In fact, there was little reason for the Home Rulers to oppose Behrman other than his association with the Regulars.

✦ ✦ ✦

William Parkerson organized and led the Home Rulers. In 1891, he had also led the lynching of eleven Sicilians in retaliation for the murder of New Orleans police chief David Hennessy. At that time, there were about fifteen thousand Sicilians living in New Orleans, a handful of whom were believed to be the first Mafia members in the United States. Chief Hennessy, who became involved in a dispute between the Mantranga and Provenzano families, was attacked with sawed-off shotguns in October of 1890 but lived long enough to whisper that it was "Dagoes" who shot him.[22]

On March 13, 1891, a jury refused to convict several Sicilian men based on lack of evidence. The *Daily Item* ranted that murder had "struck at the law itself" while other papers wrote scathing reports of the impotency of the judicial system and the threat posed to society by "oath bound assassins."[23] Rumors began to circulate that the Mafia planned to take over New Orleans. A mass meeting was organized at the statue of Henry Clay. Many prominent leaders joined the gathering, including William Parkerson and John Parker.

Parkerson, Parker, and others riled the angry mob. Parkerson asked his agitated listeners, "What protection is there left for us when the very head of our police department—our Chief of Police—is assassinated in our very midst by the Mafia Society, and his assassins [are] again turned loose on the community?"[24] Parkerson promised the crowd that he had "no desire for fame or prominence" but that "when courts fail people must act!"[25] Thousands left the Clay statue with Parkerson and Parker and headed for Orleans Street, between Tremé and Marais Streets, where the Orleans Parish Prison stood. A young but politically active Martin Behrman did not speak at the Clay statue, but he did follow the crowd at a safe distance and saw one of the victims "hanging to a tree."[26] This may have been Antonio Bagnetto, who was found shot but still alive in a pile of bodies, then hung from a tree and shot again multiple times. Emmanuele Polizzi met a similar fate except that he was hanged from a streetlight on Tremé Street before the crowd began firing at his body.[27]

One newspaper called the murders the "greatest event of the year," and the *American Law Review* said they were "conceived by gentlemen and carried out by gentlemen."[28] Parkerson, who carried a Winchester rifle and a revolver, supposedly did not fire a shot. He did, however, take credit for the killings, announcing, "I have performed the most painful duty of my life today."[29] Asked later if he regretted the murders of the defenseless men at the Orleans Parish Prison, Parkerson responded that, although it wasn't the bravest act he could imagine, the unarmed Italians were "reptiles" and the situation was an emergency requiring severe action.[30] John Parker continued leading the reform movement in New Orleans and went on to become president of the Board of Trade in New Orleans, later a vice presidential pick of Theodore Roosevelt in his failed 1916 campaign, and governor of Louisiana in 1920.

✦ ✦ ✦

A dozen years after lynching the Sicilians, Parkerson launched a political assault on Behrman, alleging that he gave the Algiers Electric Light and Waterworks Company favorable tax treatment while he was on the payroll of its parent company, the Edison Electric Light Company.[31] The *Daily Picayune* wrote expansive front-page stories on the Parkerson charges, reporting that while Behrman was on the city payroll as assessor of the Fifth District of Louisiana, he was also "on the payroll of the Edison Electric Light Company for $100 per month."[32] Parkerson and the Home Rulers soon hurled a series of new allegations at Behrman and the Regulars, alleging they were unfit to run the city. They promised a full-fledged attack on the reputation of "Honest Martin Behrman."[33]

The Home Rulers accused Behrman of cutting Edison Electric's tax assessments in half while he was on the company's payroll. According to Behrman, Edison Electric's assessment was not cut in half; moreover, it received no reduction whatsoever. Describing Parkerson's accusations as "confused," "incorrect," and "impossible," Behrman asserted that, in fact, Edison's assessments were increased. Describing the differences between the assessor's tax rolls and the comptroller's books, Behrman highlighted the carelessness of Parkerson's research and provided a point-by-point refutation of the allegations that was printed by the *Daily Picayune*.[34]

The Regular counterattack against the Home Rulers included a massive rally in Algiers where Behrman spoke only briefly, leaving the harshest rhetoric to his surrogate speakers. However, Behrman did take the opportunity to call Parkerson a "moral coward." The rally included "a parade of the seven precincts of the ward, each precinct being headed by a brass band."[35] There were men on horseback, fireworks, and all manner of celebration for Behrman throughout Algiers. Homes were decorated along a parade route adorned with colorful lights and Chinese lanterns. Marchers passed by Behrman's home on Pelican Avenue in a show of respect and admiration for their hometown favorite, winding their way along Opelousas and Elmira Avenues.

The parade lasted until well into the evening, when a series of speakers finally launched their collective defense of their mayoral candidate. As Behrman himself approached the podium, a thunderous reverberation came from the crowd. He could not speak over the enthusiastic cheers. The people refused to quiet down until the band began to play loudly "There'll Be a Hot Time in the Old Town Tonight." As had become his custom, Behrman was brief. He thanked the people for their "magnificent demonstration" and excited them against "the slanders and aspersions that have been most unjustly cast upon me by that moral coward, W. S. Parkerson." Playing up the favorite-son angle, Behrman expressed appreciation for such a warm reception "from the people amongst whom I have lived all my life." If you want to know the true nature of a man, said Behrman, find out where he stands with his neighbors. Subsequent speakers targeted the Home Rulers' attack dog, Parkerson. Above the shouts and cheers of the crowd, one person yelled, "Parkerson is all right!" Speaking on stage at that moment was Assistant District Attorney St. Clair Adams, who replied, "Parkerson! That is what the devil will say when he reaches hell."[36] The Regulars also charged that Parkerson colluded with Republicans. This was, in fact, a serious charge. Regular leader Colonel John P. Sullivan asserted that Parkerson cut a political deal with the carpetbag governor, Henry Clay Warmoth, back in the campaign of 1888—treason against white Louisianans who suffered through the Civil War and Reconstruction.

The Home Rulers nominated Congressman Charles F. Buck to run for mayor against Behrman. Buck, a previously loyal machine Democrat, lost a campaign for mayor in 1896 during the backlash against the "Boodle Council" controversies.[37] He was an experienced campaigner, having held a seat in Congress and the Louisiana state legislature.

The Regulars sought to turn Buck's experience against him, portraying him as an "office chaser" and a flip-flopper. According to them, Buck abandoned the Regulars and his principles to obtain the nomination of the Home Rulers: "Mr. Buck today is with a crowd of slanderers—slanderers and libelers." Buck and Parkerson were now making "preposterous, libelous" accusations against Behrman and the Democratic Party.[38] Many years later, Behrman paid Buck the high compliment that he had never heard a better speaker.[39]

Clearly, the Home Rulers were poised to make a serious challenge to the Regulars with the cutthroat Parkerson steering their ship and Buck as their standard-bearer. Yet, Behrman possessed many assets in 1904. Behrman not only had the Get Out the Vote (GOTV) machinery of the Regulars at his disposal, but he also enjoyed the support of organized labor. The Democratic Labor League recognized Behrman as having "risen from the ranks of labor" and as a man of "integrity." According to the *Daily Picayune*, there were some working men who opposed their leadership and supported Buck.[40] However, this appears to have been the exception rather than the rule.

Days before the election, the *Times-Picayune* reported on an incident that took place at Lauro's barber shop on Bourbon Street, next to the Cosmopolitan Hotel. Behrman encountered Judge Patrick F. Hennessy, a candidate for judge of the Second City Court. According to the *Times-Picayune*, the two men cared for each other the way a "Piccolo player likes the sight of lemons when playing on a reed." It was reported that, if they "happened to cross the river on the same boat at one time, passengers would make mental note of the life preservers." According to the *Picayune*, Hennessy planted "his heavy fist upon the jowl of the political boss of Algiers" while Behrman "was having his locks made shorter."

Accounts of the incident differ, but apparently when Behrman greeted Hennessy, he gave the reply, "I don't want to talk to you."

"I thought you were a gentleman," Behrman replied sharply.

The barber stopped clipping the judge's hair, perhaps out of caution or surprise, and Judge Hennessy repeated his remark, escalating with the undiplomatic phrase, "I don't want to talk to you or your kind" and closing with "Go to hell."

"Are you serious?" Behrman questioned.

"Yes," came Hennessy's reply, as he stood up and moved his fists from behind the white barber's linen covering his body.

"Then you can go to hell too," Behrman responded.

Judge Hennessy answered with his fist. Rather than retaliating, Behrman alerted the police to the assault. Whether this constituted an act of restraint or cowardice on the part of Behrman cannot be known. However, it demonstrates Behrman's cautious nature—a trait that served him well throughout his life. Behrman told the *Daily Picayune*, "Being a candidate for Mayor of this city, I could not enter into a personal difficulty with Hennessy, although he had struck me."[41]

Physical altercations aside, the Home Rulers were confident their attacks on Behrman were eroding his support. Still, as election day approached, they held a rally at Liberty Place and warned their supporters the Regulars might try to steal the election. If guns were required to protect a free and fair election, then so be it, they said.

Election day was tense. Poll watchers working for the Home Rulers alleged they were forced to leave multiple precincts. Reports of "rowdyism" and troublemaking abounded and, in one case, a riot nearly broke out.[42] The Home Rulers complained loudly, and Parkerson warned that his supporters might turn into a howling mob if Mayor Capdevielle could not restore order. Capdevielle responded by sending the Louisiana Guard to the Second, Fourth, Fifth, Sixth, and Tenth Wards.[43] Fortunately, there was no substantial violence at the polls—at least not compared to some problems New Orleans had witnessed in the past. Behrman and the Regulars prevailed in the election of 1904, receiving 13,962 votes to Buck's 10,047.[44] While the *Times-Democrat* alleged the Regulars stole the election, patronage likely helped Behrman more than any other single factor, with about 2,000 city and state workers owing their livelihood to the Regulars.[45]

George M. Reynolds published a comprehensive study of Behrman's election and the Regulars' turnout machine. His interviews with precinct leaders reveal an expertly run operation. Stationed at the precinct's polling place, the captain ensured that opposition voters were qualified and paid up on their poll taxes. He also tracked his committed voters and sent his assistants to their homes and businesses to "request" that they come and vote. Committed Regular machine voters who didn't come to the polls by 3 p.m. had transportation sent for them. Ward leaders distributed election-day money for "signs, transportation, assistants, drinks and other effective election day practices."[46] No reporting was required, and no report was given, so long as he won his precinct. The money was used strategically to secure as many votes as possible, hiring assistants with the largest families or paying for the use of their automobile for transportation.[47] The term for this element of campaign strategy in modern parlance is "walking around money."

With the formidable Regular turnout apparatus behind him, Behrman's victory was perhaps a forgone conclusion. But his sincere nature and friendly disposition were no less important. Behrman exuded an affinity for the people of the city and a desire to improve their quality of life. Shortly after noon on December 4, 1904, Gallier Hall at St. Charles and Lafayette Streets was filled with flowers. Congratulatory supporters gathered to watch as Martin Behrman was sworn into the office of mayor for the first time.[48] He was now forty years old and mayor of the largest city in the South. In his inaugural speech, Behrman set a positive tone, proclaiming, "We must clean this city and keep it clean; law and order and security for life and property must prevail; and wise and vigilant sanitation must make this the city of long lives."[49]

+ + +

Behrman's election signaled the birth of a new era of domination for the Regulars. They controlled the city and played an outsized role in congressional and statewide elections. With approximately 20 percent of the state's voting population residing in New Orleans, the Regulars heavily influenced gubernatorial elections between 1900 and 1924, including those of William Heard, Newton Blanchard, J. Y. Sanders, Ruffin Pleasant, and Henry Fuqua.[50] Regular allies in the oil, agriculture, shipping, gambling, and alcohol industries helped to cement a powerful coalition. While there were allegations that New Orleans's infamous brothels played a role in this alliance, little evidence was ever produced to prove such allegations.

New Orleans elected nearly two dozen members of the state House and eight members of the state Senate, most of whom were loyal to the Regulars and chosen by the machine's board of directors—a body composed of the ward leader from each of the city's seventeen wards.[51] City as well as some state and federal patronage jobs were the source of much of the machine's power and were allocated by the board of directors. Often, such appointments were to the Dock Board, Conservation Department, tax administration, and Charity Hospital.[52] In addition, Regular ward leaders determined the group's city and state policy positions via the board. Prior to 1912, ward leaders also frequently served on the city council. Finally, ward leaders supervised the precinct captains, who did the real grassroots work of turning out voters.

Membership in the Choctaw Club significantly overlapped with the Regulars, although the two were technically separate organizations. The Choctaw rolls ranged between 3,000 and 6,000 people. Many of these individuals were city employees who paid dues of one dollar each month to belong to the Choctaw Club.[53] In the absence of regulatory controls, government funds were often used for the reelection of incumbents. Politicians provided jobs and business contracts to build support networks. Government employees frequently worked directly on the political campaigns of their superiors. In addition, precinct leaders were typically municipal employees and members of the Regulars who devoted a significant portion of their time to political activity.[54] Regular machine operations and the affiliated Choctaw Club therefore resembled dozens of other powerful urban political organizations.

A precinct captain's duties included registering voters and ensuring their poll taxes were paid—a task that required knocking on the door of every likely Regular supporter. Precinct captains could be found working out of saloons and other high-traffic, community-centered businesses such as drugstores. Always quick to advise newly arrived immigrants and help families in need, the precinct captain funneled such information to his ward leader and made certain these voters got the help they needed. He might even, on occasion, get someone out of trouble with the law. The precinct captain's notes listed those who benefited from Regular support, and when necessary he reminded them of such assistance. He also informed residents about Regular candidates and when to vote.[55]

The average precinct in New Orleans during this period held about 400 voters. The task, then, was to get a minimum of 201 votes. In order to ensure they could meet this goal, and to make the election as predictable as possible, the precinct captain counted heads. This amounted to a kind of whip operation with a small group of 40 or 50 workers responsible for recruiting 4 or 5 votes each. The group of 50 might include paid precinct election officials, the police, various municipal employees, and elected or appointed officeholders. Using this method, captains could accurately assess whether their precinct was won or lost days before voting occurred.[56] Such knowledge provided Regular leaders with a tremendous strategic advantage. According to most newspapers in the city—both opponents and supporters of the Regulars—outright election fraud did not occur on a large scale, although some irregularities did arise in 1904.[57]

Behrman scholar Robert W. Williams notes that Behrman was a new kind of machine leader: "He realized that an obviously crooked machine dealing out ill-considered patronage could not last; that a do-nothing 'boodle government' like that of former boss James Fitzpatrick was a detriment to the organization; and that positive civic achievements could be reconciled with and could strengthen machine politics."[58] Indeed, Behrman's genius was in delicately balancing the legitimate needs of the people of New Orleans with the pragmatic decisions necessary to consolidate machine power.

✦　✦　✦

On July 22, 1908, as his own reelection approached, Behrman returned from the Democratic National Convention in Denver. Delegates there had just nominated William Jennings Bryan for president at the first major party convention held in a western state and only the second to include female delegates.[59] Few of those Democrats who trekked to Denver perceived the thumping their party would endure in November. On the Republican side, retiring incumbent president Theodore Roosevelt was influential in the nomination of William Howard Taft, his secretary of war. The Independence Party emerged, with the backing of newspaper publisher William Randolph Hearst, who claimed to have proof that both major parties were corrupt and under the control of Standard Oil.

Hearst's candidate, Thomas L. Hisgen, scraped together only 82,537 votes, far less than the Socialist, Prohibition, and Populist party candidates. Taft prevailed, garnering 7,676,258 votes to Bryan's 6,406,801, making Bryan a three-time loser in presidential contests. The Electoral College spread was significant, with Taft winning 321–162. Republicans maintained control of both houses of Congress. Roosevelt saw Republican victories as an affirmation of his own presidency. He was particularly invested in the presidential campaign but incorrectly celebrated Taft's ascendancy to the White House as a signal of "four more years of Rooseveltism."[60]

Behrman arrived in New Orleans just four days prior to the deadline to file for reelection. He told the *Times-Democrat* that it was not in his personal interest to run for a second term because of the financial strain it put on his family. However, Behrman claimed he was beseeched to seek reelection by supporters and many converts who had opposed him in 1904.[61] He did run again and went unopposed in the Democratic primary. The *Times-Democrat* asserted that "no mayor has worked harder or longer" than Behrman. The newspaper quoted leading citizens who praised the incumbent mayor for his performance. One referred to the young mayor as "the best" in the city's history. The newspaper tempered its praise of Behrman by asserting that all Regular candidates would ultimately be put in the position of choosing between the machine and the people. In this struggle, said the newspaper, the people always lost.[62]

Behrman won the 1908 general election for mayor by a wide margin over admittedly weak candidates from the Republican, Socialist, and Independence parties. Behrman garnered 25,914 votes while the other candidates combined earned fewer than 300 votes.[63] This was the first election in which municipal candidates were selected by primaries rather than party nominating conventions—a piece of election reform that was high on the priority list of Louisiana Populists and anti-machine reformers.[64] A new faction of apparently incompetent Democrats known as the Independent Democratic League attempted to use the same set of signatures to qualify all of their candidates for the ballot—an express violation of the campaign law requiring each candidate to have unique signatures. The group consisted of some leftover Home Rulers who lost to Behrman and the Regular Democratic Organization in 1904. They fought the ruling all the way to the Louisiana Supreme Court and lost, leaving Behrman and the Regulars with the aforementioned insignificant opposition in 1908.[65]

At his inauguration in December, Behrman sat with Louisiana's newly elected governor, J. Y. Sanders—later one of Behrman's fiercest and most able opponents. Sanders was a colorful and famous character in Louisiana politics. The former Speaker of the Louisiana House of Representatives and reform candidate for governor in the Democratic primary earned his law degree at Tulane. He was the youngest member of the Louisiana House of Representatives when first elected on the anti-lottery ticket in 1892.[66] Sanders signed several pieces of moral and social legislation that became part of the broader reaction against a growing saloon and brothel culture in Louisiana. He supported saloon licensing, child labor laws, and gambling reforms.[67]

While Behrman and Sanders stood on opposite sides of many issues, both men lost their fathers at an early age and quickly became high achievers. And their distaste for each other was trifling compared to the hatred between Sanders and Huey Long, who once fought each other in the elevator of Huey's favorite haunt, the Roosevelt Hotel. Huey famously called the aging Sanders "Old Buzzard Back" while Sanders referred to Huey as a master of "vituperation" and "demagoguery."[68]

4

CIVIC DEVELOPMENT
Fighting the Saffron Scourge

In the twenty-first century, challenges associated with flooding and infrastructure became front-page headlines across the United States—especially in major cities such as New Orleans and Houston. This long-standing problem can be traced back to the development patterns of urban and suburban America, all the way to the post-Reconstruction era, when many of the same cities suffered punishing revenue shortages.

After the Civil War, damaged buildings, roads, and docks in southern port cities remained in disrepair and harbors often stood empty.[1] New Orleans was one of the few ports where shipping increased, thanks primarily to the nation's consumption of cotton and sugar. Yet, the city faced unique challenges, including streets that remained "cesspools and open sewers for years."[2] Tackling such problems helped Behrman win reelection in 1908 and contributed to his national reputation for infrastructure development. He justifiably resented criticism of the city's wealthier reform class—those to whom he referred as the "silk stockings." Historian Terrence Fitzmorris notes, "The leading anti-Regular reformers of New Orleans, men like John Parker, Charles Allen Favrot, Esmond Phelps, James M. Thomson, and Donelson Caffery formed a self-conscious social and civic elite, bitterly resentful of its declining political power and the ascendency of professional politicians like Martin Behrman."[3]

The milieu of reform in New Orleans included not only efforts to control prostitution and alcohol consumption, but also new construction of water and sewer facilities, street paving, and much more. Still, the silk stockings gave Behrman little credit for his accomplishments in any of these areas. In the view of anti-machine reformers, Behrman's opposition to high license fees on saloons and resistance to closing the city's red-light district overshadowed everything else. The silk stockings, he decided, simply sought control of the levers of power. In this sense, to understand Behrman's record of accomplishment in the sometimes tedious policy area of civic development is to know the man and his opponents.

✦ ✦ ✦

Along the Gulf of Mexico, summer heat brings storms swollen with heavy rain. Big soakers blow in sideways and collide with the coastline, filling the skies with thunder and lightning. In Behrman's day, these storms filled residential cisterns—rain barrels that provided cleaner water than Lake Pontchartrain. But when the storms were too intense or lasted for too many days, city streets turned to mud. Open sewers tended to overflow, bringing diseases such as cholera, dysentery, and yellow fever.

Yellow fever was a particularly persistent problem in New Orleans. No element of society was insulated from the dreaded disease, which came to be known as the "saffron scourge" due to the yellowing of victims' skin. Some referred to it as "yellow jack" because yellow quarantine flags often flew over affected areas. In 1804, Louisiana governor William C. C. Claiborne lost his wife and daughter to yellow fever. He wrote at the time that "more than a third" of Americans in New Orleans had perished and "nearly every person from Europe who arrived in the City during the Summer Months had died."[4] Five years later, in 1809, Claiborne lost his second wife to yellow fever.[5] The deadly epidemics dated all the way back to 1796.

Even Thomas Jefferson, who espoused the strategic value of New Orleans and advocated for the Louisiana Purchase, stated there was "no spot where yellow fever is so much to be apprehended."[6] According to medical historian John Duffy, "In twelve of the thirty-five years from 1825 to 1860, no fewer than 1,000 deaths a year were attributed to the disease. . . . In each of four yellow fever seasons from 1837 to 1843 no less than 1,500 to 2,000 persons were swept away, while still another outbreak in 1847 killed 2,700."[7] Sadly, for much of the nineteenth century, the cure for yellow fever was often worse than the disease, with patients subjected to "treatments" that induced vomiting, sweating, blistering, or bleeding, and even mercury poisoning.

Unfortunately, the path to identifying the source of yellow fever and preventing additional outbreaks proceeded irregularly. Serious investigation into the cause of yellow fever began in 1871 when Dr. John Perry Wall studied the disease after losing his wife and young daughter in Tampa, Florida.

Wall was the first to conclude that the *Aedes aegypti* mosquito was the culprit and carrier of yellow fever. Dr. Carlos Juan Findlay in Havana confirmed this finding in 1881.[8] These studies were largely ignored, however, until an American commission to study yellow fever was organized. Major Walter Reed, Dr. James Carroll, and others demonstrated conclusively that mosquitos spread yellow fever. In New Orleans, the *Aedes aegypti* was found not only in urban water barrels but also in latrines, and just about anywhere water collected.

◆　◆　◆

Soon after Behrman was sworn into his first term as mayor in 1904, reports of a yellow fever outbreak came from the hospital Hotel Dieu on Tulane Avenue. The fortunate few who gained access to the hospital received the best medical care available in Louisiana.[9] Nonetheless, hundreds more became ill and death certificates piled up on the desks of health workers.[10] In the midst of the epidemic, a stranger approached Behrman during his morning ferry crossing from Algiers to city hall and said, "Buck up, Mr. Mayor. . . . show 'em a grin. If you let them see you in the dumps, some of these galoots will think things are worse than they really are."[11]

As mayor, Behrman held the weight of the city on his shoulders. Having lost both parents when he was young, and later his two-year-old daughter, Behrman had a unique perspective on life and death. He was astonished as the man joked about the body count and bragged, "I've got a bet of ten dollars next week will be higher than last week. I made the bet just to scare the fellows at Bertucci's saloon." Behrman later reflected on the conversation, remarking that there were many like the man who "seemed to think yellow fever was close to a sporting event," but it was "no laughing matter for the city as a whole."[12]

Behrman reacted quickly to news of the outbreak, meeting with public health officials, business owners, and Regular machine leaders. Together, they distributed flyers, purchased newspaper advertising, and conducted direct community outreach, block by block. Their public education campaign disseminated information regarding the newly understood causes of yellow fever. It encouraged citizens to oil and screen their water-collection cisterns to help kill mosquito eggs and larvae, and to install screen doors on the entrances to their homes.[13]

Letters poured into Behrman's office from across the state and nation. Governor Newton Blanchard wrote from Baton Rouge on September 23, 1905, asking Behrman to help his son, a doctor, who planned to visit the city "to seize this opportunity to acquire a knowledge of the disease." In his note, the governor requested that Behrman "go to see him and give him such aid as you can in the way of facilities to accomplish the object of his sojourn in the city."[14]

One concerned citizen wrote to Behrman, reporting that a neighbor on the corner of Jackson Avenue and Magazine Street had not yet screened his cistern. The block, he explained, was one of the more "conspicuous" in the Tenth Ward, and "it would be well, under the circumstances, to make an example" of the offender."[15] Other notes were more helpful than fearful, offering financial support and general expressions of concern. Many people volunteered their time, including one dutiful nurse. Upon reading of the epidemic, she wrote to Behrman, "I see from today's paper that there is a shortage of nurses to nurse yellow fever patients. If you can make use of me in the field, I will be glad to be of use."[16] Such was the spirit of a city that battled against more than a century of yellow fever epidemics.

The 1905 yellow fever epidemic was the last in New Orleans's history, and it tells the story of a city that reinvented itself, not only to fight disease, but to defend its economy. When the origins of yellow fever were unknown, outbreaks of the disease often generated product boycotts by other states due to alleged public health concerns. This included embargoes against products such as fruit, dry goods, carbolic acid, and sulphur. Yet, few believed that a freight car full of sulphur might carry yellow fever germs.[17] Behrman argued that "even when no quarantines were established in former years, we would be threatened. . . . Many of us believed this was done merely to advertise the fact that New Orleans might have yellow fever."[18]

Efforts to contain the 1905 epidemic were moderately successful. Reports vary only slightly with Behrman claiming 3,403 reported cases and 437 deaths, while historian Jo Ann Carrigan asserts that "3,400 cases and 452 deaths from yellow fever had been reported in New Orleans."[19] Outside of New Orleans, there were 6,000 cases and 500 deaths reported. Regardless of the number of victims, the impact of the 1905 yellow fever epidemic extended far beyond its immediate human toll.

During the 1905 outbreak, Behrman and the Regulars educated the public and emphasized the need for infrastructure development and community action. In so doing, they solidified popular support for the Behrman administration. As *Aedes aegypti* breeding grounds were reduced, the overall quality of life improved. Successful research and effective public health campaigns lent credibility to the idea that people should trust government to find solutions to big problems. If this meant taxing and borrowing to build roads and develop new water and sewer infrastructure, then so be it. Southeastern states even voluntarily transferred their quarantine powers to the federal government. This trend stands out as one of the many ways in which formerly rebellious southern states willingly ceded their autonomy to the federal government in pursuit of public health and safety. "I remember," recalled Behrman, "that there was a lot of talk about 'states rights' at Washington and elsewhere when we were after Federal quarantine." But, he said, "nobody in an official position in Louisiana or at Washington paid any attention to the great dangers of over-riding such states' rights."[20]

✦ ✦ ✦

New Orleans struggled with two major water issues. The first was acquiring clean drinking water, and the second was disposing of wastewater and stormwater. There was a private water company in New Orleans at the turn of the century, but it pumped water, as Behrman described, "directly from the Mississippi . . . just as it was taken from the river—unfiltered, muddy and in such a condition as to render it wholly unfit for use for cooking, bathing or for nearly any other domestic purpose." Behrman well understood the high cost of such water, how few streets and homes enjoyed the service, and the unsafe levels of water pressure at city fire hydrants. He implemented a plan to spend $30 million on the city's sewerage, water, and drainage infrastructure to overcome the city's water-related issues.[21]

In 1915, Behrman described one solution to the city's water woes at the League of American Municipalities annual conference:

The problem in New Orleans is to obtain units of very large capacity for the prompt removal of storm water. These pumps are among the strongest in the world, being intended to discharge of at least 550 cubic feet per second, each, at lifts of, respectively, five and ten feet from basin to basin at the pumping station, and at revolutions per minute of, respectively, 75 to 83½, with 6,000 volts 3-phase synchronous motors of, respectively, 600 and 1,200-horsepower, and to work without objectionable overloads at any lift from 0 up to, respectively, 8 to 13 feet.[22]

In this manner, the city began its tradition of pumping excess water from streets and canals, using a strategy that largely remains in effect today. Behrman explained that excess standing water was a major cause of yellow fever. The city's water collection barrels, for example, were "mostly open at the top" and "prolific breeding places of the stegomyia—the type of mosquito which the United States surgeons in Cuba, in 1900, discovered to be transmitters of the yellow fever germ."[23] Drainage was also important, and Behrman described the inglorious but life-saving work undertaken by his administration, noting, "At no time was the importance of establishing proper sewerage and drainage systems and providing the city with an abundant supply of pure water in any sense disregarded."[24] The problem, he said, was that constructing such utilities involved nearly insurmountable difficulties thought to be so "complex and expensive in character" as to be unobtainable.[25]

Behrman prioritized the city's costly infrastructure projects with the foremost needs being "protection against overflow, adequate supply of wholesome water, efficient systems of sewerage and drainage, perfection of wharves and landings, and construction of [a] publicly owned and operated belt railroad."[26] He financed construction of infrastructure with taxpayer funds and believed that public ownership was "an unqualified success in New Orleans."[27] Taxpayers' willingness to finance such large-scale projects was enhanced, no doubt, by the absence of a major corruption scandal in New Orleans since the "Boodle Council" controversy of the 1890s.

On September 29, 1915, a powerful hurricane made landfall in New Orleans. The event, which took place long before storms were given names, foreshadowed many of the city's future challenges in managing the fallout from tropical storms. In the wake of the storm, George Earl, general superintendent of the city's Sewerage and Water Board, "heartily endorsed" a "recommendation by the Chief Engineer of the Orleans Levee Board looking toward more substantial and higher levees for the protection of the city against lake tides."[28] The superintendent also noted that the storm caused a record high tide and that water entered the city in significant amounts at "numerous points along the various navigation and drainage outfall canals and on the rear protection levees."[29]

Calls for "more substantial and higher levees" were only partially heeded. Consequently, the race for growth and development in New Orleans resulted in partially man-made disasters. In 1918, Behrman told the National Foreign Trade Conference: "Away back yonder in the early history of Louisiana, the utility of a commercial navigable canal, connecting the Mississippi and Lake Pontchartrain was seriously considered and ultimately took shape in what is now known as the old Carondelet and Navigation Canal. This canal, extending within three quarters of a mile of the river, in the center of the old French quarter, has made no further progress in the direction of its original destination, and the idea of carrying it to the Mississippi, has, for several reasons, long been abandoned."[30] Behrman and others were determined to maximize the benefits of New Orleans's natural environment and, while the Old Basin Canal was no longer a viable water route to the Mississippi River, construction of a new canal was in the planning process. According to Behrman, the new canal would be six miles long and two hundred feet wide. It would have a thousand feet of property along each side to accommodate "industrial activities . . . and facilities."[31]

The push for a canal leading to the Mississippi River required federal support—something local members of Congress gladly provided. Behrman noted the financial and legal aspects of the project were approved by Congress as a war measure and "the bonds have already been disposed of."[32] The work, Behrman said, would be led by General George Washington Goethals, the civil engineer who oversaw construction of the Panama Canal. This point, Behrman bragged to his audience in Cincinnati, "gives assurance that not only will the work be done, but that it will be well done, and in its operation will be a perpetual monument to the public spirit and patriotism of the people of New Orleans."[33] The canal, known today as the Inner Harbor Navigation Canal, was completed in 1923 and turned out to be five-and-a-half miles long.

Behrman asserted that the city's public utilities and infrastructure were "monuments to the courage, determination and infinite resourcefulness of a people."[34] He frequently spoke of the city's significant progress in other areas such as parks, playgrounds, and "our wharves and docks, our Belt Railroad systems, our many miles of newly paved streets, our modern public schools and other institutions of learning."[35] Behrman's leadership in these areas make him a leading figure in the development of New Orleans and all of the South in the twentieth century.

Behrman's political enemies were nonetheless determined to fight his growing power. They alleged that he incompetently managed New Orleans's infrastructure projects.[36] Some accusations were minor in character, such as the complaint that city engineer W. E. Hardee incorrectly estimated the expense of building a new viaduct in Algiers. A more serious charge against Hardee was that he approved a defective drawbridge over Bayou St. John—without reviewing flawed plans drawn up by an out-of-state firm. After the bridge collapsed, a worker died, and the city was forced to pay over $20,000 combined for bridge repairs and compensation to the family of the dead man.

Despite attacks and setbacks, Behrman would not be deterred. As he predicted, the canal project and many other improvements to the city's water, sewer, and transportation infrastructure contributed to the city's economic growth. Yet such civic development brought its own unique challenges. Businesses and jobs were created in the immediate vicinity of Behrman's new canal, for example, and people chose to live nearby in what became known as the Lower Ninth Ward. The area became a lower- to middle-class community settled mostly by African Americans. With many homes constructed immediately next to the walls of the canal, a breach of levees during Hurricanes Betsy in 1965 and Katrina in 2005 flooded the Lower Ninth, causing widespread death and destruction.[37]

Although New Orleans's pumps were a tremendous innovation in the early twentieth century, their long-term impact has become a source of controversy. One observer argues that, contrary to our modern understanding, many areas of New Orleans stood slightly above sea level prior to 1913, when engineer Albert Baldwin Wood invented the Wood-screw drainage pump and a centrifugal pump. The pumps led to "anthropogenic soil subsidence," or human-induced sinking of the land.[38] Such environmental change, whether natural or artificial, continues to plague New Orleans. While hurricanes are certainly the dominant threat, severe rains alone are increasingly problematic. In 2022, dozens of news outlets covered a summer downpour that flooded streets across the city, and in 2017, the *Washington Post* reported on a storm that "dropped as much as nine inches of rain in just four hours." The resulting flood took "14 hours to drain . . . prompting 200 'life-threatening' emergency calls."[39]

✦ ✦ ✦

Street paving in New Orleans was a secondary priority for Behrman—a fact that caused the municipality to fall behind other major cities in developing modern roadways. This was a point that Behrman himself openly acknowledged and justified as a matter of setting priorities and making tough choices.[40] Nevertheless, it was politically untenable for New Orleans to leave a preponderance of its thoroughfares unpaved. The city council met twice a month, and Behrman estimated that at least two petitions for street paving were presented at each meeting. In August of 1910, approximately one hundred such petitions were actively working their way through the municipal bureaucracy.[41]

Initially, several types of materials were used to pave the major streets of New Orleans. The earliest choices included granite blocks, cobblestones, and even boards. Residential areas sometimes used different types of shells, including oyster shells and lake shells compacted to about six inches thick on top of cypress wood slabs. Later, asphalt or a clay-gravel mixture was adopted. The clay-gravel mixture soon proved no more reliable than the shell method, leaving asphalt the paving material of choice. In 1883, St. Charles Avenue became the first modern paved street in New Orleans. By 1900, New Orleans contained approximately 27 miles of granite block roads, 31 miles of cobblestone streets, over 100 miles of shell, gravel, or plank roads—but only 23 miles of asphalt. By 1910 there were 70 miles of asphalt at a cost of approximately $6.4 million—$4.2 million paid by the city, and the balance paid by private companies or individuals.[42]

Behrman seemed to enjoy getting down in the weeds on such matters. When he launched New Orleans's paving program, he approached city officials in Boston, Dallas, and other major cities to inquire about their best practices.[43] These efforts met with mixed results when he sought advice on the use of a certain petroleum solvent (naphtha) that was said to improve mixing stability in asphalt. In one response, the city engineer of Baltimore said that he could not comment on the merits of naphtha in asphalt pavement because "I have never used anything but the binder course."[44]

Such attention to detail aided the shift away from more permeable paving materials such as gravel and shells. Under Behrman's leadership, New Orleans gained cleaner streets and, in combination with better drainage, reduced disease and made roadways more navigable, particularly during rainy season. Unfortunately, one hundred years of reducing the permeability of the urban environment exacerbated flooding problems during periods of the heaviest rains, primarily because drainage infrastructure did not keep pace with growth and development in the New Orleans metropolitan area.

II.
BEER, WAR, AND SEX

5

TEMPERANCE AND PROHIBITION
A Damnable Outrage Spurs Action

As Behrman's career unfolded, he navigated a dizzying carousel of social and political change. Locally contested issues included municipal government reform, utilities regulation, forming the Sewerage and Water Board, and street paving.[1] In addition, debates over women's suffrage, alcohol prohibition, and a barrage of interrelated progressive issues resounded in New Orleans as they did across the rest of the country. For Behrman and other politicians, it was often difficult to measure public opinion on such matters.

The escalating crusade against alcohol was chief among the complexities public officials faced. Many politicians lost their jobs because they failed to properly judge in this area. In Ohio, for example, the Anti-Saloon League defeated incumbent governor Myron P. Herrick although every other Republican running statewide won their elections. Herrick had opposed the league's efforts to pass a local-option Prohibition law in that state. These issues shaped the contours of Behrman's career and those of politicians throughout the United States.[2]

Prior to the Civil War, Father Theobald Mathew, a Catholic priest from Ireland, became an early temperance leader in the United States. He frequently visited New Orleans and joined forces there with Father James Ignatius Mullon, the pastor of St. Patrick's Church. In 1841, Father Mullon founded the St. Patrick's Temperance Association to end alcohol abuse among the Irish and German communities. As with other elements of the temperance movement, the appeal was moderation, not total prohibition of alcohol. Father Mullon's goal was to ease the symptoms of alcohol abuse, including domestic violence and poverty. Ultimately, the other temperance activists believed, this would increase the respectability and acceptance of immigrant populations in New Orleans.[3]

While opposition to alcohol was stalled by the Civil War, it began regathering momentum in the closing months of the conflict.[4] The anthem of this resurgent movement was a song entitled "Come Home Father," by Henry Clay Work. Describing an alcoholic father's neglect of his children, the song played on the idea that fathers were deserting their families for the saloon: "Father, dear father, come home with me. . . . we are alone—poor Benny is dead, And gone with the angels of light; And these were the very last words that he said—'I want to kiss Papa good night.' Come home! come home! come home! Please father, dear father, come home."[5] Work's emotional composition was used in performances of *Ten Nights in a Barroom,* the popular stage production of Timothy Shay Arthur's anti-alcohol novel, *Ten Nights in a Bar-room and What I Saw There.* That same year John Stuart Mill's essay "The Subjection of Women" was published, offering an early indicator of the changing role of women in American society.

✦ ✦ ✦

Beer began to gain popularity in the historic Tremé community of New Orleans, a former plantation acquired by the city from developer Claude Tremé in 1810.[6] It was there, contiguous to the French Quarter, that George Merz built the Old Canal Steam Brewery to satisfy the growing thirst for lager beer in New Orleans. Merz's brewery was the first in the United States to be mechanically refrigerated—a demarcation point in the growth of the beer industry. After mechanical refrigeration spread to other breweries, malt beverage consumption increased significantly, contributing to the popularity of the Prohibition movement, and ultimately stimulating support for many component parts of the progressive movement.

Lager beer was crisp, clear, and less vulnerable to spoilage. It far exceeded the quality of other malt beverages. Prior to the rise of lager, consumers in New Orleans were forced to drink "city beer." Made from fermented molasses and vermouth, the quality was so poor that many people mixed it with syrup to improve the taste. Although it was cheap, city beer was manufactured without preservatives and could not be shipped because it spoiled quickly. Five breweries grew up around New Orleans to make the product. The first such brewery emerged in 1845 on Philip and Royal Streets and was appropriately called the Stadtsbreueri (City Brewery).[7]

In 1851, six years after the Stadtsbreueri began manufacturing city beer, the first lager beer was shipped to New Orleans by saloonkeeper Christian Krost, who imported it from Pittsburgh's Schenck Brewery.[8] Later, shipments from the Lemp Brewery in St. Louis, as well as breweries in Philadelphia and Milwaukee, increased the availability of lager.[9] But shipping beer to New Orleans from these distant points presented problems in the mid-nineteenth century—freezing barrels in the winter, exploding barrels in the summer—and transporting the heavy liquid wasn't cheap.[10] Such problems stimulated interest in producing lager locally, an impossible feat for most brewers in the southern heat—but not for George Merz.

Merz's brewery stood near the Carondelet Canal, excavated in 1794 by order of Spanish governor Baron de Carondelet. Later called the Old Basin Canal or Old Canal, it provided the inspiration for the brewery name: the Old Canal Steam Brewery. Merz took up the challenge of producing lager beer using cool temperatures—between 45 and 55 degrees Fahrenheit—as required by the lagering technique. This lagering process was so temperature sensitive that the availability of large quantities of ice eventually made cities such as Chicago, Pittsburgh, Milwaukee, and St. Louis famous brewing hubs. Yet even in those climates, lager brewing was often a seasonal proposition.[11]

Merz shipped ice from Maine and brewed the first lager beer in the Crescent City in 1864.[12] The expense and unsteady supply of ice drove Merz to quickly seek an alternative cooling process.[13] Merz soon hired an engineer, F. V. DeCoppet, to convert a first-generation, ether-based ice machine to cool his brewery. Using ammonia, DeCoppet cooled a forty-thousand-cubic-foot cellar to 40 degrees Fahrenheit.[14] The steam-powered contraption and similar machines helped to change the course of history, driving massive increases in the consumption of alcohol.[15]

Large national shipping breweries understood the value of mechanical cooling but adopted it gradually as technology improved. The invention of the Windhausen Refrigerating Machine in 1879 signaled the first widespread use of refrigeration. One of the early adopters was the Southern Brewery in New Orleans.[16] Most breweries, however, did not completely abandon natural ice until the 1890s. Breweries such as Anheuser-Busch, Schlitz, Blatz, and Lemp saw massive increases in production with the advent of mechanical refrigeration. Pabst, for example, increased total output over three decades by 697 percent compared to production in the year 1877.[17]

Brewers replaced their icehouses almost entirely by the late 1880s and early 1890s. While the icehouse worked better than underground storage, it did have drawbacks. In the brewery icehouse of the mid- to late nineteenth century, cold air fell through airshafts in the icehouse, forcing warm air outside the structure through a series of vents. This process occurred naturally due to the higher density of cold air. Ice storage often required an inordinate amount of physical space, and its weight required specific and expensive construction design. If the weather was too warm, ice shortages might result. If all of these issues could be addressed, a natural ice brewery still had to fight a constant battle against wet, rotting floors, mold, and the resulting odors.[18]

Significant advances in brewery technologies, growing beer production, and higher per capita rates of alcohol consumption led to calls for Prohibition. This protest movement did for women in the South what abolition did for women in the North: it normalized their engagement in politics.

❖ ❖ ❖

By 1879, Frances Willard became president of the Women's Christian Temperance Union (WCTU) and one of the most influential reformers in the United States. She worked to protect women and families from abusive husbands and the many social ills associated with excessive alcohol consumption. The WCTU fought to pass new laws and repeal provisions insulating husbands from punishment. Willard's work helped to develop a new generation of leaders. According to historian Elizabeth Pleck, women such as Elizabeth Cady Stanton and Susan B. Anthony "became interested in crimes against women in the 1850s as a result of their involvement in the women's temperance crusade."[19] They worked unsuccessfully for nearly a decade to reform divorce law in New York.[20] Outside of New York, some states passed legislation protecting families of alcohol abusers and permitting litigation against saloons. Nevertheless, even with such provisions in place, married men often avoided responsibility for their actions due to laws that mutually protected spouses from tort actions by each other.[21]

Willard also argued for a more forceful and widespread assertion of women's rights. In 1876, the WCTU began to debate the issue of women's suffrage while it simultaneously dropped calls for moderate drinking and started advocating for total prohibition of alcohol in the states. Historian Thomas

Pegram asserts that Willard's influence on reform inspired "an organization of middle-class, mainly conservative women to take bold political action and agitate for a wide variety of reforms." According to Pegram, Willard made temperance "the centerpiece of a web of women's activism." She combined Protestant values with the "ideals of Victorian womanhood" to advance suffrage and "radical political notions" related to women's issues.[22]

Willard argued that alcohol was only one of a variety of influences that were corrupting America's sacred institutions. Others included the political interests associated with the decline of religion and the growing political power of immigrants. The only way to counter such an assault was to give women the right to vote. Willard skillfully framed women's suffrage not as a radical new idea, but a conservative notion.[23] She argued that life's circumstances, not just alcohol, destroyed the drinker. Her holistic approach resulted in "prison reform, the eight-hour working day and the kindergarten."[24]

❖   ❖   ❖

With the large national shipping breweries growing rapidly, local and regional brewers sought a competitive edge.[25] They began opening saloons and restaurants of their own in order to guarantee themselves access to consumers. Such retail outlets, known as "tied houses," could be found nationwide. The Columbia Brewery in New Orleans was one of the earliest and most successful to employ this strategy to fend off competition from large national shipping breweries and gain market share.[26]

Unfortunately, the smaller brewers' "tied house" strategy resulted in a dramatic increase in the number of bars and saloons and contributed to the backlash against the industry. Large national shippers responded by purchasing retail outlets of their own. Anheuser-Busch eventually owned or controlled more than half of the outlets in St. Louis, and nearly all the outlets in Minneapolis functioned at the direction of a brewer or brewer-related entity. As a result, by 1909 saloons outnumbered schools—one for every three hundred people in the United States.[27]

Martin Behrman once proclaimed that "beer fell in bad company for a while and people blamed it for things it did not do."[28] Many Americans agreed with Behrman that beer was the least harmful of the alcoholic beverages, a sentiment rooted in the saloon method of selling spirits by individual drinks.

Though commonplace today, it was a novel idea during the Behrman era, and widely criticized for promoting drunkenness in the late nineteenth and early twentieth centuries. Behrman opposed this "saloon system," asserting "there were very serious evils in the saloon system of selling drinks."[29]

As public sentiment against alcohol and saloons began to shift, brewers sought to exploit the view that theirs was a beverage of moderation. They argued that beer was not only less harmful than spirits but offered significant health benefits.[30] In 1886, the Brewers' Association published a pamphlet proclaiming that "brewers drink more beer, and drink it more constantly" than others and that the rate of death among brewers was 40 percent lower than the population of urban areas. The claim was made that "the health of brewers is unusually good: diseases of the kidneys and liver occur rarely among them."[31] In the decade leading up to Prohibition, the Brewers' Association published yearbooks that were planned to provide education to "those concerned about temperance and prohibition."[32]

Brewers engaged in other public relations efforts. In the fall of 1912, the acclaimed pilot Tony Jannus flew from Omaha to St. Louis in his "hydroaeroplane," a Benoist Type XII airplane rigged with pontoons and wheels, to pick up and deliver a case of Falstaff beer from the mayor of St. Louis to Behrman in New Orleans. Jannus then hopscotched his way down the Mississippi River, stopping in Cape Girardeau, Missouri, and Cairo, Illinois, on his way to Louisiana, where he personally delivered the beer to Behrman. The Lemp Beer Company paid $2,500 for the promotional stunt, and photographer W. B. Trefis traveled with him. The "Birdman," as Jannus was dubbed in newspaper accounts, executed the longest-ever flight in a "hydroaeroplane." His flight was the second-ever aerial delivery of a case of beer.[33]

❖　❖　❖

As saloons grew in number and jazz music spread among New Orleans saloons and brothels, the city became a locus of racial mixing and controversy. The city already maintained a high profile on racial issues given its historic role in determining the constitutionality of racial segregation, tested in the Supreme Court case *Plessy v. Ferguson*.[34] When Theodore Roosevelt invited Booker T. Washington to the White House, the issue of racial mixing again dominated headlines across the nation. As a passionate young reformer, Roosevelt believed that Washington could be a helpful ally in addressing nagging racial tensions. After the Associated Press newswire broke the headline "Booker T. Washington, of Tuskegee, dined with the President last evening," all hell broke loose.[35]

Senator Ben Tillman of South Carolina stated publicly, "The action of President Roosevelt in entertaining that n—— will necessitate our killing a thousand n——s in the South before they will learn their place again."[36] In New Orleans, the *Times-Democrat* wrote, "When Mr. Roosevelt sits down to dinner with a negro he declares that the negro is the social equal of the white man."[37] The *New Orleans Daily States* described the Roosevelt-Washington dinner as a "studied insult to the South."[38] Years later the sting had not dissipated. When Roosevelt invited famed New Orleans reformer and child advocate Jean Gordon to the White House, she declined the offer based on the Booker T. Washington "insult."[39] It was perhaps inevitable, then, that race would become an undercurrent in the debate over alcohol and prostitution.

In Louisiana, opposition to racial mixing extended to the saloon, where Blacks and whites were forbidden from drinking together by the Gay-Shattuck Law. However, the law was often ignored in certain parts of the city. One report of the Citizens' League noted that at "1:50 p.m., Poydras and Saratoga Streets, man in charge became very abusive to Citizens League member when told he could not serve blacks and whites at any time on a license for whites only."[40]

In an ironic twist, *Plessy* and the "separate but equal" doctrine helped to create Black entrepreneurs through saloon ownership. Like their white-owned counterparts, Black-owned watering holes offered an opportunity to enter the middle class and served as sites of political organization. This caused consternation among some whites. Fear erupted into violence and even riots in cities such as Evansville, Indiana, and Atlanta, Georgia. Meanwhile, the Anti-Saloon League (ASL) executed a full-blown public relations push against the saloon itself. Forces aligned with the ASL capitalized on the saloon's potential to empower Blacks and immigrants, asserting they could not handle their liquor. Frances Willard, Upton Sinclair, and Jacob Riis all voiced similar concerns.[41]

In America's major cities, efforts to prevent mixing of the races were increasingly challenged by the evolution of jazz and blues music. Legends like Buddy Bolden, Jelly Roll Morton, and Louis Armstrong mastered their craft in the saloons, cabarets, and brothels of New Orleans's vice district.[42] Musician Danny Barker wrote, "When them madams and pimps brought their stables of women to hear [Buddy] Bolden play, each madam had different color girls in her stables. For instance, Ann Jackson featured mulatto girls; Maud Wilson featured high browns and so forth and so on. And them different stables was different colors just like a bouquet."[43] Although racial segregation continued in most saloons, Blacks and whites slowly began mixing in a handful of such establishments. With Black participation typically highly restricted to the playing of music, it was mixing nonetheless and frowned upon by "respectable" white elites.

✦ ✦ ✦

During the early phase of the Prohibition debate, beer was viewed by many as a less dangerous form of alcohol than whiskey. Beer therefore offered a middle ground for politicians in the growing battle between the wets and the drys. Politicians like Behrman could speak in favor of beer while espousing concerns about whiskey and saloons—or at least they could try.

Behrman saw the humor in both sides of the argument when it was taken to extremes. He wrote wryly of a debate that occurred during one city council meeting, describing the brewers' defense of the "working people" and their need for beer. "The brewers claimed that a tax of even $100 would hamper the sale of beer in the outlying sections of the city where the working men 'rushed the growler.' . . . I learned then that beer, which I had always looked upon as a good drink, was also absolutely necessary as food." Apparently, a beer lobbyist from the Security Brewing Company, Frank B. Thomas, called beer "liquid bread"—a claim that so angered one councilman that he retorted, "Why don't the bakers sell it. . . . I have seen people drunk from getting full on that kind of bread."[44] At other meetings, the retail grocers argued that in-town working men, not just those on the outskirts of the city, would be required to walk long distances for a beer were such measures passed.

All sides of the alcohol debate cozied up to the average Joe. Framing its own alliance with the common man, the beer industry sought to occupy a higher moral ground than the spirits producers. The industry's public relations and lobbying efforts could not, however, gloss over the problem of hyper-competition, cheap alcohol, and marketing gimmicks such as the "free lunch." Such devices appeared to be key drivers of alcohol abuse, facts the ASL used effectively to campaign against saloons. For the ASL and others, criticizing the average drinker held limited value from the standpoint of public relations and coalition building. It was far easier to demonize the saloon and the "liquor trust" than it was to target the lowly worker struggling to make a living and feed his family.

In Louisiana, there existed a diverse array of opinions regarding alcohol consumption. Catholics in the south, particularly in New Orleans, were more tolerant of alcohol than Protestants in the north, where the state headquarters of the Anti-Saloon League was located.[45] Yet, such generalizations can be exaggerated. Upon closer examination, the politics of alcohol in New Orleans reflect many of the same concerns about saloons and prostitution as those in the northern areas of the state.

Today, most historians agree that oversimplifications popularized by scholars such as Richard Hofstadter and Andrew Sinclair left little room for understanding the subtleties of the movement against alcohol and prostitution. Michael Lewis noted this shortcoming in a study of state and local liquor laws, asserting, "We picture public marches led by Carrie Nation and speakeasies frequented by urban men and women, but there are other stories about Prohibition that, although not as well known to the general population, complicate the simplistic picture of an evangelical and rural-based policy that was doomed to fail when it was taken into urban areas."[46]

Behrman was not shy about voicing his opinion that "you cannot enforce a really unpopular law."[47] The "Sunday Law" in New Orleans was such a law. Passed in 1886, the statute forbade alcohol sales on Sunday except at hotels, restaurants, boarding houses, and a few other exempt businesses that were permitted to sell light table wines.[48] For Behrman, a policy of "unobtrusive nonobservance of the law" seemed to make sense. This was the policy of mayors before him, and he continued it throughout his first term. It seemed to Behrman that the people of New Orleans were okay with such a lack of enforcement, asserting that "the way the voters voted certainly showed this to be true."[49] Behrman was likely correct in noting that breweries were supportive of such nonenforcement, but his read on public opinion was questionable.[50] Attitudes about saloons and alcohol consumption were changing, at least temporarily, among certain segments of the electorate.

As brewing and shipping methods grew more efficient, the number of local retail outlets increased. The number of saloons and barrooms in New Orleans increased to five thousand by some accounts.[51] One undated letter from the "commissioners" of the French Market Improvement Association petitioned Behrman and the city council to deny the license for a new barroom at 517 Dumaine Street. The group alleged that "there are now too many Bar Rooms in operation in this vicinity, and that same will be to the detriment of the morality of the neighborhood, and further depreciate the value of all adjacent property."[52]

Groups such as the French Market Improvement Association and the Anti-Saloon League also opposed the "free lunch"—hot or cold meals offered to saloon patrons at no cost, so long as they purchased alcohol. The free lunch was criticized nationwide as an irresistible temptation and cynical method of convincing the working class to patronize saloons and overindulge in alcohol. So it was in New Orleans, where reformers argued the "free lunch was unfair competition to boarding houses and that many men learned to drink too much because they went to the saloons for beer and free lunch."[53]

The free lunch became entangled in the issue of saloon license fees when the Cotton Screwmen's Association argued against higher license fees because the additional expense might force saloons to cut back on hot free lunches provided for dockworkers. Behrman was for the free lunch but noted that one must not "over-do the things." He described how he enjoyed free "sausages, pickles, cold ham, bread and crackers and then drank a glass of beer."[54] This high-sodium menu was no accident. Such salty snacks encouraged higher alcohol consumption. Writing after the implementation of Prohibition, Behrman described these as "happy, happy days."[55] The fight over saloon license fees in New Orleans began when the Constitutional Convention of 1898 approved a new provision permitting localities to raise the saloon fee independent of the state legislature's tax.[56]

On November 15, 1906, the Public School Alliance sent Behrman a newspaper clipping related to the high license fee, noting the issue was "uppermost in the minds of voters."[57] The article reported that the police jury of Terrebonne, Louisiana, had raised the retail liquor license from $100 to $1,000 and fulminated on the likelihood that New Orleans might soon be "solitary and alone under the control of the liquor interests."[58] The paper further opined that it was "probable that the low license system, which has bred dives, drunkenness, crimes, and suffering, will be crushed out of rural

Louisiana this year. Whether the cheap saloon, with all its temptations, is to continue dominant in New Orleans will depend in large measure whether the overwhelming sentiment against it can make itself properly felt within the walls of City Hall."[59]

Behrman did not support the $1,000 saloon license fee advocated by reformers, but he believed some increase in the fee was inevitable. As a result, he sometimes came into conflict with those he described as "brewers and saloon people." Nevertheless, they continued to offer their political support. The fight to raise saloon license fees in 1905 and 1906 did not hurt Behrman's 1908 reelection campaign. However, his leniency on enforcement issues eventually stirred the opposition of reformers such as Jean Gordon, secretary of the Citizens' League of Louisiana. Regarding the Sunday closing law, Gordon asserted, "There is no law which gives an official the right to select which laws he will or will not enforce." She further noted that it was "very important that our citizens know the laws involved in this crusade to clean up our city—especially the Sunday law, the Gay-Shattuck law, and the very important law defining the penalty to be meted out to negligent officials."[60]

❖ ❖ ❖

Final passage of the Gay-Shattuck Law in 1908 was a significant victory for temperance workers in Louisiana. Historian Alecia Long suggests the law demonstrated "how central the saloon had become to entertainment and leisure pursuits . . . in New Orleans and throughout the state."[61] Emily Epstein Landau referred to the Gay-Shattuck Law as "the most comprehensive temperance reform legislation" in Louisiana. The law focused much of its attention on the relationship between women, girls, and alcohol.[62] Women and girls could not buy or sell liquor in saloons, cabarets, and the like. Some saloons tried to disguise themselves as restaurants or hotels because of a loophole created for such establishments. Bad food and small, dirty accommodations were often the outcome.[63] The widespread notion that saloons and prostitution were closely tied together is reflected in the Louisiana law that forbade setting apart "any apartment where intoxicating liquors are sold to girls or women, or minors, or to permit girls or women, or minors, to enter or drink in any such apartment."[64]

Alcohol reforms such as Gay-Shattuck clashed with the labor movement in the beer industry, reflecting the complexity and diversity of the progressive movement. Between 1880 and 1920, the beer industry developed a vibrant labor movement of its own. A 1902 report of the Census Bureau indicates that in 1850 there were 2,347 men employed in breweries. By 1880, that number had increased to 26,220. According to the same analysis, there were 29 women employed in the industry in 1850 and the same number in 1880. In 1870, 94 children worked in the brewing industry, and by 1880 that number grew to 190.[65] Generally speaking, brewery laborers were slower to organize than in some other industries. This seems odd given the industry's explosive growth during the period. It is at least partially explained, however, by the relatively small number of people employed at each brewery. For example, the average brewery in 1870 employed only 6 workers. By 1880, the number doubled to 12 but remained small.

Brewery trade unions frequently evolved out of mutual aid societies. An early example of this type of organization was the Brewers' Mutual Aid Society of Cincinnati, founded in 1852. In 1860, an organization called the Original Brewers' and Coopers' Guard was formed. It was out of this group that the Original Brewers' and Coopers' Sick Benefit and Mutual Aid Association of New York was created. Brewery owners participated in the organization, which was focused more on taking care of immigrants with little support structure than on improving the working conditions of laborers. By 1866, a national convention of brewery workers assembled in Baltimore, but it did not yield a nationwide union. The convention advanced an agenda focused on shortening the workday to eight hours.[66] By 1868, through the agitation of brewery workers and laborers in a wide variety of industries, the U.S. Congress enacted the Eight-Hour Law, establishing an eight-hour workday for government workers. While the law was later overturned by the U.S. Supreme Court, it focused attention on the plight of workers and demonstrated the power and popularity of labor politics.

It was not until 1879 that a Cincinnati brewery workers' union issued a call for the organization of a union that would "extend over the whole of the United States." The call apparently fell on deaf ears until five unions—one each from New York, Newark, Philadelphia, Detroit, and Baltimore—met at Neidhart's Hall in Baltimore on August 29, 1886, and created the National Union of the Brewery Workmen, calling for a reduction in working hours and an increase in wages. In October, the union published the first edition of its newspaper, the *Brauer-Zeitung*. The mission of the newspaper was to provide "truthful reports of the existing evils under which the workers have suffered so long . . . give every brewery worker in the country an opportunity to inform himself in regard to our organization and its aims . . . form a connecting link among all the fellow-workmen . . . prevent misunderstandings among our large membership . . . [and] stand in a decent but determined manner for its own and the general labor interests." According to the union itself, the brewery labor movement achieved some early success:

The excessively long working hours had been reduced by a third or even more. The burden of heavy work which had formerly bent the back of the brewery workman in a few years and crippled his limbs and made his body clumsy and awkward, had been considerably lightened. He had come to be recognized as a human being, and the unworthy treatment which had been accorded to him before had given way to a more humane relationship. His wages had been increased, and on account of the reduction of the working hours he had some free time.[67]

The history of the labor movement in the brewing industry is long and colorful. Disputes arose periodically between the brewers and the labor unions, and at the local level these conflicts were sometimes violent. However, the labor movement in America's breweries continued to grow throughout the early twentieth century until the implementation of national Prohibition. By the time the United Brewery Workmen held their national convention in New York in 1908, the organization had grown to 42,570. This sum included 373 local unions and 180 branches. Between 1908 and 1910, according to a union publication, members increased "to 45,233, which are distributed in 366 local unions and 187 branches." The same publication reported that some branches were "composed entirely of women, the members of which are mostly employed in the bottled-beer industry."[68]

The United Brewery Workmen opposed Prohibition and various restrictions on the sale of beer because it "would endanger the existence of thousands of brewery workers and their families" and "cause the government to lose a revenue of millions of dollars annually." The labor union resolved not to support any candidate for public office "if he had spoken for Prohibition." The organization determined that it must help its members become citizens "in order to assist in social and political reform of our adopted fatherland." Furthermore, the union intended to promote the welfare of its members "through active participation in the political movements of the country."[69] Saloon owners and foremen could not join the union.

As labor union participation increased, so did competition for members and money. The Teamsters and others viewed beer delivery-truck drivers as belonging to their organization rather than the United Brewery Workmen. The umbrella organization for both unions, the American Federation of Labor (AFL), first ruled in favor of the Teamsters but soon reversed itself and supported the United Brewery Workmen. Other AFL member organizations sided with the Teamsters, and legal battles broke out in various cities across the nation.

In New Orleans, the Teamsters organized a local union to compete with the United Brewery Workmen, who controlled the Beer Drivers' Union No. 215. The Teamsters subsidized their workers, offering cheaper dues in an effort to drive the Beer Drivers' Local 215 out of existence. A general strike of brewery workers ensued but met with little success. The dispute was eventually resolved with the readmission of the Beer Drivers' Union No. 215 to the AFL and recognition of its proper place in the United Brewery Workmen's union by the AFL. Such jurisdictional disputes plagued the American labor movement for decades, particularly among brewery workers.

Nonetheless, the beer industry continued to grow due to ongoing technological advances beyond the revolution of mechanical refrigeration. A growing rail network and the tied-house system gave the industry a boost. And the changing tax code permitted brewers to bottle beer without kegging it first, as had previously been required for excise-tax purposes. This drove down prices, helping increase per capita consumption from fifteen gallons per year in 1895 to twenty-one gallons per year in 1913 and 1914.[70] Beer and other forms of alcohol were cheap and easy to access.

6

REFORM
The Rising Tide in New Orleans

A brisk intellectual debate surrounds southern progressivism. Political scientist Ann-Marie Szymanski disputes the idea, popular in some circles, that southern progressives were followers, and hesitant ones at that. "Southern reformers were fully capable of devising governmental solutions to perceived problems and of providing policy templates for the more 'enlightened' regions of the country.... Southern parochialism—far from being a deterrent to centralized policies—also served as a catalyst for these policies."[1] The vigorous push for progressive reform in New Orleans is consistent with Szymanski's thesis, whether initiated by Behrman and the Regulars or the anti-machine reformers.

Differences among progressives in New Orleans and those in other parts of the country are embodied in the Gordon and Werlein families. The dynamic sister duo of Jean and Kate Gordon and the husband-and-wife team of Elizabeth and Philip Werlein were at the forefront of the reform movement in New Orleans. Behrman occasionally cooperated with such leaders, particularly in the early stages of his career. Over time, however, Behrman came to see these anti-machine reformers as power seekers, while they viewed Behrman and the Regular machine as the most significant obstacle to their movement.

In 1909, a short notice in the *Lower Coast Gazette* reported: "Misses Jean and Kate Gordon have organized a woman's suffrage club at Shreveport. All of North Louisiana is to be dotted with similar organizations."[2] Indeed, the sisters worked actively for reform at the local, state, and national levels. Among progressives, however, there was sometimes disagreement on the parameters of reform, including women's suffrage.

Many reformers believed that securing the right to vote for women was integral to moving the progressive agenda forward, but they lacked consensus on *how* to attain suffrage. Kate Gordon, for example, supported women's suffrage at the state level but opposed a federal constitutional amendment.

On June 21, 1908, she wrote to Behrman requesting his support for a resolution of the National American Woman Suffrage Association. The group hoped to have its resolution "embodied" in the Democrats' platform at the 1908 convention. The resolution called for "the extension of the Elective Franchise to the women of the United States, by the States, upon the same qualifications upon which it is now accorded to men."[3] Gordon opposed many of Behrman's policies, but the two developed a working rapport in areas such as factory inspections, street paving, and more. On this occasion, the influential reformer requested Behrman's support in the event that he was appointed to the Democratic Party's Resolutions Committee, "These women are not like the women of the less fortunate States—peers of the idiot, insane and criminal,—but they are equal in the sight of their State with the men. . . . the only way women can be of service to their State and their kind, is to have a voice and equal representation to demand and command protection. [We are] earnestly hoping that you will give consideration to our request, and thanking you again for your timely help in all personal requests for the protection of women and children."[4]

Gordon's reference to "peers of the idiot" is a harsh attack on those who supported a constitutional amendment for women's suffrage. Gordon's letter highlights the states' rights emphasis, which often accompanied reform in the South, as well as a broader division over Black voting rights within the women's suffrage movement. Gordon believed it would be "a glad, free day for the South when the ballot is placed in the hands of its intelligent, cultured, pure and noble womanhood. . . . the negro as a disturbing element in politics will disappear."[5]

This was not a passing sentiment for Gordon, who was appointed to speak on behalf of those opposed to a federal constitutional amendment at an emergency convention of the National Woman Suffrage Association held in Atlantic City in 1916.[6] Her support of women's suffrage laws at the state level and opposition to federal involvement in the matter offers insight into progressivism in the South. If the federal government could mandate women's suffrage, it could also guarantee Black citizens the right to vote—an idea Gordon and many other Louisiana reformers opposed. In their view, there was nothing inconsistent or hypocritical about supporting women's rights while opposing the rights of Black voters.

Kate Gordon's legacy, like that of many progressives in the early twentieth century, is stained by racism. Without overlooking this fact, a critical consideration of her accomplishments reveals great influence in the local, state, and national reform movements of her day. For example, Gordon served as chair of a statewide campaign of the Louisiana Anti-Tuberculosis League. She led a crusade to improve ambulance service, a campaign to provide affordable drugs to the poor, and worked diligently on other public health issues affecting Louisianians. Gordon even assisted in organizing the Louisiana Society for the Prevention of Cruelty to Animals. She was instrumental, along with Behrman, in the installation of new sewers in New Orleans.[7] Although she opposed a federal suffrage amendment, Gordon was described by the *New York Times* as "the power before the throne, the medium between the head of the National Woman Suffrage Association—Miss Carrie Chapman-Catt, its president—and the outside world."[8]

Jean Gordon, Kate's sister, also engaged in expansive social work. Jean was involved in the Milne Home for destitute girls and worked for the admission of women to Tulane Medical School.[9] She also worked for the protection of child laborers. In 1906, Jean became the first woman factory inspector under the state's Child Labor Act—a bill she helped to push through the legislature.[10] Social historian Mara Keire mentions Jean Gordon as a key figure in the fight against segregated vice, along with more widely recognized figures John D. Rockefeller Jr., Jane Addams, and others.[11] As a factory inspector she encountered women that came to be known as "repeaters" who had difficulty keeping jobs and frequently turned to prostitution out of financial need.[12] Witnessing the impact of Storyville on the lives of such women fueled her opposition to the vice district.

A renowned reformer in her own right, Elizabeth Werlein differed from fellow activists Jean and Kate Gordon on women's suffrage. She supported an amendment to the U.S. Constitution giving women the right to vote. In this respect, Werlein belonged to a minority of suffrage supporters in New Orleans. Most other local reformers wanted the matter settled in the states.[13] Werlein's father was a successful businessman with the means to send his teenage daughter to Europe for an education. She studied music in Paris, enjoyed the instruction of private tutors, traveled to Russia and Africa, and rubbed elbows with royalty. She even took aviation lessons and earned a pilot's license. This was no ordinary woman by the standards of any century.

Werlein credited herself with being the first woman to fly in a plane—a plausible claim given that the New York Aero Club awarded her a set of wings, in part for her work in identifying landing fields across the state of Louisiana for the governor and the U.S. Army.[14] She served as Louisiana state chair of the National League for Women's Service and financial chair of the Women's Committee of the Council for National Defense in Louisiana, and she was the first commandant of the Red Cross in New Orleans.[15]

Elizabeth's husband, Philip Werlein, was a tireless opponent of the vice district. He led the New Orleans Progressive Union and joined with Jean Gordon to create "The One Hundred For Law Enforcement," a group of reformers, pastors, and others dedicated to vice suppression. One project involved redrawing Basin Street to hide Storyville from tourists arriving by train, thereby improving their first impressions of the city. Despite these efforts, promotional brothel directories known as Blue Books and newspaper stories in major cities across the nation increased Storyville's visibility.

✦ ✦ ✦

By 1912, the saloon and brothel had become symbols of immoral and unhealthy desires in American society—at least among many reform-minded citizens. The twin evils contributed to Behrman's first serious electoral challenge since 1904 and became issues in the campaign for mayor. Anti-machine reformers alleged that Behrman and the Regulars "ignored charges of gambling, prostitution, graft and waste in the city administration."[16] One of the city's most prominent reformers, John M. Parker, sensed an opening and organized the Good Government League. Parker enjoyed enormous goodwill among reformers in New Orleans, in part because of his long history of opposing machine politicians, dating all the way back to 1888.

Parker was Theodore Roosevelt's hunting buddy and ideological kindred spirit. And he was Behrman's constant rival for decades. Unlike Behrman, who was the orphaned son of European immigrants, Parker's family roots reached deep into the American South. One grandfather was chancellor of the Mississippi Supreme Court, and the other was a large landowner who deployed slave labor for profit. Emblematic of the fleeting consensus among white Democrats in the South, his father was a successful entrepreneur and cotton broker who participated in the anti-Republican White League until the splintering of the Democrats' coalition in the 1880s.[17]

Parker was born in Bethel Church, Mississippi, on March 16, 1863. He was educated at the Eastman Business School and employed in his father's cotton brokerage house, where he became president of the company in 1893. He served on the powerful New Orleans Cotton Exchange and managed the federal food administration program in Louisiana during World War I. Parker was a leader of the business-oriented progressive movement in New Orleans dating back to the late nineteenth century.[18] He and the anti-machine reformers condemned the Regulars for poorly managing the city's affairs, accumulating too much debt, and increasing taxes. They criticized Behrman despite his support for the Public Belt Railroad, improvements to the system of sewerage and water disposal, and new street paving."[19] Because Behrman acted as a faithful steward of many such priorities, he was not shaken by his critics.[20] He referred to Parker as one of the "outs" trying to get "in."[21] Nevertheless, when Parker organized the Good Government League immediately prior to the election of 1912, Behrman took him as a serious threat.

Behrman and the Regulars faced other concerns. Colonel Robert Ewing, the man who first recruited Behrman to run for mayor, withdrew his support over a dispute regarding the governor's race. Ewing sided with the Leaguers and took his newspaper, the *New Orleans States,* with him. The influential legislator J. M. Generally also switched loyalties after failing to gain the support of the Regulars for his campaign for district attorney.[22]

In the heat of campaigning, voters learned of an investigation of Behrman and his administration by a New York–based detective agency. When asked, representatives of the William J. Burns detective agency said only that its findings would be "sensational" and involve "prominent citizens."[23] Most Regulars viewed the investigation as a campaign ploy funded by Good Government League supporters, but Behrman handled the situation with skill.

The Burns agency was famous for exposing corruption in cities such as Detroit and San Francisco as well as bribery among state and federal officials.[24] Behrman knew it would be fruitless to attempt to discredit the agency or defend himself against as yet unnamed charges. Instead, he simply welcomed the investigation, declared his administration's transparency, and stated that he would support a grand jury if necessary.[25]

When the Burns agency finally announced its findings, supporters of the Good Government League were disappointed. No scandal emerged. There were a few minor accusations against the police for, among other things, alleged payoffs from brothels, but the promised "sensational" evidence against "prominent" citizens was underwhelming at best. The results of the investigation were revealed to the public, perhaps not coincidentally, the same week the Regulars announced their slate of candidates for the city election.[26]

Announcement of the Regular candidates overshadowed the release of the Burns agency findings. Much to the chagrin of the Good Government League and its allies in the press, the Regulars named a group of citizens with sterling business credentials. Their executive experience included service on the New Orleans Cotton Exchange, the Public Belt Railroad, and the New Orleans stock exchange. Regular candidate recruitment simply overwhelmed the Good Government League.

Stunned, the league and its allies in the press sought to combat the growing momentum behind the Regular ticket. They attacked Behrman for abandoning popular ward leaders like Alex Pujol in favor of more electable candidates and sought to discredit Regular-backed candidates who "set themselves below" Behrman on the ticket. That fact alone, said the *Item,* was "reason enough to vote against them all." League speakers further complained that the Regular ticket did not sufficiently represent all parts of the city and that there were no Irish Americans among the Regular candidates.[27]

Behrman reacted to league attacks with a calm steadiness that had, by now, become his public habit. He rested his case on the accomplishments of his first two administrations. Behrman invited voters to review his record and to consider his character and "purpose" in service to New Orleans. There was no significant rhetorical counterattack against the league's mayoral candidate, Charles Claiborne, grandson of W. C. C. Claiborne, the first territorial governor of New Orleans. The league was pleased to have a candidate of Claiborne's stature. He had previously served as vice president of the city council and chair of the city budget committee. Despite his qualifications and stance against patronage, Claiborne garnered the support of only 13,917 citizens compared to Behrman's 23,371 votes.[28] The election passed quietly and without violence or charges of voter fraud. Even Behrman's old foe from the 1904 campaign, Charles Rosen, endorsed Behrman in the waning days of his campaign.[29] The Regulars' dominant showing and their selection of candidates in the municipal election of 1912 stand as further evidence of Behrman's reform tendencies. Historian Terrence Fitzmorris notes that on the 1912 ticket "all four [candidates] were businessmen of substantial social and commercial reputations ... not tied formally to the RDO."[30]

Anti-machine reformers did have one bit of good news in 1912—winning the governor's mansion with Luther Hall. Even this victory was diminished, however, when Hall cut a deal with the Regulars in Baton Rouge and municipal reforms were watered down in New Orleans. Things would get worse for the reform faction of Democrats in Louisiana. On July 3, 1912, Theodore Roosevelt Jr. asked league leader John Parker to support his campaign for president of the United States as a member of the new Progressive Party. Describing Roosevelt as a friend of New Orleans, Parker deserted the league and accepted Roosevelt's invitation to switch parties. Within weeks Parker became Roosevelt's acknowledged Progressive political front man in the South.[31]

Parker's move was a calculated gamble—and one that he lost when Woodrow Wilson defeated Roosevelt in the presidential election of 1912. The Progressive Party was equally unsuccessful in the midterm congressional elections of 1914. Then, in 1916, Teddy Roosevelt asked Parker to be his vice presidential candidate on the Bull Moose Progressive ticket, and promptly proceeded to drop out of the race.[32] Shortly thereafter in 1916, Parker switched back to the Democrats and mounted a campaign for governor of Louisiana. Here, he suffered another disappointing loss, this time to Ruffin G. Pleasant.[33] With Parker and the anti-machine reformers' influence seemingly waning, Behrman easily won the mayoral election in 1916. Yet, Parker and the reform faction were bowed, not broken.

Roosevelt dropping out of the 1916 presidential campaign altered the dynamics of national politics. The war in Europe and Prohibition topped a long list of concerns for many Americans. In his 1916 article "The Election and Prohibition," L. Ames Brown analyzed the potential success of western progressives and their impact on the Prohibition movement. Brown's analysis, which appeared in the *North American Review,* accurately predicted that progressives would be instrumental to the success of the prohibitionists.[34] Brown noted the ideological ties between prohibitionists and progressives: "The arguments for both are of a piece, and casual study would seem to justify confidence in the expectation that the next few years will find the prohibitionist at the head of the progressive council table. He is certain to sit at the head if he is admitted at all, for the efficient political machinery which he has constructed and manipulated so skillfully will demand it inevitably."[35]

History proved Brown correct. Progressives aligned with prohibitionists to form a winning coalition that helped Woodrow Wilson win the West and another term in the White House. This coalition between progressives and prohibitionists also contributed to the congressional victories that led to national Prohibition.[36]

7

STORYVILLE
Mecca of Whores

When night fell in Storyville, inhabitants of soiled lodgings began to stir and the acrid smell of lye sometimes wafted through open windows. In the twelve-block area heralded as a "veritable Mecca of whores," prostitutes stirred the water-lye mixture and hid it under their beds for protection from violent customers. A "John" who forgot his manners might get a face full of the poisonous mixture also used to clean drains and strip flesh from animal carcasses.[1]

The Storyville vice district was home to some of the most infamous brothels and madams in the United States.[2] Its lower-end rooms, known as cribs and low dives, were usually dirty and cheap—often a basement apartment or shack. The sex offered there was fast and cheap. Sometimes intercourse could be found for as little as fifty cents.[3] On the higher end were the city's brothels and upstairs rooms in bars such as Tom Anderson's Fair Play Saloon.

The Fair Play opened in 1901, four years after Storyville was created. It quickly became the talk of New Orleans, not for the prostitutes who resided upstairs, but for its one hundred electric lights—allegedly the first such display in any saloon in the United States. Opening night drew a crowd of celebrities that included stars of film, athletics, and big-city politics. Famous and infamous patrons included Babe Ruth, Ty Cobb, and Big Tim Sullivan from Tammany Hall.[4] Anderson's saloon was a modern technological marvel and a high-profile symbol of the nexus between prostitution and alcohol in the early twentieth century.

Anderson earned the nickname "mayor" of Storyville because he controlled much of the vice there and represented the district in the state Senate.[5] Although an extraordinary figure, he was by no means unique. There was a Tom Anderson–type leader in virtually every major city in the United States. In Chicago, Mike McDonald owned a large saloon and gambling establishment that helped him to retire a multimillionaire. "King Mike," as he was known, ascended the political ladder with the election of Henry Colvin as mayor in 1873 and subsequently came to rule the city in both criminal and political enterprise.[6] In San Francisco, "Blind Boss" Buckley owned a saloon that earned the nickname "Buckley's City Hall." In 1902, the Milwaukee City Council included thirteen saloonkeepers; in Chicago nine saloon owners became aldermen; and in New York the number serving on the council was eleven.[7]

Anderson's road to the "mayorship" wound through the brothels and saloons of New Orleans. If attainment of financial and political power was the only measure of achievement, he became wildly successful. Anderson did not face exceptional trials on his way to the top. Tom Anderson was born Thomas Christopher Anderson in the Irish Channel district. Despite its name, the Irish Channel was also home to many first-generation immigrant families from Germany and Italy.[8] It was a working-class community populated by shotgun houses and dockworkers. The Irish Channel district predated the Potato Famine, but like other urban areas of the United States, it experienced an influx of Irish immigrants during that era.[9] The docks and warehouses were hangouts for some of the roughest characters in New Orleans. Originally constituting much of the city of Lafayette, the area was incorporated into New Orleans in 1852.[10] Its early inhabitants included members of the Original Dixieland Jazz Band, "the first jazz band to make a phonograph record and to go to Europe."[11]

According to Al Rose, an early scholar of Storyville history, Anderson seemed to have an innate understanding of how to work the system in his favor, and by the age of twelve, he had ingratiated himself with local law enforcement by acting as an informant. He also made money delivering newspapers, cocaine, and opium. After warnings from his friends in the police department, he apparently ceased delivering drugs to some of the early New Orleans madams, including the brothels of Kate Townsend and Hattie Hamilton.[12] Anderson must have been impressed by the operations of these houses because, by the time he was in his twenties, he was invested in the brothel of a young madam named Josie Arlington and became her frequent escort.

Anderson opened his first restaurant and bar in 1892 and a few years later unveiled a saloon called the Astoria Club in an African American section of town. The Astoria quickly earned a reputation for vice of all types and became a popular attraction for Black patrons—who remained separated from brothels in the white section through cultural and social, rather than legal, barriers. When Tom Anderson spoke, people listened. The word came to "Close all the houses 'till the heats off" or "No gambling, the police's gonna raid all the joints!"[13] By 1897, the Astoria investment with his partner, Billy Struve, had generated enough cash for him to invest in the Fair Play Saloon, which he spent several years remodeling before opening for business in 1901.[14]

At the peak of his power, Tom Anderson became a boss-like figure in the tradition of more widely studied big-city politicians of the early twentieth century. He ruled the Fourth Ward as a member of both the state Senate Ways and Means Committee and the Committee on New Orleans Affairs, never relinquishing his powerful hold over Storyville.[15] Anderson's Fair Play Saloon was unique for its electric lights, but not for its unconcealed marketing of women and girls for sex.

So-called "concert saloons" were a hallmark of Storyville and many vice districts across the United States. In such establishments, women referred to as "waiter girls" or "beer jerkers" often engaged in sex for money.[16] As payment for sex increased, so did awareness of the many "unregistered" prostitutes operating in saloons. Eventually, many reformers believed there was little to distinguish the saloon from the brothel. Opposition to the saloon brought Tom Anderson and other operators into the crosshairs of anti-prostitution activists.

In 1905, for example, there was a literal fusion of the saloon and prostitution in New Orleans when a fire in Josie Arlington's brothel displaced her employees. She relocated the girls upstairs at Tom Anderson's saloon, creating a hybrid saloon-brothel. Anderson's saloon-brothel was dubbed "the Arlington Annex," and the nickname was painted on the front of the building. Lulu White's Mahogany Hall was another fusion saloon-brothel and one of the few spaces in New Orleans where races mixed openly. Lulu's place operated from 1908 until 1920 and was one of the earliest jazz scenes in the United States. Black jazz legends such as Jelly Roll Morton could be found in many of Storyville's saloons and bordellos.

The madams of New Orleans ran some of the best-known brothels in America. Josie Arlington owned one of the higher-end brothels on Basin

Street in Storyville. She was a fixture not only among the top madams from the 1880s onward but also on the arm of Tom Anderson. In fact, it was Anderson who eventually constructed the brothel that she would run until her retirement in 1909 and that would bear her name.[17] Arlington's early days were particularly sketchy. One story describes the time she fought with a prostitute, biting off half of her opponent's ear and a portion of her lip.[18] After surviving her rough-and-tumble younger years, Arlington rose up the ladder of vice in New Orleans. She eventually purchased one of the finest houses in New Orleans. The Blue Book directory of brothels in New Orleans described her brothel, the Arlington, this way:

> Nowhere in this country will you find a more complete and thorough Sporting House than the Arlington. Absolutely and unquestionably the most decorative and costly fitted-out sporting palace ever placed before the American public. The wonderful originality of everything that goes to fit out a mansion makes it the most attractive ever seen in this or the old country. Miss Arlington, after suffering a loss of many thousand dollars through a fire, has refurnished and remodeled the entire place at an enormous expense and the mansion is now a palace fit for kings. Within the great walls of the mansion will be found the work of great artists from Europe and America. Many articles from various Expositions will also be seen and curios galore.[19]

Among the madams of Storyville, there were other equally brassy brothel owners, including Lulu White. White's famed Mahogany Hall was considered one of the elite establishments in the vice district. Al Rose describes her operation as "the most celebrated brothel in America."[20] Lulu White became known for holding elaborate formal dinners in which a single girl appeared stark naked before dinner guests—except for a pair of stylish heels—and for her "circus" performed acts of bestiality with a pet dog. Another well-known madam and acquaintance of Tom Anderson was Gertrude Dix. According to Rose, Dix served as "ex-officio administrator" of the Arlington after Miss Josie's retirement.[21] In 1928 Dix and Tom Anderson were married.

The mayor's office received many complaints about brothels and prostitution spreading throughout the city. On April 8, 1907, for example, a group of property owners and residents petitioned Behrman to force the occupants of

823 Orleans Street to vacate the premises. The group alleged that the house was "occupied by five women . . . leading an immoral life. . . . therefore, in virtue of their occupation, the said women have no right to reside in this respectable neighborhood."[22]

As the saloon morphed into the bordello, a new body of literature began to focus on the links between alcohol, prostitution and public health.[23] In New Orleans, Jean Gordon described Storyville as a "vile and shameless marketplace of fallen humanity."[24] This sentiment worked its way into political campaigns in Louisiana and across the nation as the reform impulse reached a fever pitch.

❖ ❖ ❖

Vice districts existed for several practical reasons. Although scholars do not entirely agree on the cause and effect, one explanation for the vice district's existence was a permissive attitude inside the institutions of local law enforcement. Some believe such permissiveness was tied to a quid pro quo. Prostitutes could operate but only in exchange for financial kickbacks. Others theorize that police departments found vice easier to control when it was limited to a specific district. And some in the public health community favored creation of vice districts for precisely this reason. This group saw the vice district as a kind of containment strategy permitting medical examination of prostitutes and preventing the spread of sexually transmitted disease.

Some elected officials bought into the strategy of containment. Behrman himself favored this approach, believing the orderly licensing and regulation of prostitution would prevent its spread and limit its social impact. There is also a purely economic explanation that suggests that red-light districts existed because market demand was highest in areas near downtown business and entertainment districts. That is to say, the prostitutes followed the men—and the money.[25]

When prostitution began to spread beyond its designated boundaries, calls for reform erupted. Red-light districts such as Storyville often included or were adjacent to "respectable" restaurants, theaters, and other entertainment establishments. The scholar Neil Larry Shumsky writes, "Located in and among the cribs and parlor houses, French restaurants and hot-sheet hotels, were dance-halls, variety shows, theatres and gambling dens. Respectable restaurants and cabarets adjoined brothels and low dives." According to Shumsky, "slumming" became a widespread form of amusement in middle-class America, with reputable members of the community venturing into red-light districts such as Storyville for "visual thrills."[26]

During the Behrman era, the evils of prostitution were nevertheless viewed as too great to ignore. Voters and elected officials sought to regulate prostitution because it commoditized sex. They were concerned about its demeaning and damaging effect on women. Like alcohol, prostitution destroyed marriages and families while degrading entire communities. In turn, prostitution threatened individual and public health and resulted in human trafficking and other crimes. And most important to many of the reformers of the Behrman era, prostitution eroded the morals of their sons and daughters.[27] In the late nineteenth and early twentieth centuries, such threats to children and families were taken particularly seriously. Frequent newspaper reports of children falling into the clutches of pimps and madams accelerated the push for reform.

Soon, the red-light district came to be seen not as a "reform" but rather as the source of the prostitution problem. Opponents began passing laws permitting use of civil courts of equity to hold property owners legally responsible for the use of their property. The goal was to prevent use of a property for the purposes of prostitution in the future, rather than to punish for an act that had already occurred.[28] There were several advantages to this course of action. First, it relieved prosecutors of the burden of demonstrating that the property owner had knowledge of the illicit use. Second, the consequence was immediate—the eviction of the tenant and filing a monetary bond. Third, in the event the property owners were slow to react to an injunction, the state might "oust the current tenants, auction off the furniture and fixtures, padlock the property for up to a year, and permanently prohibit its use as a brothel or saloon."[29]

These "abatement laws," as they were called, were effective because they typically permitted individual citizens to initiate legal proceedings. This prevented corrupt politicians and police departments from protecting madams and saloon owners who permitted prostitution in their establishments. Reformers pursued the strategy relentlessly, forcing property owners to abandon the practice of prostitution, whether directly or with tacit permission. The penalty for ignoring the orders of a judge in such a civil case was often the loss of one's property. Mara Keire notes, "By making landlords, real estate agents, furniture companies, and breweries responsible for the use of their property, anti-vice reformers cut into the profits of prostitution and pushed the old-fashioned parlor house into near extinction."[30] Using this line of attack, vice reformers closed segregated districts in Buffalo, Omaha, Portland, and dozens of other cities across the nation.

Madams often attempted to relocate as red-light districts began to close—a phenomenon reformers called "scatteration." However, because individual citizens could bring legal action and cases were adjudicated by a single judge rather than a jury, it was difficult to move a brothel business from place to place.[31]

Whatever the reasons for their existence, red-light districts helped to bind the anti-alcohol coalition together. Lobbyists favoring an outright ban of alcohol, including Wayne Wheeler and the Anti-Saloon League, benefited from the real and imagined association between saloons and prostitution in ways the temperance movement of the nineteenth century did not. As public awareness of the situation increased, calls for a national prohibition of alcohol grew louder.

8

AMERICAN EXPANSION
The Algiers Navy Yard

The evolution of the New Orleans Navy Yard parallels the political history of the city and the nation as a whole. America grew more powerful over the course of the nineteenth century and eventually began to project its power across the world. But that was a later development. Earlier in the century, the United States spent surprisingly little on its military, including its naval forces, relative to nations of similar size. Almost nothing was done to protect the nation's vast coastline from foreign adversaries. This began to change as the twentieth century approached, with New Orleans and Martin Behrman playing a significant role.

As settlers moved into the interior sections of the North American continent, New Orleans began to grow. Multiplying farms and plantations produced tobacco, grain, sugar, and cotton—much of which made its way downriver to New Orleans. This river traffic transformed the city into a focal point of trade in the Mississippi Valley. As the nineteenth century approached, the number of sugar plantations and enslaved persons increased in lower Louisiana, exacerbating southern reliance on slave labor—a phenomenon compounded by the growth in cotton exports. New Orleans thus became not just another slave-trading venue, but an epicenter of the slave trade.[1]

The convergence of migration, slavery, and river trade elevated New Orleans to prominence in the national economy.[2] Noting the city's status, Secretary of State Thomas Jefferson emphasized that America had a "right to some spot as an entrepot for our commerce."[3] As president a decade later, Jefferson told his ambassador to France, Robert Livingston, that "one spot" on earth would make its possessor an automatic enemy of the United States— New Orleans. "It is New Orleans through which the produce of three-eighths of our territory must pass to market, and from its fertility it will ere long yield more than half of our whole produce and contain more than half our inhabitants."[4]

For Thomas Jefferson, the strategic value of New Orleans was both economic and military in nature. He well remembered the French and British competition for land in the Ohio Country and virtually all of the Mississippi watershed. That expensive contest led to British taxation of the colonists and ultimately to the American Revolution.[5] Jefferson also had not forgotten King George's attempts to regulate colonists' access to land west of the Appalachian Mountains. In 1763, the king had asserted that "no Governor or Commander in Chief in any of our other Colonies or Plantations in America shall grant Warrants of Survey, or pass Patents for any Lands beyond the Heads of Sources of any of the Rivers which fall into the Atlantic Ocean from the West and North West, or upon any Lands whatever, which, not having been ceded to or purchased by us."[6] Complaints against such limitations on westward expansion were expressed in the Declaration of Independence, authored by none other than Jefferson himself.

James Madison, Thomas Jefferson's secretary of state, described the Mississippi River as "the Hudson, the Delaware, the Potomac, and all the navigable rivers of the Atlantic States formed into one stream."[7] Thus, when France secretly took control of Louisiana from the Spanish with the Third Treaty of San Ildefonso in October of 1800, there was great concern inside Jefferson's administration. Napoleon was ambitious, and the thought of France using New Orleans to reestablish a foothold in North America filled Jefferson and his cabinet with anxiety.[8]

In the near term, Spain continued to administer New Orleans and closed the navigation of the Mississippi River to American citizens. It cut off trade and withdrew the right of deposit—the freedom to send goods down the Mississippi River and off-load them at Spanish New Orleans for later shipment to overseas ports. This prompted Jefferson to instruct Ambassador Livingston and James Monroe to ask the French about purchasing New Orleans. The inquiry ultimately led to a transaction many historians have called the greatest real estate deal in history, the Louisiana Purchase of 1803. Napoleon's ambitions in Europe, his need for cash, and his belief that he could not have defended New Orleans against British warships all helped to secure the sale. Soon afterward, the federal government established a naval facility in New Orleans to help protect the city.[9]

The Louisiana Purchase helped to secure the commercial backbone of the central United States, and by 1822, New Orleans had one of only thirteen naval stations in the nation. Moreover, it was one of only seven naval stations with an actual navy yard and ship repair capabilities. Over the next twenty years, military planners continued to consider ways to harden New Orleans's defenses even as they unwound the navy yard and reduced the number of troops. Then, in 1846, the vulnerabilities of Gulf Coast states were accented by the Mexican War, and on February 17, 1849, 31.12 acres were purchased near Algiers Point on the Mississippi River with the plan of reestablishing a navy yard.[10] In 1852, a report by the secretary of the U.S. Navy noted that during the Mexican war "millions" could have been saved on repairs and many delays avoided if the U.S. government had owned and operated an adequate navy yard in New Orleans. A lack of funding, however, prevented construction of the facility. Many factors, including the Civil War, delayed the establishment of a navy yard near Algiers Point until near the turn of the century.[11]

After the Civil War, concern about political turbulence overseas and the preparedness of the U.S. Navy intensified. In 1880, international experts ranked America's Navy twelfth in the world, spurring Congress to approve funds for new steel ships.[12] At the same time, Louisiana congressman Adolph Meyer led an effort in Washington, DC, to refocus federal planning away from the Trans-Mississippi Indian wars toward the protection of national borders. While Congress realized that it must fund the construction of new facilities, it disagreed on the details of implementation. Challenges opening the Algiers Naval Station were compounded by lobbying from other cities such as Mobile and Pensacola seeking federal funding for their own ports and naval facilities.[13]

After studying the question of new naval facilities, a congressional commission chose New Orleans as the site for a new navy yard in 1889—a decision hailed by the *Times-Picayune* and others as a victory for "the principal commercial port of the Gulf States," demanding "protection at any cost."[14] After further delays, the federal government finally purchased an additional 212 acres in Algiers in 1893. However, construction of the new navy yard was further delayed until the beginning of the Spanish-American War, a conflict hastened by the demise of the *Maine*.

When President McKinley sent the U.S. battleship *Maine* to Havana in 1898, the U.S. Navy had already undergone significant upgrades from its lowly status in 1880. Undersecretary of the Navy William Whitney led an effort to reorganize the naval bureaucracy, destroy ships that were long past their prime, and construct twenty-two steel ships that helped the United States move its international ranking from twelve to three, behind Germany and Great Britain.[15] The United States now asserted itself in places such as Cuba, where a harsh regime was propped up by the Spanish. As rebellion spread across the island, Cuban revolutionaries became popular with the American press, and calls for intervention increased. Then, on February 15, 1898, the *Maine* exploded and sank in Havana Harbor, killing 266 sailors. The cause of the explosion was presumed to be a mine laid by the Spanish. Although definitive evidence was never found, war broke out in April.[16]

One month later, Congress authorized funding for the navy yard and dry dock in Algiers. The Maryland Steel Company was awarded the construction contract, and by June of 1899, both man and machine were finally on-site to build the Algiers Navy Yard. Congressman Meyer continued to work diligently to ensure funding of the yard and secured $689,000 in appropriations for the facility. Total spending on the Algiers yard during this initial phase was nearly $750,000, and by 1901, the Naval Dry Dock YFD-2 began its journey down the Atlantic coast of the United States to Algiers.[17]

President Theodore Roosevelt saw the need to modernize America's defenses. Around the turn of the century he proclaimed, "I believe we intend to build up a good navy, but whether we build up even a respectable little army or not I do not know; and if we fail to do so . . . we shall have to learn a bitter lesson."[18] Roosevelt initiated a major shift to reliance on a "standing battlefleet" away from coastal defenses fortified primarily by artillery. This change effected yet more modernization as consensus grew among military and civilian leadership that the continental defense of the United States alone was an insufficient strategy.

International power politics contributed to the increasing complexity and competency of the U.S. Navy. Much of this change was driven by events in Asia.[19] As Japan grew, the island nation prioritized confronting European and American hegemony, setting its eyes on China and the Philippines.[20] Such goals placed Japan squarely in opposition to the United States, which controlled the Philippines and intended to play an active role in the Pacific theater.[21]

For the United States, competing militarily and economically with Europe, China, and Japan proved an expensive endeavor. The nation's strategic quandary was how to project its power "across six thousand miles of ocean to defend interests its citizens probably regarded as insufficient to fight for."[22] Roosevelt himself did not doubt the need for a powerful, two-ocean force. He sent the Great White Fleet, a flotilla of sixteen battleships, on a circumnavigation of the globe from 1907 to 1909. Roosevelt's purpose was to impress upon Japan and the European powers that America was committed to a significant new presence on the world's oceans.

According to one account, "the President, and indeed the throngs of onlookers gathered on shore, felt a great sense of pride and exhilaration as 16 battleships of the US Atlantic Fleet, all painted white, save for gilded bows, steamed in a long, majestic column out of Hampton Roads to the open sea, flanked by their attending auxiliary ships."[23] Other ships joined various legs of the journey, and ultimately an estimated fourteen thousand sailors participated in a peaceful and impressive display of power. Unfortunately, due to the rapid evolution of naval warfare, the ships of the Great White Fleet were obsolete by the time they returned home to the United States.[24] Roosevelt's vision for America's military defenses nonetheless gained popularity. In cities such as New Orleans, community leaders argued for their share of the federal spending to transform Roosevelt's dream into reality.

❖ ❖ ❖

In October of 1901, the *Daily Picayune* remarked, "Although there has been a naval reservation at this port, just below Algiers for many years, it is only recently that the Government has decided to utilize it, and within a few days, the great floating dry dock now on its way from Baltimore, will be permanently located there." Announcing that "full-fledged" operations of the naval station would begin in less than one year, the newspaper bragged there was no doubt the New Orleans Naval Station would be "the most important on the Gulf of Mexico."[25] Its arrival on November 6, 1901, was cheered by a throng of eight thousand citizens. Some estimated that a much larger crowd of up to twelve thousand people gathered on the Mississippi River banks to greet the new dry dock.[26] The dry dock itself became a piece of American history when it was moved to Pearl Harbor and, on December 7, 1941, supported the USS *Shaw*, a Mahan-class destroyer hit by several Japanese bombs.[27]

The Algiers Naval Station's new Dry Dock YFD-2 could raise ships weighing as much as fifteen tons out of the water. In combination with the construction of housing, storage, power plant, and other facilities, it elevated New Orleans's role in America's national defense. In 1902, the federal government acquired additional land to accommodate new facilities at Algiers. In 1903, Captain J. P. Merrell, commandant of the New Orleans Naval Station, requested nearly $4 million for repairs and improvements. Of this, the Naval Station received about $3 million over the next five years.[28] In February of 1904, Congressman Meyer, a longtime supporter, passionately argued in the House of Representatives for continued funding of the yard. "The appropriations herein incorporated are very moderate," he argued. The funds were "by no means what could properly be appropriated for the speedy completion of the station but they are ample to continue the work of construction for the next fiscal year in a reasonable way," asserted the congressman.[29] Meyer, a respected Civil War general and senior member of Louisiana's congressional delegation, had led the fight for the navy yard at Algiers for decades.[30] When Meyer passed away in 1908, the Algiers Navy Yard lost its biggest advocate in Congress. When President Theodore Roosevelt left the White House that same year, the entire U.S. Navy lost its most influential ally.

After winning the presidential election of 1908, William Howard Taft promoted George von Lengerke Meyer, a patrician from Boston, to secretary of the Navy. Meyer soon called into question the usefulness of the Algiers Navy Yard. It was not lost on New Orleans's newspapers that Taft and Meyer questioned the usefulness of southern navy yards more frequently than others. Taft's Republican administration was soon accused of partisanship in allocating federal spending on naval bases, a charge that likely held some merit. Yet, irrespective of geographic considerations, problems with naval expansion dating back to Roosevelt's administration were widely acknowledged. During the tour of the Great White Fleet, critics attacked the quality of the Navy's shipbuilding programs and the administration of America's naval yards.[31] William S. Sims, a confidant of Theodore Roosevelt, was critical of the ships of the Great White Fleet: "Freeboards were too low to fight in stormy seas. Transfer conditions between powder rooms and turrets lay open, vulnerable to sparks that could accidentally ignite the charges. Turrets, though heavily armored, had ports too wide to protect the guns or their crews."[32] Sims broke informal protocol by doing much of his complaining through the press.[33] Thus, in 1907, the *Daily Picayune* editorialized, "The Navy Department has been more or less severely criticized recently on a good many points, and it must be confessed that some of the criticisms have been merited."[34] The paper argued for the adoption of modern business methods both in ship construction and in the overall management of the navy yards. In a not-so-subtle call for more work for the New Orleans Navy Yard, the newspaper suggested another problem was that the yards of other nations were supplied with projects on a consistent basis, allowing them to keep a skilled workforce gainfully employed year-round, whereas the United States failed to do so.[35]

❖ ❖ ❖

The Algiers Navy Yard remained a hot topic in New Orleans politics well into the twentieth century. As early as 1908, the argument for increased federal spending in New Orleans assumed a more parochial and defensive posture. The *Daily Picayune* claimed, "Navy Yards and Stations are not located with a view to their usefulness in time of peace, but with reference to the needs of war as far as they can be foreseen."[36] Indications from the nation's capital were that the Gulf Coast stations should be scaled back to minor repair stations and only a handful of navy yards would remain on the Atlantic. Over the next few years, the partisan siren would sound to save the New Orleans Navy Yard from such growing threats.

Late in the winter of 1911, Secretary of the Navy Meyer gave an interview to *McClure's Magazine* in which he continued his campaign for a more efficient Navy and closing southern navy yards. The *McClure's* article elicited a harsh response from the *Daily Picayune:* "While he advocates the dismantling of all the Southern yards, he asks Congress to spend huge sums of money in building up an utterly useless naval station at Guantanamo."[37] And, the paper queried, if there were truly too many yards, why not close Boston or Philadelphia, which were located so near the giant yard in New York? The bias against the South was now clearly stated. Two months later, the newspaper was openly contemptuous of a proposed $14 million expansion of the Brooklyn Navy Yard:

> The reason why the yard at Brooklyn gets the lion's share of the work is purely political. The expenditures of large sums of money there will do the dominant political party more good than would the expendi-

ture of the same amount of money elsewhere. It is this matter of expediency that explains the utter neglect of the Southern yards. These
yards could repair many of the cruisers and some of the battleships
as well as the work that could be done in the New York yard, but if
that were done the Eastern yards would lose some of the money, and
consequently, some of the political power, which they now wield in
the interest of the Republican Party.[38]

It was believed that the presence of a significant Democratic majority in the
House of Representatives would prevent closures of the southern navy yards.
All that was required, according to the *Daily Picayune,* was that southern
Democrats defend their yards as energetically as the northern Republicans
attacked them.[39] In August of 1911, the southern yards began closing. In Pensacola, half the Marines left for Honolulu and the other half for Port Royal,
and the tugboats, heavy machinery, and naval officers were all transported
to places like Guantanamo and Boston.[40] In the end, the navy yard in New
Orleans suffered a similar fate. It would not survive the Taft administration.
However, although the Algiers Navy Yard closed in September of 1911, its
future was not so grim as many were led to believe.[41]

Politicians, newspapermen, and other influential types took to calling the
idle military installation at Algiers the "Reservation," "Government Pasture,"
"Forest Reserve," and "The Old Hermitage."[42] With fierce competition from
Pensacola and Mobile, the pressure was on New Orleans's elected officials
and business leaders as well as Louisiana's members of Congress to reopen
the base. It was not only an important commercial issue but a point of civic
pride. Louisiana congressmen Henry Garland Dupré and Albert Estopinal
applied pressure to the Washington establishment while urging local leaders
to help "make the Algiers Navy-yard a great naval base" or risk losing out
to another city such as Pensacola.[43] In the face of such pressure, critics in
Washington, DC, argued that it was simply "too hot in New Orleans to get
good work the year around."[44]

Several factors suggested the South might finally receive a larger portion
of U.S. military spending. The election of Woodrow Wilson in 1912 bright-
ened the prospects of the New Orleans Navy Yard only a year after it was
closed. Wilson faced intense pressure from Senator Henry Cabot Lodge to
get the United States on a war footing.[45] In addition, the support of southern

states was imperative to Wilson's reelection. Finally, several key cabinet members hailed from southern states. Navy Secretary Josephus Daniels was from North Carolina, and Secretary of War Newton Baker was born in West Virginia, although he later moved to Ohio. In short, President Wilson and the senior leadership in his administration had every reason to give the New Orleans Navy Yard a long, hard look. The pending opening of the Panama Canal seemed to seal the deal.

Both Theodore Roosevelt and Franklin Delano Roosevelt advocated for easier access between the Atlantic and Pacific Oceans. In May of 1913 Secretary of the Navy Daniels toured the closed naval station at Algiers. In September of the same year, a front-page, above-the-fold headline of the *Daily Picayune* screamed, "ROOSEVELT IS TO VISIT NAVY-YARD AND GIVE RULING," referring to Franklin Delano Roosevelt's upcoming visit to the city. Roosevelt, then assistant secretary of the Navy, soon announced his support for the navy yard. He went further, arguing the New Orleans Navy Yard should be converted to a full-blown naval and army base "where troops destined to the Philippines, Hawaii, and the Panama Canal Zone could have temporary quarters, and from which they could embark for foreign possessions of the United States via the Panama Canal."[46] Roosevelt was of the opinion that half of the 225-acre navy yard could be used by the War Department without negatively impacting the productivity of the proposed naval base. The *Daily Picayune* reported, "If New Orleans is made a troop base there would be a large number of transports at the docks at all times, and a big business would be done in army supplies and ship repairs."[47]

Finally, in June of 1914, the state legislature authorized the Board of Commissioners of the Port of New Orleans to provide "full and exclusive use and control" of approximately 130 feet along the river for the navy yard.[48] Two months later, on August 15, 1914, the Panama Canal opened. And on January 7, 1915, the *New Orleans Herald* enthusiastically reported on the reopening of the navy yard. Under the headline "Opened Again at Last," the paper reported, "The Naval Station is finally officially declared opened and Naval Constructor H. T. Wright of the United States Navy is to take charge of the Industrial Department and is the advance guard of the official force selected to direct the operations of the Algiers plant."[49] Wright had been responsible for building the Puget Sound Navy Yard and had also recently worked on the yards in Philadelphia and Mare Island, California.

The Navy Yard Commission limited the function of the Algiers Naval Station to maintaining the Navy's New Orleans class cruisers and other boats patrolling Gulf of Mexico and Caribbean waters. Calling New Orleans "an unlikely location for a first-class naval base," the commission cited a series of arguments against locating a "base" in New Orleans, including a strong current, low elevation relative to the nearby levee, water depth, and distance from the yard to the Gulf of Mexico.[50] Even with such criticisms, the commission ultimately concluded that "New Orleans could render an important service by serving as a supply center and base for repair and refit for destroyers, submarines, light cruisers, auxiliary merchant cruisers, supply ships, transports and other auxiliaries."[51]

Shortly after the navy yard reopened, Behrman was pulled from a meeting of the Sewage and Water Board. The Louisiana Navy League was in a panic because Congressman Estopinal was prepared to kill the Navy bill. The controversial legislation increased Navy spending in the name of preparedness and funded the Algiers Navy Yard. Behrman sent a telegram to Estopinal imploring him to change his position and vote for the bill: "I urge your support, as a member of the House conference committee, of the construction program and the increase in the number of officers and men provisions in the Senate Navy Bill. The sentiment here is, in my opinion, overwhelming for preparedness along all lines and I am sure you feel as we do about it."[52] Behrman and the Regulars were at the peak of their power and wielded considerable influence with the New Orleans congressional delegation. Estopinal, who had been helpful to Behrman and the navy yard in the past, agreed to support the bill.

Behrman helped the city win back its valued navy yard and played a central role in preserving congressional funding for its ongoing operations. Not coincidentally, public satisfaction with Behrman and the Regulars was at its peak in 1916. During that year's municipal election, Behrman earned 27,466 votes with no opposition except a Socialist candidate who earned fewer than 1,000 votes.[53]

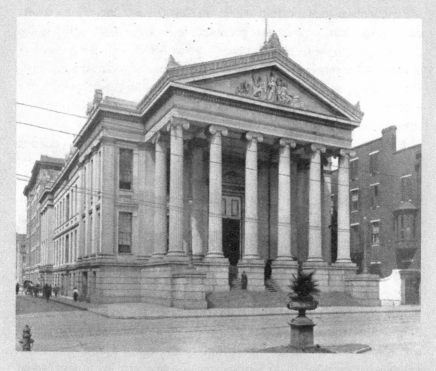

Gallier Hall served as New Orleans City Hall during the Behrman era. It was designed by New Orleans architect James Gallier and constructed between 1845 and 1853. Known for its Greek Revival architecture, it is considered one of Gallier's finest buildings. Reproduced from *Martin Behrman Administration Biography, 1904–1916* (1917).

Martin Behrman at his desk in the mayor's office, New Orleans City Hall. The Historic New Orleans Collection, Gift of Mrs. Jeanne Rabig, acc. no. 1994.115.16.

Sts. Peter and Paul Church, where Martin Behrman and Julia Collins were married. The church was erected in 1860 by its first pastor, Cornelius Moynihan. Courtesy Archdiocese of New Orleans.

Early twentieth-century pumping station drainage system. The Historic New Orleans Collection, Gift of Joel Jergins and Mrs. Eugene Delcroix, courtesy of the New Orleans Museum of Art, acc. no. 1984.189.1838.

DISCHARGE FROM ONE 12-FOOT WOOD SCREW PUMP.

TWELVE-FOOT WOOD SCREW PUMPS.

INTERIOR OF NEW DRAINAGE STATION NO. 1.
TYPICAL OF THE SIX STATIONS OF DRAINAGE SYSTEM.

The now-infamous wood screw pumps are pictured here at Drainage Station No. 1. Reproduced from *Martin Behrman Administration Biography, 1904–1916* (1917).

The Old Canal Steam Brewery, where George Merz became the first brewer in the United States to produce lager-style beer using artificial refrigeration. *Graham's Crescent City Directory 1867*, Earl K. Long Library, Louisiana Collection, University of New Orleans.

Tom Anderson, the boss of Storyville. Courtesy Hogan Jazz Archive.

Tom Anderson's Arlington Annex Restaurant in Storyville, a hybrid saloon-bordello. Courtesy Hogan Jazz Archive.

"Head of the Class." The cartoon depicts Woodrow Wilson as teacher, Secretary of War Newton Baker as a schoolboy, and Secretary of the Navy Josephus Daniels as a schoolgirl. The two men worked closely with Raymond Fosdick, head of the Commission for Training Camp Activities, to close Storyville. *St. Louis Globe-Democrat,* October, 24, 1916.

Raymond Fosdick, who launched investigations into workplaces throughout New York as a young city inspector, wrote one of the first studies on police reform in the twentieth century, and led the fight to close Storyville. He also coauthored a study that remains, even today, the foundation of alcohol regulation in much of the United States. Library of Congress Prints and Photographs Division, Washington, D.C.

TO THE PUBLIC

The Congress of the United States has prohibited the selling or giving of intoxicating liquors to the officers and men of the Army and Navy.

The undersigned, Breweries domiciled in the City of New Orleans, will not serve or sell their product to any person, firm or corporation guilty of violating this law or resorting to any subterfuge having for its purpose an evasion of liability under the Statute.

We reaffirm our belief in law enforcement, and to that end tender our services to the Department of Justice or other proper authority.

American Brewing Company
Columbia Brewing Company
Consumers Brewing Company
Dixie Brewing Company
JacKson Brewing Company
National Brewing Company
New Orleans Brewing Company
Standard Brewing Company
Union Brewing Company

Advertisement with brewers offering their "services" to the U.S. Justice Department. *New Orleans Times-Picayune,* April 10, 1918.

Mardi Gras, 1925. A child in costume with a Choctaw hat and pro-Behrman decorated wagon. Charles L. Franck Studio Collection at The Historic New Orleans Collection, acc. no. 1979.325.3889.

A PROPHECY IN 1904
—Retold After Sixteen Years of Behrman—

HERE IS A CARTOON, drawn sixteen years ago, on the day after the election of 1904, when because the free citizens of Orleans had neglected to pay their poll taxes or register Martin Behrman slipped into office by a meager majority.

The cartoon was not published.

From the depths of the artist's desk it has been brought out. Today it is shown you, as a picture of a fact that has endured for sixteen years, hindering, hampering, holding down, impeding, hurting the city of New Orleans. The city's growth has been in spite of its political system, its progress over obstacles inevitably set by Ring Rule.

The Thumb of Behrmanism will be knocked off the map of New Orleans . on September fourteenth, the city's Second Day of Independence.

"Behrmanism" cartoon. *New Orleans Times-Picayune*, 1920.

Campaign posters were plastered across the city on election day, September 14, 1920. The Historic New Orleans Collection, Gift of Waldemar S. Nelson, acc. no. 2003.0182.285.

Longtime Behrman foe John Parker addresses a crowd in the 1920 campaign for governor. Parker, with his hand on rail, debated the machine-backed Colonel Frank P. Stubbs at Jefferson Race Track. Parker made Behrman the centerpiece of his successful campaign against Stubbs. Eight months later, Parker and his allies propelled Andrew McShane to victory over Behrman in the mayoral campaign. The Historic New Orleans Collection, Gift of Waldemar S. Nelson, acc. no. 2003.0182.405.

The *Times-Picayune* front page on election day, September 14, 1920, with O.D.A. candidates featured prominently to promote the "rebirth of New Orleans." *New Orleans Times-Picayune.*

A portrait of Martin Behrman taken on November 24, 1925, approximately six weeks before his death. The Historic New Orleans Collection, Gift of Allan Phillip Jaffe, acc. no. 1981.324.7.8.

"Papa's-Gone-Home"

Late in his career, Behrman earned the nickname "Papa." Upon his death, many of Behrman's friends, and even former enemies, looked back upon his service to the city with fondness and nostalgia. The Historic New Orleans Collection, Gift of Mr. John Churchill Chase and Mr. John W. Wilds, acc. no. 1979.167.23c.

III.
LOSS AND REDEMPTION

9

A GATHERING STORM
The Commission on Training Camp Activities

John Parker and Raymond Fosdick enjoyed close relationships with powerful national allies— Parker with Theodore Roosevelt, and Fosdick with Woodrow Wilson. Working separately but toward the same end, the two men shifted the previously firm ground on which Behrman and the Regulars once stood. To know these men and their long battle with "vice" is to understand one of the major forces shaping Martin Behrman's career. They proved the maxim that what the federal government gives, it can also take away.

❖ ❖ ❖

On November 5, 1912, Woodrow Wilson became the first Democrat elected to the presidency since 1892—and one of only three Democrats to occupy the White House between 1861 and 1933. The former college professor and Princeton University president promoted his "New Freedom" agenda, narrowly defeating Theodore Roosevelt on the strength of a four-thousand-vote margin in California.

After securing the Democratic nomination in 1912, the fastidious Wilson sought to implement a strict budgetary process and clear lines of accountability for the financing of the Democratic National Committee. Who better to implement Wilson's new system of audits and accounting than his old friend Raymond Fosdick, a former examiner of accounts and commissioner of accounts in New York City? Wilson wrote to Fosdick, "I should myself feel greatly honored that a former pupil of mine, who has so distinguished himself in a position of trust, should turn to me at this time."[1]

Fosdick soon moved into DNC headquarters at the old Fifth Avenue Hotel in New York, where he assumed the position of comptroller and auditor, gaining access to Wilson's political network. Fosdick worked with future secretary of the Treasury William McAdoo. He was introduced to Josephus

Daniels, who played a central role in the reorganization of the U.S. Navy. As Navy secretary, it was Daniels, along with Secretary of War Newton Baker, who later directed Fosdick's work with the Commission on Training Camp Activities. Fosdick also met a "tall, slender, handsome young fellow of great charm—a year older than I was—a man of whom we were all deeply fond."[2] Some people called him Frank, others called him Franklin, Fosdick recalled. "Twenty years later we called him Mr. President."[3]

Fosdick was a prototypical reformer in the era historian Richard Hofstadter described as an "Age of Reform."[4] He came from a long line of reform-minded New Yorkers, including his maternal grandmother, who he described as a "born leader . . . active in the women's suffrage and temperance movements."[5] Fosdick recalled meetings "at her house, where all the women wore little bows of white ribbon as badges of the temperance cause."[6] Fosdick's paternal grandfather developed a prison-outreach ministry in Buffalo, gave lectures on temperance, and helped enslaved people in the United States escape across the Niagara River to Canada. His parents, Frank and Amie Fosdick, were dedicated Republicans. One of Fosdick's earliest childhood memories was staying up late one night in 1888 to watch his father march in a torchlight parade for presidential candidate Benjamin Harrison.

Fosdick began his collegiate career at Colgate, but unhappy with the curriculum, he soon transferred to Princeton, where a chance encounter with Woodrow Wilson changed the arc of his career. Walking across campus, Fosdick recognized Wilson and tipped his hat to the university president. Wilson returned the gesture and spoke to the unfamiliar young man, asking, "You're new here, aren't you?"[7] Fosdick replied that he was, and after exchanging niceties, the future president of the United States said, "I wish you would drop in to see me."[8] Fosdick did go to see Wilson and took advantage of the opportunity to develop a relationship with him. He also enrolled in at least one of the classes Wilson taught. The Princeton days were the beginning of a long friendship that endured beyond Wilson's White House years and lasted until the time of his death.

Woodrow Wilson's biographer, John Milton Cooper Jr., suggests the basis for the relationship between Wilson and Fosdick was Wilson's fondness for the more "serious and personable" students. "In them, Wilson could see a later generation's embodiment of himself," writes Cooper.[9] Wilson was drawn to students like Fosdick because he was working to reform the curriculum at Princeton, raise university standards, and attract more serious students.

During his college years, Fosdick had read *How the Other Half Lives,* written by the muckraking journalist and reformer Jacob Riis. He decided to explore the Lower East Side himself and witness the circumstances of the unfortunate souls who subsisted in its slums. Fosdick left some of the most poverty-stricken neighborhoods in the United States in "hot anger that life could be so ignoble and cheap."[10] He incorporated this sense of injustice into his upcoming speech for Princeton's commencement day. Standing before a "distinguished audience of trustees and guests" in Alexander Hall, including Wilson and Grover Cleveland, Fosdick condemned the "hideous inequalities" in New York City. Leaving the dais, Fosdick caught the disapproving gaze of university president Wilson. Unbeknownst to Fosdick, New York City mayor George B. McClellan, son of the Civil War general of the same name, was present to receive an honorary degree. The mayor had been forced to sit through the brash young undergraduate's harangue. McClellan apparently took no offense, approaching Fosdick and congratulating him on the speech. "I really think conditions are not quite so bad as you believe," said Mayor McClellan.[11]

Fosdick spent a year in graduate school after raising Wilson's eyebrows with his diatribe against poverty on the Lower East Side. The height of excitement during his graduate experience appears to have been the nonacademic exercise of campaigning against Tammany Hall. Standing in a horse-drawn truck across the street from the machine's headquarters, Fosdick saw a crowd pour out of the building and approach him. After cutting Fosdick's horses loose, Tammany workers lit the truck on fire and pushed it over. In taking on Tammany, Fosdick had jumped from the ivory tower without a parachute.

Soon after his scrape with Tammany Hall, Fosdick entered New York University Law School and reconnected with Lillian M. Wald, the reformer who ran the Henry Street Settlement and assisted him with his senior oration. Working with the legendary reformer, Fosdick was immersed in the world of New York progressivism, supporting Wald's efforts to help the poor of the Lower East Side at the peak of unrestricted immigration into the United States. They directed their energy to improving the medical care of schoolchildren, labor reform, and protections for immigrants.[12]

With twenty thousand immigrants per day arriving at Ellis Island, the challenges seemed overwhelming to Fosdick. Looking back, he called it the "era of the sweatshop in the garment industry" and a time when "whole families toiled during long-hour working days in disease-ridden tenements."[13] Fosdick described "narrow streets, made narrower still by endless lines of pushcarts and jostling, shoving crowds." His ominous portrayal of immigrant life included "exorbitant rents for dark and odorous tenements where health and decency were corrupted and betrayed." In such a vulnerable state, Fosdick said, new residents were oppressed and manipulated by private companies, politicians, and police. Even their fellow countrymen found them easy to exploit.[14]

Fosdick recognized his work at the Henry Street Settlement as "a kind of education I could nowhere else have obtained."[15] Through Wald and the settlement, Fosdick met leading reformers such as Jane Addams, Florence Kelley, Julia Lathrop, and Mary McDowell. He encountered Russian revolutionaries exiled by the czar and worked with young Jewish boys who were pouring out of that country with their parents into New York. "They were an engaging group," Fosdick said of the young Jewish immigrants who constituted his boys' clubs at the settlement. "I could never entice them into the gymnasium because their whole interest was in discussion and debate, and their talk ranged over a wide field of contemporary social and economic topics." He recalled the boys' desire to debate politics late into the night. Later, as successful professionals, they reminisced with Fosdick about their experiences at the Henry Street Settlement. Fosdick also joined the district Republican club for a brief period because he believed an affiliation with the Democrat-run Tammany organization was out of the question. He nonetheless took a paid position with the city of New York and was later appointed commissioner of accounts.

Fosdick was immersed in fighting corruption in New York City when 147 employees of the Triangle Shirtwaist factory died tragic and avoidable deaths while he was only blocks away. "It was a Saturday afternoon," said Fosdick, "and I happened to be in the neighborhood. Nothing that I saw at the Front in the First World War seven years later surpassed in horror that dreadful scene. It has haunted me all my life."[16] Americans were outraged. Many of the exit doors were locked, and fire escapes failed or did not exist. The fire and gruesome deaths—many of them young girls—acted as a kind of break in the dam that had been holding back reform in many parts of the nation.

It was believed that bribery among construction inspectors, compounded by the hubris of the factory owners and management, was behind the fire and the deaths. Although Fosdick was not involved in the investigation of the factory, he was motivated to do everything in his power to prevent a repeat of such a horrible event. As commissioner of accounts, Fosdick immediately began corruption investigations of the Bureau of Buildings in Manhattan. He quickly found that payoffs to building inspectors were common. One witness he subpoenaed told Fosdick that bribing inspectors was such a habit that "our men would let it go in as expenses on the time sheets."[17]

◆ ◆ ◆

Raymond Fosdick brought many new ideas about law enforcement from Europe to the United States. This was a period one scholar has labeled the "Political Era" of policing. In New Orleans and other large cities, the appointed commissioner, captain, and beat cop were often closely connected to the city's governing elite and beholden to those who controlled the levers of power. As the first decades of the early twentieth century passed, civil service reforms led to changing police principles emphasizing expertise and professionalism. This led to the Professional Era in the 1930s, which later morphed into the Community Policing Era of the 1960s and 1970s. Fosdick's research was on the cutting edge of this evolution in law enforcement.[18]

After Wilson prevailed in the general election of 1912, a new world of opportunities opened up to Fosdick. He could start his own law practice, accept an opportunity to serve in state or local government in New York, or become involved with any of several business propositions. Fosdick's contemplation of these prospects was interrupted when John D. Rockefeller Jr. called to ask for help with a study of law enforcement in Europe. Fosdick agreed. In January of 1913 Fosdick and his wife, Winifred, departed for Europe.[19] With a home base in Scotland Yard, Fosdick visited more than twenty major European cities.[20] He went on patrols, witnessed arrests, observed investigations, and participated in raids. Much of this activity related to prostitution and gambling.

Upon returning from Europe, Fosdick published his study *European Police Systems*. The book was initially published at the end of 1914 and became highly regarded in policy circles as one of the first studies of its kind. It later became part of a larger project on human trafficking in Europe, supervised by the Bureau of Social Hygiene. The study included chapters entitled "The Purpose and Function of the Police," "The Place of the Police Department in the State," and "The Organization of the Police Department," among others.[21] Fosdick concluded that a key element of European police systems' effectiveness was that "the European police are not called upon to enforce standards of conduct which do not meet with general public approval. There is little attempt to make a particular code of behavior the subject of general criminal legislation."[22]

In England, for example, a law banning the sale of liquor on Sundays would be opposed by the public, said Fosdick. To illustrate his point, Fosdick quoted an unnamed source in the Metropolitan Police Force, who asserted that such a law "would mean the demoralization of the force" because leadership could not "guarantee the integrity of the police against the vicious influences arising from unenforceable laws."[23] Fosdick soon tested this theory.

Fosdick's book served as his initial high-profile foray into questions of law enforcement and prostitution. His chapter entitled "The Integrity of the European Police" notes that "wherever the control of prostitution by regulation has been attempted it has been accompanied, if not by open corruption, at least by grave suspicions that such corruption exists."[24] Thus, well before he took on the challenge of closing Storyville, Fosdick opposed efforts to regulate prostitution as a legal or quasi-legal activity due to the likelihood that it could lead to police corruption, or suspicion of such.

In hindsight, Fosdick said, "if I had realized that this specialized interest would lead in turn to a government assignment on the Mexican border, and ... similar duty in Washington in the First World War ... I doubt if I would have had the courage or the desire to wander so far from my original pattern."[25] Indeed, the path that led Fosdick to a position of influence in national politics began, somewhat ironically, in one of the most remote regions of the country.

✦   ✦   ✦

Encamped on the Mexican border, Thirteenth U.S. Cavalry soldiers were jolted from a deep sleep by gunfire. They scrambled for their weapons and, recovering from the haze of a late-night drinking binge, fought off Pancho Villa and five hundred of his revolutionaries, or "Villistas." As the Mexicans withdrew, they attacked the town of Columbus, New Mexico. The Villistas burned, looted, and shouted, "Muerte a los Americanos!" (Death to Americans!). The smoldering remains of the town held seventeen dead Americans, and the murders were front-page news across the nation.[26] Villa and the Mexicans lost one hundred men.

Crouching in his Chihuahua, Mexico, jail cell, Pablo Lopez, the "chief lieutenant" to Pancho Villa, told an Associated Press reporter that Villa "was convinced that the United States was too cowardly to try to win Mexico by arms and believed that it would keep pitting one faction against another until we are all killed off, when our exhausted country would fall like a ripe pear into their eager hands."[27] The factions Lopez described resulted from a bloody civil war Mexicans had endured since 1910, when President Porfirio Díaz broke his promise to step down after a fraudulent election. Díaz claimed to have garnered an incredible 99 percent of votes cast. The violence that followed forced the United States to move thirty thousand troops to the border under the direction of President Taft.[28] Continued instability in Mexico resulted in further civilian and military casualties in the United States, and eventually President Wilson sent the entire U.S. Army Second Division to the border.[29]

Duty in the desolate border area brought long stretches of boredom. With few places soldiers could spend their paychecks except saloons and bordellos, newspapers soon published shocking reports about excessive drinking, patronization of prostitutes, and an alleged increase in socially transmitted diseases. In response, Secretary of War Baker called Fosdick to Washington, DC, in July of 1916 and requested that he travel to the Mexican border, acting as a personal representative of the secretary of war, to investigate the situation.[30]

Fosdick complied, first traveling to San Antonio, Texas, where he received final orders. General Frederick Funston treated Fosdick respectfully and ensured him that he would have unlimited access to the troops. Fosdick nonetheless felt that Funston and other officers in Texas viewed the mission and its leaders with skepticism. Their attitude, according to Fosdick, was that "men were men and 'sissies' were not wanted in the army."[31] The officers took to calling Fosdick "Reverend"—in a polite but mocking jest.

Fosdick was so deeply disturbed by what he found on his five-week trip that it was easy to ignore the jabs. In one month in Laredo, Texas, ten new saloons were opened. In Douglas, Arizona, liquor was sold openly to soldiers in violation of the state's dry law. Fosdick reported that "crib buildings, similar to a vicious type which I had seen in San Francisco and New Orleans during my study of police systems, were being erected in many red-light districts, and according to the police large numbers of prostitutes from all over the country were flocking into San Antonio, Laredo, and El Paso."[32]

In one town, Fosdick reported there was nothing for the soldiers to do—no movies, pool tables, libraries, books, or magazines. Only "a few disreputable saloons and a red-light district" were available to occupy their free time. "The American soldiers used to come across the railroad track in huge droves out of sheer loneliness, and resort to those institutions because there was nothing to take their place."[33] As the situation deteriorated, riots broke out around crowded brothels and saloons, and incidents of venereal disease continued to rise.

While some commanders used military police and physical space to create barriers, most officers did very little to address the proliferation of saloons and houses of prostitution near soldiers stationed along the Mexican border. Fosdick reported that many local citizens were increasingly alarmed at the situation. He cited El Paso as a specific case where locals "were concerned about the growing demoralization of their communities and looked in vain to the top army command for light and leadership."[34]

Returning to Washington, DC, Fosdick called for a comprehensive policy, issued directly from the highest levels of civilian leadership. He "advocated that all 'crib' sections be put out of bounds."[35] In a policy recommendation that foreshadowed future moves against cities such as New Orleans, Fosdick recommended "close cooperation between the army and municipal authorities in enforcing existing laws."[36] If cities and towns resisted efforts to control alcohol and prostitutes, Fosdick said, the troops should be moved to another site.

Baker approved Fosdick's recommendations, including removal of troops, where necessary, to protect them from negative influences. He issued a general order implementing the changes while Fosdick worked with local law enforcement and elected officials on the border to educate them on the War Department's new policy. The YMCA even created specific Army and Navy branches to get athletic equipment to the troops on the border. Their efforts paid off, and the situation on the border improved.

Fosdick and Baker thus created a model for one of the greatest and least known social experiments of World War I—controlling the behavior of American troops and restricting vice in the communities in which they were located. Reflecting on events at the Mexican border, Fosdick wrote to Baker to tell him the "cribs" and "fly-by-night saloons" near most camps were closed. He nonetheless cautioned the secretary that "you have had enough experience in city government to know that this *Verboten* approach isn't going to accomplish a great deal. . . . We're up against a pretty competitive situation here, and something on a pretty ambitious scale will have to be done."[37] Indeed, something grand was undertaken, but the "*Verboten* approach" remained a central tenet of their strategy.

Less than a year later, Fosdick listened inside the U.S. Capitol as President Wilson delivered his war message to Congress. The president promised the nation would fight for "the rights and liberties of small nations, for a universal dominion of right by such a concert of free peoples as shall bring peace and safety to all nations and make the world itself at last free."[38] Wilson's concept of a "universal dominion of right" introduced a new era in American foreign policy that divided his fellow progressives.

Fosdick soon departed Washington, DC, for a study of military camps in Canada. On his way out of town, he bumped into his old friend Lillian Wald of the Henry Street Settlement in New York. She was returning from a visit to Wilson at the White House, where she pled for continued neutrality on the war in Europe. Standing beside their mutual friend Jane Addams in Union Station, Wald gripped Fosdick's two arms in her hands. With watery eyes, she implored him, "Raymond, this is wicked, wicked. It must somehow be stopped."[39]

✦ ✦ ✦

On Canal Street in New Orleans, young boys excitedly distributed newspapers to businessmen and dockworkers. "PRESIDENT ASKS FOR DECLARATION OF WAR," screamed the headline. The date was April 3, 1917. The nation had been forced into the fight only after a "long series of outrages against Americans," said the *Times-Picayune*.[40] Just weeks beforehand, after months of German U-boat warfare against American shipping, a German proposal to draw Mexico into the war against the United States was discovered. The so-called Zimmerman Telegram tilted American public opinion in favor of entering the war against Germany.

Eight months after the United States entered the war, on December 4, 1917, Captain William Stanley Behrman, son of Mayor Martin Behrman, boarded the USS *George Washington* for a sixteen-day voyage across the rough winter seas of the Atlantic Ocean.[41] Traveling as part of the 313th Labor Company of American Expeditionary Forces, Captain Behrman was one of two million soldiers the Navy carried safely across the Atlantic.[42] It accomplished this task with great success—not one ship under Navy escort was torpedoed, nor any soldier injured by a German ship on the journey overseas. To accomplish the feat, 9 million tons of ships were built or purchased, and another 900,000 tons of Dutch and German ships were pressed into service by the Emergency Fleet Corporation.[43]

For the first time, all the world's great powers were engaged in simultaneous large-scale, interstate industrial warfare.[44] One expert notes that technological advances such as the development of the steam locomotive and telegraph, combined with advances in projectile design and new manufacturing processes, gave industrial warfare many unique qualities.[45] The ability to build bigger, more powerful ships and weapons, expansive railroad systems, and far-reaching communications networks required additional money. Government therefore needed the authority to enact new taxes. It also needed healthy soldiers and workers to build the weapons of war. Such needs gave progressives increased leverage to push for the suppression of prostitution and alcohol, and for new taxes.

But even with early success, the path to war was rutted with conflicting passions. The war created a schism in the progressive movement that began its demise. Lillian Wald and Jane Addams, for example, abhorred the death and destruction of war. They viewed the historic event as a course reversal for humankind. In contrast, Herbert Croly and Walter Lippmann, editors of the influential *New Republic* magazine, viewed the war as a crusade for progressive ideals. They intended to use their support for the war as leverage with the Wilson administration to implement progressive programs in the United States. Wald, Addams, and pacifist groups such as the American Union Against Militarism were on the losing side of this debate.

Indeed, for better or worse, the war's impact was felt far beyond the battlefield. The 1917 Immigration Act imposed a literacy test and a tax on immigrants. It forbade the entry of "idiots" and banned alcoholics and polygamists. German Americans, meanwhile, faced discrimination and beatings. Prostitutes were also banned from entering the United States.[46] At the same time, women's rights took a leap forward with the creation of the Women in Industry Service, and female participation in the workforce increased. During this period, eight additional states gave women the right to vote in whole or in part, and President Wilson announced his support of women's suffrage. One of the first acts of the new Congress in 1918 was to pass a women's suffrage amendment. Such changes led the president of the National Women's Trade Union League to describe the period as "the woman's age!"[47]

There were also improvements in sanitation, education, and mental health. Sanitation was directly linked to the physical health of the broader population from which America drew its soldiers. The war produced "shock" at the poor health of draftees. According to one source, 29 percent of draftees were rejected as unfit for military service.[48] On this side of the Atlantic, however, many viewed the saloons and brothels of America's vice districts as the greatest threat to America's fighting men.

✦ ✦ ✦

As war commenced, Fosdick discovered the circumstances at many Army camps were similar to those he had witnessed on the Mexican border. He noted the isolation of Camp Funston in Kansas, observing, "The nearest town has a population of three thousand." Recreation included only "a dirty moving-picture show and a dirty restaurant. All the facilities that the town could possibly develop by itself would not begin to take care of the sixty thousand men in their leisure time."[49] Contemplating his experience on the border, Fosdick was convinced that simply banning saloons and brothels was not enough to deter soldiers from engaging in risky and immoral behavior.

The proposed solution for this dilemma was the Commission on Training Camp Activities (CTCA). Secretary of War Baker credited Fosdick with the idea for the CTCA, but in his memoirs Fosdick demurred, suggesting that he served more as a contributor to the idea through his investigations of camps near the Mexican border and also in Canada. As a former mayor of Cleveland, Ohio, Baker dealt with many of the problems created by alcohol and prostitution. He was eminently capable of devising an effective strategy for the CTCA—both political and operational—particularly with Fosdick's assistance. However, Fosdick's reluctance to take credit for the creation and operation of the CTCA is likely more an act of humility toward a man he greatly respected than a matter of historical fact.

Secretary Baker told Fosdick, "We will accept as the fundamental concept of our work the fact that . . . young men spontaneously prefer to be decent, and that opportunities for wholesome recreation are the best possible cure for irregularities in conduct which arise from idleness and the baser temptations."[50] The pair took their plan for a nine-member commission to President Wilson, who not only approved of the idea but suggested the creation of a second commission for the U.S. Navy. Fosdick became chairman of both commissions. Combined, they grew to include thousands of employees.

In July of 1917, Secretary of the Navy Josephus Daniels sent a telegram to football legend Walter Camp at the Lenox Hotel in Boston. Today, Camp is considered the "father of American football." He instituted the line of scrimmage and the system of downs, modernizing the sport and contributing to its immense growth in popularity. Camp was acclaimed even in his own day, and Daniels wanted to know if he would serve on "a Navy committee with special reference to athletics and welfare work" in coordination with the Army Commission on Training Camp Activities.[51] Camp told Daniels that he would be "delighted to render any service" he could and that he would be in Washington, DC, soon. Camp's involvement became central to the CTCA's athletic work as well its promotional and public relations efforts.

Fosdick described the "two phases" of the CTCA's work. The first was positive—the construction of recreational facilities and provision of boxing tournaments, books, movies, and other activities. The second phase was negative—the suppression of "things that for years have been traditionally associated with armies and army camps."[52] Boxing was emphasized for its utility as well as its entertainment value. Fosdick believed that boxing carried obvious benefits as a form of hand-to-hand combat training: "I have seen a boxing instructor stand up before a group of two thousand men and put them through a series of evolutions that would later be tried out in sparring contests, and eventually be invaluable to them in hand-to-hand encounters out in no man's land, for there is a close relationship between boxing and bayonet fighting."[53]

Fosdick also believed that soccer developed physical skills and coordination essential to combat. He described how "a man must be ready constantly to strike the ball with either foot. In this way he naturally acquires the short gait and balance that will serve him in good stead when he comes to crossing furrowed and shell-torn stretches of devastated land."[54] The CTCA promoted other sports, including baseball, fencing, swimming, and even games of tag. According to Fosdick, these activities were helpful in developing the soldiers' "self-control, agility, mental alertness and initiative."[55]

Where possible, the CTCA relied on private organizations to help provide recreational alternatives to drinking and prostitution. The American Library Association raised $1.5 million to build and supply camp libraries.[56] Fosdick viewed libraries as an important element of the program because "on the Mexican border the men wanted books about Mexico. Now the soldiers are beginning to demand books about France; they want to know what sort of a country they are going to." In many cases it was necessary to invest taxpayer funds in CTCA endeavors. According to Fosdick, the federal government invested $500,000 in theaters and booked "the best Broadway attractions."[57]

The "hostess house" was another important CTCA project. Established in coordination with the Young Women's Christian Association, the first hostess house was apparently not popular with soldiers.[58] Cynthia Brandimarte describes hostess houses as "shelters" that "mediated public and private space . . . between soldiers and their female friends and relatives."[59] Eventually, the utility of hostess houses became self-evident and each of the thirty-two army camps in the United States contained one.

Fosdick described a hostess house at Camp Meade as "a big affair, with huge fireplaces," offering "facilities for the women visitors in camp to meet their men relatives and friends." Women previously had nowhere to meet friends, husbands, and sons, he claimed, except the "windy corners of the military base," forcing them to "parade the streets."[60] Such concern for women did not extend to protection of their civil rights because during World War I, "any American woman could be detained legally and medically examined if, in the opinion of officials of the CTCA or the Interdepartmental Social Hygiene Board, her life-style or observed or rumored sexual behavior indicated that she might be infected."[61]

Describing the CTCA's work, Fosdick asserted that, "As a result of our work, thirty-seven red-light districts in thirty-seven cities have been eliminated, and scores of cities have been cleaned up because of the attitude of the War and Navy Departments." Even New Orleans, Fosdick asserted, "which from a modern social point of view seemed almost hopeless so far as moral conditions were concerned, has been cleaned up."[62] Ironically, the CTCA's more enduring influence had little to do with illicit sex. Encouraged by Fosdick, Daniels, and Baker, Walter Camp's sports programs fostered healthy diets and daily calisthenics. High schools and colleges across the United States later used his methods to develop their own athletic programs. The CTCA is also credited with the legitimization of boxing, which, prior to the war, had been outlawed in many states.[63]

Survey Magazine called the CTCA the "the most stupendous piece of social work in modern times."[64] Yet, there were hurdles in protecting the honor of innocent women and safeguarding the morals of soldiers and sailors. Recalling the beginnings of the CTCA, Fosdick noted that "the complexion of our early work was determined—unexpectedly for me—by two sections of the Military Draft Act: sections 12 and 13, which were to have far reaching and unforeseen consequences."[65] In New Orleans, Mayor Behrman experienced those consequences firsthand.

❖   ❖   ❖

President Wilson's declaration of war brought a new level of intensity to activities at the Algiers Naval Station. The facility repaired vessels at its dry dock, functioned as a signals-intelligence gathering center, and served as a hospital. The station added new shops, storage, barracks, and more. Over one hundred officers resided there, and approximately seven hundred enlisted men utilized its firemen's and machinist's mate school for training.[66] Though Storyville was by now in decline, the declaration of war also brought the vice district into focus.

Storyville maintained its national reputation as a "veritable Mecca of whores" and survived legal challenges all the way to the U.S. Supreme Court in *L'Hote v. New Orleans.*[67] But several of the most notorious madams had moved on, and nearly every major city, and many smaller ones, now boasted its own vice district. The most significant threat to Storyville, however, was embodied in the person of a representative from Fosdick's Commission on Training Camp Activities. This gentleman appeared in Behrman's office demanding the closure of Storyville or loss of the navy yard. Behrman told the CTCA representative: "I think you'd better hold this up a while . . . until you hear further from the Secretary of War [Newton Baker]."[68] He understood, nonetheless, that Storyville's status was in danger.

To address the situation, Behrman called a meeting of key influencers in New Orleans, and behind the neoclassical columns of Gallier Hall, the city's most powerful men sat in Mayor Behrman's office. Perennial reformer John M. Parker was there. One year earlier, in 1916, Parker briefly teamed up with Teddy Roosevelt on the Bull Moose ticket. The editors of New Orleans's most widely circulated newspapers were there too—Daniel D. Moore of the *Times-Picayune* and Marshall Ballard of the *Item*. During an age when newsprint was the dominant source of information, their influence exceeded that of most politicians. The group convened to address an unusual convergence of beer, sex, and war threatening the existence of the city's cherished navy yard.

A plan was devised by the men in Gallier Hall on that August day in 1917. Mayor Behrman would take a train to Washington, DC, and make a direct appeal to Secretary of War Baker to keep Storyville open and save the treasured navy yard in the process. No objections were raised—privately or publicly— nor was dissension expressed by any of the meeting attendees during or immediately afterward. John Parker personally conveyed his faith in Behrman, and Frank B. Hayne proposed a motion of confidence. Ballard offered the motion and Moore seconded.[69] The vote was unanimous in favor of Behrman's idea for a meeting with Secretary Baker.

Behrman's trip to meet Baker took place that same month. In Baker's office sat U.S. Senators Joseph Ransdell and Robert Broussard, as well as Congressmen Henry Dupré and Albert Estopinal. Mayor Behrman argued that, rather than closing the vice district, police and military guards could patrol the perimeter of Storyville and prevent soldiers and sailors from entering its saloons and brothels. He further asserted that closing the vice district would scatter prostitutes around the city in a manner that would be impossible to control or monitor. Secretary Baker, a former mayor himself, disagreed with the scatteration theory, but consented to wait and see if Behrman's plan could succeed.[70]

It is not entirely clear what impact Behrman's trip to Washington had on Secretary Baker. We do know that, in the same month Baker met with Behrman, he refused a request by Fosdick to close Storyville. He told Fosdick the army presence in New Orleans was insufficient to order Storyville closed—and he did so even as he put the rest of the nation on notice that their vice districts were expected to close. On August 10, 1917, Baker wrote a letter addressed to "The Mayors of the Cities and the Sheriffs of the Counties in the Neighborhood of All Military Training Camps."[71] Their cooperation was expected in the enforcement "of the suppression of prostitution and the sale of alcohol to soldiers in uniform within a given radius of military posts and camps."[72] Baker emphasized that the implementation of five-mile zones increased the enforcement burden on local officials, stating, "While we have fixed a five mile radius about the camp, in which prostitution is strictly to be put down, the War Department will not tolerate evil resorts of any kind within easy reach of the camp, even though such resorts lie without the five mile zone. If places of bad repute spring up outside the five-mile limit, but fairly accessible to the camp, I shall not hesitate to insist upon their elimination."[73]

After Baker refused to order Storyville closed, Fosdick turned to Navy Secretary Daniels. In a letter dated September 12, 1917, Fosdick revealed the somewhat flimsy and highly technical nature of Baker's decision to leave Storyville open. "I tried to get the district closed because of its proximity to an army camp located nearby," Fosdick wrote to Daniels, but "the army camp was only a temporary affair, and Secretary Baker felt that action of this kind should be taken only in case the camps were of a permanent nature."[74] In a bow to the power of Mayor Behrman, Fosdick advised Daniels: "Because of the peculiar political situation in the state, I think it would be much more effective if you took this matter up with the Mayor, rather than the Governor. Only the other day the Mayor said that if you would ask him, he would close the district."[75] Going forward, the Navy secretary would play the central role in the unfolding drama surrounding the closure of Storyville, but a hitch in the federal government's plan soon revealed itself.

✦   ✦   ✦

Shortly after his election in 1912, Woodrow Wilson appointed Josephus Daniels to lead the U.S. Navy. An influential former editor of the *Raleigh News and Observer*, Daniels believed that too much thought was given to weapons of war and not enough to the well-being of individual soldiers and sailors. Daniels asserted that "every ship should be a school" where a sailor could "improve his mind, better his position and fit himself for promotion."[76]

Secretary Daniels was equally passionate about the emotional and spiritual needs of the Navy's sailors. He increased the number of chaplains and instituted Sunday religious services. On June 1, 1914, Daniels issued an order banning alcohol from Navy ships—making the U.S. Navy officially dry. According to Daniels's wife, a single incident triggered his decision to implement the ban. A young Navy officer "who had never before tasted liquor became drunk and was court martialed," she told a group of Navy and Marine Corp officers and their wives during an informal gathering.[77] Apparently, the young man's uncle was a friend of Daniels and, upon learning the news of his nephew's fate, lashed out at Daniels for confirming the court-martial. Asked if her husband was a total abstainer himself, Mrs. Daniels asserted, "Mr. Daniels does not even know the taste of any intoxicant. He is a broadminded man who took a course he thought absolutely essential to the moral and well-being of the men he loves."[78]

Mrs. Daniels told the group that her husband said to her, "If this action will save one young man from becoming a drunkard it will be worth all the criticism that will come to me from this act."[79] Such changes did not sit well with Republicans in Congress and many Navy officers who wanted the Wilson administration to focus on preparedness. While opponents saw Daniels's actions as a willful distraction from more important issues, much of the nation agreed that alcohol was a major social problem, in part because it was linked to other evils, such as prostitution.[80] Daniels had a plan to deal with both.

The Navy secretary's plan to protect America's fighting men was anchored in the recently passed Selective Service Act, which provided for war preparations, including the draft of 500,000 men. It was initially believed the act permitted both the Army and the Navy to close red-light districts near their bases. However, in May of 1917, the Navy's top lawyer, W. C. Watts, notified Daniels that the act did not, in fact, authorize the Navy to close vice districts such as Storyville.[81] A wave of confusion swept through communities across the nation, where it was unclear how the new law could apply to soldiers but not to sailors.

Reading the memo from Watts, Secretary Daniels contemplated the bad news. The problem, Watts explained, was in sections 12 and 13 of the act. The language applying to vice districts could only be construed to apply to the Army—not to the Navy.[82] Section 12 of the act authorized President Wilson to "make such regulations governing the prohibition of alcoholic liquors in or near military camps and to the officers and enlisted men of the Army as he may from time to time deem necessary or advisable."[83] This provision outlawed the sale of any intoxicating drink to military personnel in uniform and also banned the sale of "intoxicating or spirituous liquors" at any "military station, cantonment, camp, fort, post, officers' or enlisted men's club."[84] Regarding prostitution and the nation's red-light districts, section 13 provided that "the Secretary of War is hereby authorized, empowered, and directed during the present war to do everything by him deemed necessary to suppress and prevent the keeping or setting up of houses of ill fame, brothels, or bawdy houses within such distance as he may deem needful of any military camp, station, fort, post, cantonment, training, or mobilization place."[85] Notably, this section mentions only the secretary of war, not the secretary of the Navy. Analyzing this section, Judge Advocate General Watts indicated, "I have made the foregoing summary to see whether there are any provisions in the act that would indicate whether it was intended to apply to the navy or the naval forces, and it does not appear to me that it does."[86]

Watts believed that even the title of the act was a problem: "To increase temporarily the Military Establishment of the United States."[87] In *Church of the Holy Trinity v. United States,* the court held that, "Among other things which may be considered in determining the intent of the legislature is the title of the act. The court does not mean that it may be used to add to or take from the body of the statute, but it may help to interpret its meaning."[88] Concentrating on the words "Military Establishment," Watts urged that the act should apply only to the secretary of war, and therefore, only to the Army. It was the secretary of war alone who presided over the "Military Establishment." Congress had given jurisdiction over a distinctly separate "naval establishment" to the secretary of the Navy in 1798. This policy, argued Watts, gave the term "Military Establishment" in the title of the law a "signification of its own."[89]

Watts noted other distinctions between "military" and "naval" service and areas of the act where the secretary of war was mentioned but not the secretary of the Navy. For example, the punishments prescribed in sections 12 and 13 were not made applicable to Navy personnel. Watts further observed that a different piece of legislation, Senate Bill 1829, explicitly identified the "Secretary of the Navy" and "naval forces," conveying clear legislative intent. Watts concluded his lengthy analysis with these parting thoughts:

"Sections 12 and 13 of the act of May 18, 1917, have no application to the naval service. However, as it is understood that the Secretary of the Navy entertains doubt in the matter and desires an opinion of the Attorney General it would seem that the Attorney General might render an opinion."[90] Watts's conclusions about the applicability of laws protecting recruits against alcohol and prostitution were quickly submitted to the U.S. attorney general for his opinion.

✦ ✦ ✦

Secretary Daniels wrote to Attorney General Thomas Watt Gregory, describing his support for the substance of the act. "I am in full accord with the purposes of this law," Daniels told Gregory, "and would be glad if it could be held to apply, in whole or in part, to the naval forces of the United States." He continued, "Acting upon the opinion of the Judge Advocate General of the Navy, who is of the opinion that it does not so apply, I have asked the Congress to enact similar legislation that will clearly refer to the naval forces."[91] In closing, Daniels asked if sections 12 and 13 of the act applied to the Navy and requested the attorney general's response "as promptly as may be practicable."[92]

Thomas Watt Gregory began his service as President Wilson's attorney general in 1914. As the nation's top law enforcement officer during World War I, Gregory administered laws related to espionage, sedition, and trading with the enemy, and he represented the Wilson administration in Supreme Court cases involving child labor and railway labor.[93] Gregory, who later declined a nomination to the U.S. Supreme Court because he believed he lacked the temperament for the job, offered a curt reply to Daniels's inquiry. Without responding to the prostitution question, Gregory flatly stated, "I regret that I am not able to comply with your request for the reason that the question involved does not, in my judgment, arise in your department, but in the administration of my own."[94] The attorney general did offer one important opinion, however: "This department has administratively construed the provision in question [section 12, related to alcohol] as covering the entire military establishment of the United States, including the Navy and Marine Corps."[95]

In receipt of Attorney General Gregory's clipped response, Secretary Daniels followed up a week later, asking again if the prostitution provisions applied to the Navy. Gregory never answered Daniels's repeated inquiries about the applicability of the prostitution provision to the Navy.[96] The attorney general merely repeated his interpretation of the section related to alcohol "as covering the entire military establishment of the United States, including the Navy and Marine Corps."[97] Secretary Daniels and Fosdick would have to find a new path to eliminate Storyville and other vice districts.

Just days after the Selective Service Act was approved on May 18, 1917, municipal court judge E. L. Guptil sat in his chambers in Portsmouth, New Hampshire, and crafted a telegram to Secretary Daniels. He wanted to know if the sale of liquor to uniformed naval personnel had been outlawed. Guptil closed with urgency: "Important to know much confusion here."[98] Guptil was not alone in wondering what the recent orders from Washington meant for his local community. Judge Guptil received a prompt reply: "Question raised has been referred to Attorney General."[99]

Other letters and telegrams soon began pouring into Navy headquarters. On June 9, 1917, William Sheafe Chase, superintendent of the Prohibition advocacy group the International Reform Federation, wrote to Daniels on behalf of the Episcopal Church of Brooklyn, asking whether a prohibition on the sale of liquor to men in U.S. uniforms applied to the Navy as it did to the Army. Chase told Daniels, the "situation outside New York Navy Yard serious."[100] Around the same time, a Brooklyn lawyer named Adam Christmann Jr. wrote Daniels on behalf of "a few saloon keepers" requesting more information regarding the sale of intoxicating drinks to soldiers and sailors.[101]

Finally, on June 8, 1917, the judge advocate general sent an "Alnav," a telegram informing the entire U.S. Navy of the attorney general's ruling that section 12 of the Selective Draft Act (relating to alcohol) covered the "entire military establishment, including the Navy," and by June 9, the office of the judge advocate general replied to William Sheafe Chase and saloon lawyer Adam Christmann, informing them of the attorney general's interpretation: section 12 did, in fact, apply to the Navy.[102] Sailors in uniform could no longer be served alcohol. The rest of June and July of 1917 passed without much progress on the question of prostitution as it was addressed in section 13 of the Selective Service Act.

As days turned into weeks, and weeks into months, Fosdick's desire to close Storyville grew. The Citizens' League in New Orleans regularly contacted him to complain about the vice district. Around the time of Behrman's trip to meet with Secretary of War Baker, one of the group's leaders, William Railey, wired Fosdick asking "what answer" Secretary Baker had given.[103] In a later communication, Railey added, "The Naval Station at Algiers ... is the darling of the Mayor's heart."[104]

Writing to Navy Secretary Daniels in August, Fosdick emphasized that "the Army law has not been made applicable to the Navy." He included key language from a presidential order on the matter: "The President directs that the term 'military camps' employed in the regulations ... shall be construed to refer only to cantonments or camps established for the mobilization and training of divisions of the National Army or divisions composed of members of the National Guard."[105] In other words, President Wilson himself confirmed in writing that the U.S. Navy had no legal authority to shutter Storyville. Fosdick told the president that, if Congress passed new legislation "in New Orleans, we shall be able to close the segregated district."[106]

According to Fosdick, President Wilson was "deeply and personally interested" in the work of the CTCA.[107] Wilson often wrote to Fosdick, either to inquire about the commission's progress or to make suggestions. Although Fosdick worked directly for Secretary of War Baker and Secretary of the Navy Daniels, he frequently met privately with the president at the White House. Fosdick declared that "the President never bothered about official channels" when it came to the CTCA.[108] Frequently typing on his own personal typewriter, Wilson alerted Fosdick to his concerns about issues such as discrimination against Black soldiers or the commission's neglect of "moving pictures" as a source of entertainment for soldiers and sailors.[109]

Secretaries Baker and Daniels well understood the close relationship between President Wilson and Fosdick. When Prime Minister Georges Clemenceau expressed interest in "the creation of special houses" of prostitution in France to reduce the transmission of socially transmitted diseases, Fosdick shared the letter with Secretary Daniels. After reading Clemenceau's letter twice, Daniels told Fosdick with "a half smile," "For God's sake, Raymond, don't show this to the President or he'll stop the war."[110]

10

THE TRICKS AIN'T WALKING
Closing Time in Storyville

As the first American soldiers landed in France, Fosdick still had not overcome Behrman's resistance to closing Storyville. Seeking additional leverage over the mayor, he asked Secretary Daniels to seek new federal legislation applying the Selective Service Act's prostitution language to the Navy. On September 4, 1917, Secretary Daniels complied, ordering Judge Advocate General Watts to prepare a letter to President Wilson requesting Fosdick's proposed legislation.[1]

After corresponding with President Wilson, Secretary Daniels wrote to Louisiana governor Ruffin Pleasant, asking him to intervene in the matter of closing Storyville.[2] He began, "I am sure you will agree with me that we should see to it that the young men who have enlisted in the military and naval services of the country should be shielded from these temptations to immoral conduct which, in some instances have done more to undermine the fighting strength of an army than the bullets of the enemy." Daniels went on to describe efforts to "safeguard the morals" of soldiers and sailors and the efforts that had been undertaken to preserve them. He informed Governor Pleasant of the CTCA investigation of New Orleans and the "vicious" nature of the situation in that city. It was one of the worst in the nation, Daniels observed. He said that he was appealing to the governor "to close the restricted district because of its proximity to the Navy Yard," accounting for the great number of sailors who patronized the brothels. Daniels included a report showing addresses and dates when sailors were observed patronizing such houses of prostitution "and drinking in them." Telling Governor Pleasant of his "intense" desire to close Storyville, Daniels relayed his intention to send Behrman a copy of his letter, hoping for "immediate action." As promised, Daniels forwarded a copy of the letter to Behrman, suggesting that New Orleans "co-operate."[3]

With federal legislation empowering Secretary Daniels to close Storyville imminent, Behrman penned his response on October 1, 1917. He explained to Secretary Daniels that, because Storyville was created by city ordinance, it would also have to be dissolved by ordinance. "I will cause to be introduced, tomorrow night, the necessary ordinance of abolition."[4] Behrman's order closing the district was presented to the city council on October 2. Four days later, on October 6, 1917, Congress approved "An Act to Promote the Efficiency of the United States Navy," giving Secretary Daniels congressional authority to shutter Storyville. The act amended the Selective Service Act approved five months earlier, construing sections 12 and 13 of the previously passed selective-draft act to mean that:

> the word "Army" shall extend to and include "Navy"; the word "military" shall include "naval"; "Article of War" shall include "Articles for the Government of the Navy"; the words "camps, station, cantonment, camp, fort, post, officers' or enlisted men's club," in section twelve, and "camp, station, fort, post, cantonment, training, or mobilization place," in section thirteen, shall include such places under naval jurisdiction as the President may prescribe, and the powers therein conferred upon the Secretary of War with regard to the military service are hereby conferred upon the Secretary of the Navy with regard to the naval service.[5]

The ordinance abolishing Storyville passed the city council on October 10, 1917.[6] A short, one-paragraph story in the *Times-Picayune* noted, "Closing of District Is War Measure," and "the request of Secretary Daniels is taken to mean the local naval station is to become a more important post. Already there are 1400 skilled workman and 600 enlisted men of the navy there."[7]

According to legend, Tom Anderson told the denizens of Storyville, "the handwriting is on the wall. . . . the tricks ain't walking and the johns are squawking."[8] Storyville, the most visible vice district in the United States, was closed, and a message was sent to cities such as Philadelphia and San Francisco that resistance to pressure from the armed forces was futile. They should immediately close their own vice districts. Fosdick reflected on the closing of Storyville as a watershed moment for the CTCA and took a jab at Behrman: "New Orleans, whose notorious red-light district, covering twenty-eight city blocks, had not been disturbed in more than half a century, put up a strenuous fight, and the mayor of the city made two trips to Washington to argue with us about 'the God-given right of men to be men.' It was not until November 1917 that the district was ultimately closed, and the incident was noted through the country as a final and complete indication of the government's attitude. Never thereafter was its sincerity questioned."[9] The government's argument for this unprecedented social experiment was built on the catch phrase "Fit to Fight." In the near term, it was an effective strategy. Through its Social Hygiene Division, the CTCA was able to drive the rate of venereal disease in training camps to the lowest in the military's history. And drunkenness "no longer represented a serious situation," according to Fosdick.[10]

On October 18, Navy Secretary Daniels responded to the closure of Storyville with a letter to Behrman, claiming: "The last session of Congress, as you know, passed an act which would prevent the location of any houses of ill-fame near any camp, and also giving large powers to the Secretary of War and Secretary of the Navy. I need not tell you that it is most gratifying to me that you have acted in this matter so promptly that it has not been necessary for me to act under Sections 12 and 13 of the Act of Congress."[11] Daniels's muscle flexing was an act of deception because the act was not amended to include the Navy until after Behrman closed Storyville. It is true, however, that Behrman saw the "handwriting on the wall." Ultimately, he could not withstand the weight of the U.S. military in a time of war.

Behrman's compliance in closing Storyville came only after months of resistance. This must have annoyed Secretary Daniels, who had worked with New Orleans's congressional delegation and Behrman for several years to build up the Algiers Navy Yard. In previous years, Secretary Daniels had been attacked by politicians and newspapers alike for his support of the navy yard in New Orleans. For example, Woodrow Wilson's enemies alleged he moved Navy jobs from Portsmouth, New Hampshire, to New Orleans in retaliation for his defeat in the Granite State during the presidential election. Daniels retorted that Portsmouth employed more people under Wilson than it had under Taft.[12] Nevertheless, such accusations constituted a frequent Republican line of attack against the Wilson administration, perhaps making Behrman's reticence to acquiesce to the demands of the CTCA all the more frustrating to Daniels and Fosdick.

Fosdick and Daniels used the Storyville template across the United States. According to one government official: "Ninety-one red-light districts have been wiped out of existence through representatives of the Law Enforcement Division [of the CTCA] acting in cooperation with the Department of Justice. It should be added, however, that a large proportion of these have been abolished simply by local action after the request or *pressure* had come from representatives of the War Department."[13] "Pressure" is the operative word. Army and Navy bases injected cash into communities, bending local leaders to the will of Washington officials such as Fosdick, Daniels, and Baker. This fact was alluded to by Fosdick himself, as well as by William Zinsser, a director in the Section on Men's Work of the Social Hygiene Division of the CTCA, and by Walter Clarke, a first lieutenant in the Sanitary Corps of the U.S. Navy.[14] Another official proclaimed, "Even that Gibraltar of commercialized vice, notorious not only on this continent but abroad, the New Orleans district, which comprised twenty-four solid blocks given over to human degradation and lust and housing six to eight hundred women, has gone down with the rest."[15]

Fosdick hoped the CTCA would forever change the cities and towns where its reforms were implemented. The South, including New Orleans, was a particular focus for Fosdick and the CTCA. He believed that the South lacked "cohesiveness" and needed to implement meaningful community programs that might serve as alternatives to the saloon and the bordello. He wrote, "I cannot help thinking that through this community work in the neighborhood of military camps, we are making a permanent addition to the life of the towns that will last long after our war camps have been forgotten."[16] Whether Fosdick attributed the South's supposed lack of cohesion to its history of racial division, its strong agricultural tradition, or something else is not clear. Regardless, his comments appear to betray some common prejudices against the region.

Fosdick's leadership of the crusade against vice districts contains within itself an unexplained contradiction. In his memoir, Fosdick recalled a class taught by Woodrow Wilson at Princeton. "Morality," Wilson said to his students, "is a great deal bigger than law." He continued: "The individual morality is the sense of right or wrong of one man. The social morality must strike an average. This is where reformers make their tragic mistake. There can be no compromise in individual morality; but there *has* to be a compromise, an average, in social morality."[17] Contemplating Wilson's words, Fosdick asked, "Is it any wonder that a man who taught this kind of doctrine . . . described the proposed prohibition law as unworkable and sent it back to the Congress with a stern veto?"[18] Yet, Fosdick and Wilson together imposed the same unflinching reform on American troops and communities from coast to coast.

✦ ✦ ✦

Closing Storyville did not end the fight over prostitution and alcohol. The battle raged across the nation. On the East Coast, for example, Senator Park Trammell of Florida wired Secretary Daniels seeking a revocation of what he believed was the order to close Tampa's saloons. There was no regular naval station in Tampa, he reminded the Navy secretary. Furthermore, Trammell argued, a naval reserve office in the city had only nine men. A radio station at Palmetto Beach had only seven—meaning that "in all only sixteen men" would dramatically impact a population in Tampa of more than sixty thousand. Finally, Trammell claimed that thirty-five liquor dealers held over $500,000 of inventory and a combined total investment locally of $3 million.[19] The Exchange National Bank and the Citizens Bank and Trust Company also sent telegrams to Washington, DC, asking for assistance in keeping the saloons open. The effort must have been highly coordinated because the parties had nearly identical talking points. Congressman Herbert Drane of Tampa received a similar telegram signed by dozens of Tampa-area business and political leaders.

Favoring restrictions, the Reverend R. A. Smith, president of the Florida Ministerial Union; A. F. Turner, general secretary of the YMCA; and D. C. McMullen, head of the Florida Anti-Saloon League, all put their names to a telegram asserting that "public sentiment" approved of a dry zone forcing saloons to close.[20] On May 6, Secretary Daniels responded directly to Reverend Smith and his compatriots, informing the trio of prohibitionists, "I have not felt that I could take action except at places where we have large numbers of sailors or marines under training."[21]

Resistance to five-mile bans took many forms—including appeals to common decency. In Chicago, John Sherwin sent a petition to Assistant Secretary of the Navy Franklin Roosevelt, asking for relief from Daniels's dry order. Sherwin was president of the Chicago Hardware Foundry Company, located near the Great Lakes Naval Training Station. Three-hundred-thirty-nine molders working for Sherwin signed the petition, which requested one case of beer per week for each person. "You will note," said Sherwin, "that these men, who in the past have always been used to having a certain amount of beer, especially during the summer months, when their work is especially arduous, are making a request for a minimum supply.... It is for their own private and individual use."[22]

On the West Coast, in Vallejo, California, the fight to keep the town's saloons and brothels cost one Navy doctor his job. Speaking about vice suppression at a public meeting in San Francisco, Dr. T. A. Berryhill allegedly criticized the CTCA's repressive measures. In a letter to Daniels, Fosdick complained of the incident, relaying accounts of Berryhill's public statement that "men were animals and needed sexual activity, that the only sensible way was to have a red-light district with the women examined periodically," and further that he opposed the order "abolishing the 'individual prophylactic packet."[23] Notably, Berryhill made many of the same points that constituted scatteration theory as advocated by Behrman in New Orleans.

The Navy secretary's response to Fosdick's letter was brief. "My Dear Mr. Fosdick," he began, "in reply to your letter of October 10th, I write to say that I have issued instructions that Commander Berryhill be assigned to some other position."[24] Dissent in the ranks, even from medical professionals, would not be tolerated.

California senator Edwin G. Grant led the fight for the abatement act in the state legislature. He wrote to Secretary Daniels on October 5, 1917, urging that "the chief obstacle in the way of a clean-up of vice conditions ... is Henry Widenmann ... whose brewery leased the notorious bawdy house at 229 Georgia Street, which debauched United States sailors, and which escaped prosecution ... [and] has never been proceeded against under any Redlight Abatement Act." Furthermore, said Grant, he was "strongly convinced that the closing of Mr. Widenmann's [sic] brewery and the saloons he controls ... would be a great victory toward winning the war against Germany." For good measure he added that the efforts of brewers and vice peddlers in working to "break down the morale of the American troops, is unquestionably looked upon in Berlin as an important victory for the Kaiser."[25]

Widenmann, who owned multiple saloons and brothels near the Mare Island Navy Yard, became so angry with Senator Grant that he brutally assaulted the legislator. Two pastors reported that Grant encountered Widenmann on the street when the big German brewer growled, "I have looked it up and find that I cannot get redress against you for what you have done to me, whether civilly or criminally by law, but I am going to get you now." Widenmann proceeded to punch Grant twenty-five times in the presence of the mayor and the police commissioner, who took no action to stop the beating. The pastors, Henry G. Porter of the Methodist Church of Vallejo and William B. Phillips of the Christian Church of Vallejo, asked Secretary Daniels to "intern Henry J. Widenmann and his brother . . . the German Brewers for the rest of the war."[26]

Sometimes regulations intended to protect soldiers and sailors ended up causing them serious grief. In Philadelphia, Quartermaster Second Class Larry Albert Byers wrote to Josephus Daniels from his bed in the Pennsylvania Hospital. On Tuesday, June 8, 1918, about 1:00 a.m., three detectives went to Byers's home at 1034 Laine Street in Camden, New Jersey, and arrested his wife on the charge of running a house of prostitution. According to Byers, the detectives showed no warrant and did not know his wife's name until she was asked and responded to questions about who resided in the home. The police did have a document of some sort with the name of "Elizabeth Horner or a name similar to that, and while my wife was dressing they changed the name." The detectives escorted Byers's wife and her unnamed caregiver to the prosecutor's office and forced them to make a statement covering a period of their lives for about six years. Byers's wife was locked in a cold cell without blankets and denied medical care by authorities. Unable to find out if a complaint was filed against them, they never learned why their home was targeted. Aside from the obvious embarrassment of the situation, Byers complained that "our money is gone and we are forced to fall back on my wife's parents for a living."[27]

Byers emphasized that neither he nor his wife had ever been arrested for any reason. He closed by asking Daniels to "bring justice" to the parties causing the situation and seeking "advice as to what can be done to those men that have so deliberately and shamefully insulted both my wife and friend." The sad tale of Quartermaster Byers and his wife highlights the need to balance vice suppression with due process and other constitutional rights.

While pleased with the outcomes of the CTCA's work, Fosdick recognized there were problems. Even after closing many red-light districts, prostitutes could often be found around the Army and Navy camps. Referred to as "charity girls," the women were often unanchored to an identifiable brothel or red-light district. Efforts to rid the camps of such women resulted in overcrowded prisons. In at least one case, "every single inch of floor space on three floors was covered with mattresses in an attempt to provide for the inmates."[28] President Wilson had to provide $250,000 from the war emergency fund to help alleviate the problem of overcrowding in women's prisons and detention centers.[29]

11

REPERCUSSIONS
The Election of 1920

In 1920, the United States navigated a postwar economic crisis that put more workers out of jobs than any previous recession in U.S. history. The downturn began shortly after the conclusion of hostilities in Europe, when stock prices began cratering in the second half of 1919. Economist W. S. Woytinsky notes that, as a result of this industrial depression, "Factory employment dropped 30 percent from March 1920 to July 1921. . . . Unemployment rose above 4 million."[1]

The economy was only one of the Democrats' many challenges heading into the 1920 election. Equally menacing was the internecine warfare created by Woodrow Wilson's exit from the national stage. Widespread party infighting was finally resolved with the selection of a compromise presidential nominee—Ohio governor John M. Cox.[2] Republicans, who had previously taken control of both the House and the Senate in the 1918 midterm elections, stood to gain further from Democrats' disunity.

Republican presidential primary candidates included Senator Hiram Johnson of California, Governor Frank Lowden of Illinois, General Leonard Wood (a commander of Rough Riders fame), and Senator Warren G. Harding of Ohio. While Harding was the least known and arguably least experienced, he hailed from the key swing state of Ohio. His nonconfrontational style made him the Republicans' default choice after multiple ballots at the nominating convention.[3]

In a campaign that featured some of earliest uses of radio in politics, a growing sophistication in advertising across the board, and increasing retail politicking, Harding and the Republicans dominated Democrats. In the presidential contest, Harding smashed Cox, winning over 60 percent of the popular vote and 404 electoral votes. Republicans also won 10 seats in the US Senate, giving them a commanding 59–47 majority in the upper chamber. In the House, Republicans gained 63 seats.[4]

✦ ✦ ✦

The nationwide recession and poor showing of Democrats nationally also impacted Behrman's prospects for victory in the New Orleans mayoral election of 1920. In addition, for many locals, passage of the Eighteenth Amendment banning the sale of alcohol contributed to the malaise. After passing Congress on December 18, 1917, national Prohibition was ultimately approved on January 16, 1919. Ratification in Louisiana was not without controversy. The state Senate's efforts to approve the measure during its 1918 regular session ended in a 20–20 tie. A special session was called later that year and the amendment passed 21–20. The House voted 69–41 to approve, and Louisiana became the thirteenth state in the Union to notify Congress of its approval, on August 21, 1918.[5] After the state House vote, one member of the Louisiana House of Representatives sarcastically pronounced, "Now, Mr. Speaker, I move that the House take a recess in order to give the prohibitionists time in which to 'get tight' and celebrate their victory."[6] Behrman's fight to protect Storyville added to the negative atmosphere.

Cumulatively, these factors bred a desire for change among anti-machine reformers, the press, and many voters. Their goal was to win the governor's mansion in January and leverage that control in New Orleans's mayoral election the following September. Those who wanted Behrman gone were cautiously optimistic.

✦ ✦ ✦

In preparation for the gubernatorial election of 1920, anti-machine reformers founded the Orleans Democratic Association (ODA). Like its predecessors, the Citizens' League of 1896, the Good Government League of 1912, and the Louisiana Progressive Party of 1916, the ODA was a collection of "silk-stocking reformers and renegade Regular Democrats."[7] With the cooperation of virtually every newspaper in the state, the ODA turned the gubernatorial contest between John M. Parker and Colonel Frank Stubbs into a referendum on Behrman and the Regulars. While the four-term mayor's name appeared nowhere on the January ballot, the problem of "Ring" control regularly appeared in front-page above-the-fold headlines. Voters were divided into the "bossed" and "unbossed," depending on whether they supported Stubbs (the machine candidate) or Parker (the ODA candidate).

New Orleans lawyer Charles Rosen was appointed to lead the attack on Behrman for the ODA. Rosen was a frequent speaker during a series of Parker rallies in the weeks leading up to the primary election. The *Times-Picayune* covered the events in great detail with splashy headlines, eagerly reporting on Parker's increasing momentum. On January 6, 1920, a crowd of six hundred voters endured a cold and wet evening to cheer on anti-Regular speakers until past midnight at the Sacred Heart Hall in New Orleans. Signaling a key message of the coming weeks, one speaker, Donelson Caffery, alleged that Colonel Stubbs, the Regular-backed candidate, would bring back "Tomandersonism," a reference to the former state senator and boss of Storyville prior to its closing. Caffery sarcastically suggested that Behrman and the chief of police should accompany Billy Sunday on his cleanup campaigns, mocking with hyperbolic rhetoric: "What animated city disinfectants, what vice-extinguishers in boots and what human vesuviuses for pouring out burial lavas upon Storyville."[8] This was the foundation of the Parker strategy—conflating the New Orleans machine and Colonel Stubbs. A vote for Stubbs was a vote for Behrman and the hated machine. A vote for Parker was a vote for reform and freedom from the Regulars.

At another campaign event, Congressman J. Y. Sanders, Rosen, and other ODA speakers unleashed new attacks on Behrman. Rosen criticized the mayor for raising taxes and fees and for his influence with the Public Belt Railroad. He pounded on Behrman's so-called "secret mission" to save Storyville and further alleged that poor management of city resources had resulted in inadequate schools and facilities for education. Citing Philadelphia and New York, Rosen asserted that other major cities had overthrown machine rule, and New Orleans could do the same, liberating its citizens and business owners from the "yoke of the ring."[9] Congressman Sanders, a former governor himself, urged the crowd to think for themselves and not be directed by Behrman and the Regulars. His vote, said Sanders, was all a poor man owned, and it was equal in value to that of a wealthy person. Sanders also attacked Behrman for supporting an increase in streetcar fares and gas rates.[10]

In Shreveport, Rosen told a crowd that he was campaigning for Parker to "save the city as well as the state."[11] Parker's vision, said Rosen, was to

destroy the power of the Regular machine, which had "New Orleans completely in its grasp; and is now striving to clutch in its hideous talons the body
politic of the entire state."[12] The tone of the campaign got hotter as election
day approached, and the emphasis on Behrman's support of the closed vice
district increased. On January 17, just days before the election, Rosen ham-
mered Behrman's support of Storyville and his trip to Washington, DC, to
appeal to keep the vice district open. Three times in his speech Rosen posed
the rhetorical question, "Who sent you to Washington, Martin Behrman?
Was it Tom Anderson?"[13] The *Times-Picayune* reported, "Mr. Rosen spoke
of vice conditions that have permeated the city under Ring protection, and
pointed out that Tom Anderson's ward in New Orleans had more vice and
crime than any other similar area in the United States."[14]

Democrats supporting Parker were described as "unbought." Inside an
Alexandria, Louisiana, theater, Sanders shouted to the gathered masses that
Behrman held all the power of the New Orleans machine, appointing all city
officials, elected and otherwise, as well as other city and state jobs. Sanders
himself bellowed to the enthusiastic crowd, "I tell you that after his election
there will be no secret marriage with King Martin but instead there will be
a public funeral."[15] The *Times-Picayune* reported that Sanders's speech was
"a scathing attack upon the usurping of power which has caused the Democratic Party to be spelled B-E-H-R-M-A-N." In reporting Sanders's attacks
on Behrman, the *Times-Picayune* was careful to highlight its own righteousness: "Mr. Rosen said that for years *The Times-Picayune* had been calling
attention to gambling halls along Royal and other streets of the city, dens
where young manhood of New Orleans was being broken and degraded and
yet never a word from Behrman or the chief of police. The same paper, he
said, had revealed the truth about questionable resorts of Jefferson and St.
Bernard parishes and still no response from the mayor or his lieutenants."[16]

On election day, January 20, 1920, T. Semmes Walmsley, a Regular loy-
alist, held three important posts. He was a captain with the New Orleans
Police Department, assistant attorney general of the State of Louisiana, and
not coincidentally, deputy campaign manager of Behrman's reelection campaign.[17] At Behrman's request, Walmsley assembled a squad of eighteen men
to "settle differences at the polls and make the election as peaceable and fair
as possible."[18] The *Times-Picayune* reported that, aside from a handful of
minor accusations to the contrary, the vote was accurately recorded in a free

and fair election.[19] There were fifty-three problems reported to Walmsley, including thirteen arrests and several fistfights. Most conflicts were related to poll watchers who did not reside in the ward of the polling place where they chose to volunteer. Violations tended to be technical and did not result in the invalidation of ballots. A handful of more complex cases involved questions related to payment of poll taxes and confusion over sample ballots.[20] In the end, Behrman's precautions against fraud appear to have resulted in a relatively clean election with Parker beating the Regular candidate Stubbs by a comfortable margin—77,686 to 65,685, or 54 percent for Parker to 45 percent for Stubbs.[21]

Among the many reasons for Stubbs's loss was a sense that the entire state of Louisiana, not just New Orleans, had fallen under the thumb of "Behrmanism." The allegation appeared to be substantiated by reports of Behrman's strong-arm tactics in Tangipahoa Parish, where Stubbs was losing badly to Parker. Ostensibly, Behrman threatened to halt the construction of a planned highway between New Orleans and Tangipahoa if parish leaders did not support Stubbs. Tangipahoa leaders claimed Behrman himself issued the order: "Not a spade of dirt will be thrown on the New Orleans–Hammond Highway unless Tangipahoa parish gives the candidacy of Colonel Stubbs more consideration."[22] The *Times-Picayune* asserted that Tangipahoa leaders had personally "declared that coercive methods had been resorted to by the ring in its endeavor to make Tangipahoa parish get right."[23] It's certainly possible that, as mayor of New Orleans and leader of the Regulars, Behrman engaged in such hardball politics. On this particular occasion, however, it's also possible that his enemies at the *Times-Picayune* exaggerated the story. Their sources were all anonymous, making it difficult to gauge the extent of his effort to squeeze the parish.

✦ ✦ ✦

Parker's victory gave reformers and the press hope for defeating Behrman and the Regulars in the coming city elections to be held in September of 1920. With their first genuine prospect of victory in decades, Behrman's opponents launched an all-out assault. The *Times-Picayune* seized on Parker's gubernatorial victory as a call to arms. It described Parker's win as a "verdict of guilty against the ring and a declaration for decent government."[24] In late January, just days after Parker's victory, the mantra among ODA politicians was "Death to the Ring: A final smashing, knockout blow in municipal campaign in September."[25] In the coming days and weeks, torchlight parades and rallies were held by celebrants who reveled in the Parker victory over Stubbs. Rally speakers included the usual anti-Behrman personalities such as Charles Rosen. New Orleans's local newspapers also stepped up their support of the ODA and opposition to Behrman.

Daniel D. Moore, publisher of the *Times-Picayune,* and James M. Thompson, publisher of the *Item,* spoke against Behrman and the Regulars at several rallies. The two publishers also bitterly attacked Behrman in print, intensifying their feud with him. As the focus turned from Parker's successful gubernatorial bid to the September municipal campaign, the *Times-Picayune* ran a story that Behrman was indeed planning to run for reelection for what would be his fifth consecutive term. The column, entitled "Behrman's Hat Again in Municipal Arena, Is Persistent Rumor," asserted that Behrman held a conference of his closest friends and advisors after which he made the decision to run. Stoking doubts about the mayor's future, the *Times-Picayune* alleged that his associates were alarmed: "Mr. Behrman's decision to run is expected to cause another panic among his associates. The word has been passed among them that the mayor was doomed politically. All they can see with Mr. Behrman dropped as their leader is a great blank wall of defeat, but with him in the race the wall grows to a mountain."[26] This, of course, is from the same newspaper whose publisher spoke against Behrman at the ODA rally in Lafayette just hours before.

As the idea of a potentially historic city election settled over the political and chattering classes in New Orleans, Behrman departed for a Cattlemen's Convention. Speculation swirled around his potential opponents in the Democratic primary. Colonel John Sullivan, president of the ODA, had already bowed out of a challenge to Behrman, announcing at the Lafayette Square rally that he would not run. Those rumored to be eyeing a run included Charles Rosen, Behrman's most vociferous critic, and E. M. Stafford, a state senator who had considered running for governor but backed out when Parker announced his candidacy.[27]

By mid-July, Behrman officially announced his candidacy for mayor of New Orleans, and by August, both sides were ready to launch their campaigns.[28] The ODA announced that its mayoral candidate was the relatively unknown Andrew McShane. McShane was an underwhelming candidate, but there was great concern among the Regulars regarding voters' apparent desire for change.

Behrman and the Regulars attempted to sate the public's appetite for change by running all new candidates for city commission.[29] The replacement Regular candidates were Maurice DePass, Thomas Harrison, Paul Maloney, and C. S. Barnes. In addition, Walter J. Verlander, longtime leader of the Regulars in the Twelfth Ward, was ousted.[30]

The *Daily States* skewered Behrman for the housecleaning, asserting that he had cast incumbent Regular commissioners Ricks, Glenny, Stone, and Monrose "to the wolves." The editorial sarcastically suggested they had been "unceremoniously" abandoned by "the appreciative and loyal Mr. Behrman." It also questioned Behrman's strategy: "In short, doesn't he realize that the popular demand for change applies to the head of the ticket rather than the rest of it, inasmuch as, under the commission form of government, he has made himself the whole government and the political organization as well—so much so indeed that when he is absent the City Hall ceases to function, and politics goes on vacation?"[31] The editorial was soon reprinted in the more widely circulated *Times-Picayune*.[32]

Virtually every newspaper in New Orleans opposed Behrman and the Regulars in 1920. The *Item* called for a changing of the guard, and the *States* and its editor Robert R. Ewing withdrew their occasional support for Behrman and the Regulars. The *Times-Picayune* had been a longtime critic of the city machine and had become fervent in its opposition during the recent gubernatorial election. Benjamin T. Waldo, a *Times-Picayune* reporter, regularly attacked Behrman and the Regulars in the months leading up to election day.[33] In August of 1920, the *Times-Picayune* reminded readers of Behrman's support of Storyville, noting, "And, by the way, who was it who used his influence in efforts to keep open a moral pest district to lure our soldiers and sailors to misery and death?" The column alleged a close relationship between the Regulars and "gamblers and touts and steerers that Behrmanism and Ringism breed."[34]

Behrman punched back against the *Picayune*–ODA alliance and attacked the ODA nominee fiercely. He mocked the "luminous minds" of the ODA who selected the relatively unknown Andrew McShane to head their municipal ticket. Describing McShane as a "mouse," Behrman asserted that he had "kept the faith" with voters.[35] From Electric Park in Algiers, the same spot where he kicked off his first mayoral campaign in 1904, Behrman defended his record and asked voters to judge him by it alone and not the attacks of his opponents in the press:

My Friends and Neighbors:

On these very grounds, sixteen years ago, I appeared for the first time a candidate for mayor of this great city. Well do I remember that occasion, and often have I recalled with a thrill of pleasure how gallantly you cheered me on to one of the most notable victories in the annals of political contests in this city. . . . you will remember the bitter vituperation employed and the abuse heaped upon me. . . . With reckless disregard for truth or justice, they pictured me a mental and physical monstrosity, accused me of high crimes and misdemeanors, referred to me as illiterate and uncouth, and appealed eloquently to the electorate to forever repudiate my absurd pretensions.[36]

Behrman noted how the press had historically opposed him. Reviewing his major accomplishments, Behrman defended himself against the charge of "bossism." He said that he refused to be bossed himself by institutions such as the press and by the man who sought "to acquire power and office to serve his own ends."[37] Behrman alleged that his opponent hid "behind the name of reform" in order "to gain qualifications for public office."[38] Although Behrman delivered his speech to a rally of thousands of supporters, it was reported by the *Times-Picayune* with far less fanfare than the ODA rallies of the recently concluded Parker campaign.[39]

Immediately after Behrman's kick-off speech, the *Times-Picayune* responded with an article entitled "Our Reasons." Acknowledging its opposition to Behrman, the newspaper emphasized that it was using "utmost restraint" in its effort to defeat Behrman, contending, "No right hearted, clear-thinking voter in this city, who has a spark of thought for the human welfare of any child or woman or honest man in all New Orleans—could by any possibility if possessed of the information now in the hands of the *Times-Picayune,* justify a ballot cast to continue for an instant the Behrman ring that now rules and is wrecking this municipality."[40] The paper further editorialized that Behrman failed to effectively administer the city's affairs and blocked, by legal maneuver, an investigation alleging that he and others ignored the activities of drug dealers, illicit gambling operations, and houses of prostitution.

The *Times-Picayune* allegation related to a highly political piece of legislation pushed by Governor Parker in Baton Rouge. The act created a special commission to investigate the affairs of the Behrman administration—an effort Behrman successfully postponed until after the election by asking the judiciary for an injunction.[41] Behrman complained about the investigation to a crowd of more than forty-five hundred supporters: "You have seen a good deal of commotion raised by the newspapers and our opponents during the past week because the gentlemen who compose the city administration have declined to allow the Orleans Democratic Association to squander $25,000 of the taxpayers' money, and create hundreds of jobs for the next month, with an illegal probe commission. . . . the Spanish Inquisition never enjoyed greater power than was given this probe and when you picture how its findings would be painted by a violent and already abusive newspaper trust, you can imagine the result."[42] Behrman went on to say that one of the newspapers now aligned against him had, in 1912, bankrolled a similar investigation. Any desire for a new investigation, he asserted, could be conducted in a similar fashion using private, not public, funds. The city's books were open for inspection, proclaimed Mayor Behrman.[43]

Even as he stepped up his attacks against the "newspaper trust," Behrman sought to define his opponent, Andrew McShane, as unfit for the office of mayor on the grounds that he had no record of working for the betterment of the city or its citizens. During a speech in the Twelfth Ward, Behrman called McShane a "pitiful spectacle" and the "standard bearer" of the newspapers and a "self confessed public drone who has done nothing else in his entire selfish life but accumulate money for his own comfort and welfare."[44] Behrman attacked his wealth, lack of service to the community, failure to participate in city business organizations, and more. He said that McShane had been untouched by World War I and that "his country called but he heeded not."[45]

Behrman held nothing back in his counterpunching against McShane or the newspapers. He attempted to shine a light on the close relationship between the two, alleging that the newspaper editors told McShane, "Instead of your making speeches, we will write statements for you; we will turn Behrman's great assets to his discredit; we will misrepresent his long activity for city development; we will picture the great business exchanges to which you have been too selfish to belong as social clubs; we will appeal to and stir up class hatred; we will try to arouse the laboring people, to whose welfare you have never given a single thought in your entire life."[46] What galled Behrman the most, he proclaimed, was the "supreme effrontery" shown by the newspaper editors. They had some nerve, he asserted, to "babble about regarding their profession and their function as sacred."[47] And so went the back-and-forth of the campaign through August and the first two weeks of September.

Both sides courted organized labor, leading to some drama in the campaign. Speaking to the employees of a local shipyard, Behrman was interrupted by cheers of "hurrah for McShane." Some attendees carried signs reading "Behrman You're Doomed September 14" and "Behrman: A Friend of Scab Labor." The *Times-Picayune* reported that Behrman was repeatedly heckled and that the "noise and clamor and hoots and hisses of a Tulane–L.S.U. football game had nothing on the lusty-lunged McShane shouters when the Mayor began his speech."[48]

Labor was not the only important constituency. The Nineteenth Amendment was ratified in time for the women of New Orleans to participate in the municipal election, and both the Regulars and the ODA appealed for their support. The *Times-Picayune* ran a front-page story declaring, "Women Join O.D.A. to Crush Bossdom: Two Hundred of Fair Sex, Soon to Be Voters, Pledge Support."[49] The newspaper explained how women from every ward in the city gathered to hear from those engaged in the campaign. The women created a temporary committee to coordinate their efforts and establish a permanent group. Male speakers from the ODA told the women who had gathered for the meeting how for decades they had been relegated to joining "auxiliaries" but now they would be part of the official apparatus, allegedly with all the rights and benefits of membership enjoyed by men. Jean Gordon played a leading role at the ODA meeting. "It is pleasant to stand here," she said, "and hear you men say the dreadful things we have been saying for eight years. . . . Behrmanism is dead. If not, the people of New Orleans are rotten to the core."[50] Gordon was selected to serve as one of four women on a temporary committee to organize women's ward meetings.

Other speakers at the meeting included ODA luminaries such as Charles

Rosen and the mayoral candidate himself. Rosen asserted, "Ring rule affects the woman in the home even more than the man in business. . . . Foul streets and filthy markets, vice and debauchery attack your interests even more than they do ours."[51] Pressing for his own political advantage, McShane stressed the idea that the women of New Orleans, not Martin Behrman, deserved credit for the city's modern infrastructure. It was they who fought for such improvements while Behrman had merely submitted to their demands.[52]

Times-Picayune editor D. D. Moore's comments were intended to re-inforce the image of Behrman as anti-woman, anti-family, pro-drinking, pro-sex, and pro-gambling. Unfortunately for Behrman, he had taken several high-profile steps to bolster the depiction. His support of Storyville, the racetracks, and even his participation in Tony Jannus's aerial beer delivery all helped Behrman's enemies to paint him as a vice peddler. Such political problems were compounded by the fact that Behrman's enemies were mostly unconstrained by the truth in distorting his record.

The suffrage issue sheds light on such deceptions. For example, *Times-Picayune* editor D. D. Moore alleged that Behrman delayed women's suffrage. His own newspaper, however, reported months earlier, on May 13, that Behrman had been busily signaling to state legislators that he supported the federal suffrage amendment. Under the sub-headline "Behrman Wires Support," the newspaper indicated, "Mayor Behrman, of New Orleans, assured the ratification forces that he was doing everything possible to urge New Orleans' delegation in the Legislature to vote for the amendment."[53] In favoring the Nineteenth Amendment, Behrman chose sides against those who supported individual state suffrage laws but opposed a constitutional amendment.

During a rally for women's suffrage in Lafayette Square, Moore and Behrman appeared on the same dais together while Behrman praised the federal amendment. Behrman expressed his regret that Louisiana did not edge out Tennessee as the final necessary state to ratify the suffrage amendment. He told the audience that "no man was happier than I was when news of Tennessee's ratification was received. . . . The grant of full citizenship to women of this republic is the most significant event in history since the close of the Civil War."[54]

Like many politicians, Behrman had once opposed women's right to vote. However, as at least one other speaker noted, Behrman's recent actions in support of the federal amendment were self-evident.[55] Ultimately, said Behrman, the impact of women's suffrage could not be predicted, though the effect would certainly be positive. One speaker at the celebration in Lafayette Square was more definitive, vowing that "many a dirty hole, politically speaking, that men have simply swept around, will be totally cleaned out when women cast their ballots."[56]

Although newspapers and the ODA sought to deceive voters regarding Behrman's position on the federal women's suffrage amendment, the Regulars nevertheless boasted a strong contingent of women supporters. An incident the week before election day shows they weren't about to sit idly by while Jean Gordon and the ODA mobilized female support for McShane. During a sermon at Trinity Church, rector Robert S. Coupland noted with disappointment how many women in New Orleans were supporting Behrman and the Regulars. In the process of advocating for the ODA from the pulpit, Coupland criticized Behrman's female supporters: "These women are willing to sacrifice principles, morality, righteousness, honor and truth for the sake of petty personal revenge to satisfy an offended spleen."[57] Dr. Coupland's tirade drew a strong reaction, including a mass meeting of Regular women and a petition signed by four thousand women. The petitioners demanded an apology, asserting that the rector was a coward for not offering some conciliatory gesture. Moreover, they said, his actions were "false, contemptible," and "unworthy of a Christian minister."[58]

Election day was scheduled for Tuesday, September 14. In the closing weeks of the campaign, children returned to school. Voters were reminded of the stakes in the election alongside advertisements for "Girls Fancy Gingham Dresses for $2.98," "Boys Wool Knicker Pants for $3.95," and "High Grade Lead Pencils" for a nickel. The *Times-Picayune* spewed venom at Behrman and "Behrmanism." Front-page headlines shouted, "Enthusiastic O.D.A. Voters to Eliminate Ring Misrule Today" and "Men Whose Election at the Polls Today Mean a Rebirth of New Orleans" above smiling pictures of ODA candidates. As precincts were organized, turn-out operations targeted voters, tempers flared, and attacks grew more intense. The election-day edition of the *Times-Picayune* included a voter guide with endorsements of McShane and other ODA candidates and a ward-by-ward listing of all polling places.[59]

Surprisingly, there was little controversy on election day, especially considering the narrow margin between candidates up and down the ticket. On September 19, five days after the municipal election, a *Times-Picayune* headline announced a recount might be required. Calling the initial returns "remarkable," the newspaper speculated that the election was "probably the closest in city history."[60] Forty-eight hours later, Secretary of State James Bailey issued official returns, with McShane garnering 22,767 votes compared to 21,443 for Behrman.[61] Paul Maloney was the only successful Regular candidate for commission, squeaking out a narrow victory over his ODA opponent with a margin of just 147 votes. Regular commission candidate Morris B. DePass lost to his ODA opponent by only 54 votes.[62] The times had changed, however temporarily, and Behrman had not. The winds of reform swept Behrman out of the mayor's parlor for the first time in sixteen years.

The long hours and vicious personal attacks of the 1920 election took a toll on Behrman. Stress, countless cigars, and weight gain caused his health to decline. Behrman took only a brief rest after the defeat. He soon began calculating the barriers to political reentry—both internally with the Regulars and externally with the public. Inside the Regular organization and the Choctaw Club, there was a growing sense that Behrman had become a liability. He still enjoyed a reservoir of goodwill among his friends and longtime supporters, but everyone recognized the press had painted a target on Behrman that would be difficult to overcome. After a meeting with ward leaders, Behrman consented to give up his leadership role to the newly elected city commissioner, Paul Maloney. This setback did not deter Behrman. He remained committed to restoring the Regulars to power and rehabilitating his own reputation.[63] It wouldn't be easy with anti-machine reformers now in control of the city and state apparatus and patronage jobs.

In August of 1921, Behrman took a job as vice president of American Bank and Trust Company and announced that he would serve as director and vice president of the Appalachian Corporation—a company that owned apple farms in Georgia.[64] No longer the mayor or official leader of the Regular Democratic Organization, he nonetheless remained leader of his home ward. As such, he was elected to the Constitutional Convention of 1921. In a sign that Behrman and the Regulars were not totally defunct, Behrman's archenemy, Charles Rosen, was defeated in his campaign for a judgeship and a Regular candidate was elected to the Louisiana Public Service Commission.

12

PAPA AND THE KINGFISH
Fact versus Fiction

Martin Behrman was a rarity among urban machine mayors. For the most part, these elected city executives did not control the political organization responsible for their election. Likewise, most machine leaders did not run for office, but rather remained behind the scenes. As the *Times-Picayune* once noted, many of these machine leaders intentionally avoided the accountability that came with holding the office of chief executive. Behrman, on the other hand, "never evaded responsibility nor sought to camouflage his mistakes in any way."[1] Behrman's unique dual role contributed to his defeat at the polls and resignation from leadership of the Regular organization.

The Storyville controversy was one of the few instances where Behrman failed to properly gauge public opinion and, furthermore, where he underestimated the ruthlessness of his opponents. After the election, Behrman suggested that his biggest mistake in both the city and state campaigns was his failure to answer the Storyville attacks. Indeed, Behrman's failure to answer the charge that he endangered the New Orleans Navy Yard is perhaps the most glaring error of his political career. While Behrman's concerns about "scatteration" are plausible, the concept of regulating prostitution as a quasi-legal enterprise had fallen out of favor by 1920. Perhaps this is why he never found his footing in the debate over Storyville, how it came to be, and why it should be eliminated.

Anti-machine reformers were tireless in their attacks. Behrman asserted that Jean Gordon "would still be carrying a gun and debating constitutional points about secession had she been a soldier in the Confederate Army. . . . She has never given up even in the fights she lost."[2] The Storyville undertow pulled Behrman and the Regulars down in 1920, but it was especially strong against the backdrop of a nationwide recession and local grievances such as the railway strike. Behrman himself noted that "the big wave of discontent that followed the war" was also to blame for his loss. Parker, he said, "had made an impression of being against everything," and so was a natural fit for the political mood of the time.[3] Nevertheless, the decisive factor was the anti-machine reformers who made Storyville the centerpiece of their campaign against Behrman.

When Behrman finally defended his actions on Storyville, he told of John Parker's duplicity and the *Times-Picayune* distortion of the situation. He told of the consensus on that day in 1917 when the small group voted inside Gallier Hall. Everyone, including Parker, agreed that Behrman should go to Washington, DC, and appeal to Secretary Baker to keep Storyville open. Behrman also argued that the *Item* had historically done little to oppose the segregated district. To prove this assertion, Behrman quoted a 1910 *Item* editorial asserting that "many of the more advanced students and experts on problems of this kind thoroughly approve of the system adopted by New Orleans and it may be said truthfully that we are ahead of the times rather than behind the times in matters of this kind."[4]

Despite such private and public expressions of support, the anti-machine politicians and newspaper editors turned on Storyville and Behrman. They denied any association with the vice district or Behrman himself. They publicly accused Behrman of being sent to Washington, DC, by Tom Anderson, boss of Storyville. And yet, even in his "failure" to keep the vice district open, Behrman convinced Secretary Baker to keep his hands off New Orleans. It literally took an act of Congress for President Wilson, Josephus Daniels, and Raymond Fosdick to put Behrman in a corner tight enough to close Storyville. This was the kind of political muscle New Orleans desperately missed in future battles with Huey Long.

✦   ✦   ✦

While Behrman's post-factum defense could not change history, it could affect the next election. The political situation in New Orleans was more fluid than it had been for decades. Behrman's absence from the mayor's office led to divisions within the Regulars. A group of disgruntled Regulars separated from the machine and joined with a faction of anti-machine reformers. This latest splinter group of Democrats was dubbed the "New Regulars." Huey Long scrutinized this developing political situation. Such instability impacted the Public Service Commission, where he served as chairman, and created opportunities to expand his political relationships in the city.[5]

Behrman could not run for mayor again until 1925, the date of the municipal election having been moved to an off-year schedule. He nevertheless played a major role in city and state politics. In 1924, Behrman and the Regulars, though not as strong as in previous decades, helped to defeat Huey Long in his bid for governor. The machine supported Henry Fuqua in his successful campaign. Although Huey lost, he was a serious candidate and his insurgent campaign raised eyebrows.

Huey's natural retail political skills and the appeal of his populist message were duly noted.[6] Looking to the future, anti-machine reformers and major newspaper editors worried that Huey's populist rhetoric, and a few more votes in the city, could someday land him in the governor's mansion. Huey's enemies didn't constitute the type of statewide "oligarchy" described by T. Harry Williams and early Long scholars, but they were nonetheless united by their opposition to Huey. The best perspective on this political landscape is offered by historian Glen Jeansonne, who points out there was neither a statewide machine nor a statewide political organization standing in Huey's path to the governor's mansion: "The New Orleans machine, rather than dominating state politics, found it difficult to elect a governor."[7]

Huey's opponents were right to be worried. In the gubernatorial campaign of 1924, Long was able to capture a majority in twenty-one parishes and a plurality of the vote in seven more. He carried most parishes in the northern and central parts of the state and even three parishes in the southern region of Louisiana. All of these parishes were relatively poor and dominated by small farms—substantiating the thesis that Huey had a strong appeal among this demographic.[8] It is also true that Huey failed primarily due to the strong opposition of Behrman and the Regulars, and that he was opposed by the anti-machine reformers and the New Orleans press. This was not, however, the permanent ruling class Huey and others made it out to be. It was a temporary coalition—a marriage of convenience created in the interest of stopping Huey Long.

After his loss in 1924, Long manufactured the legend that rains across the state prevented his rural supporters from getting to the polls on Louisiana's poorly constructed roads. But privately, Long knew that he had not earned enough votes in New Orleans. He never forgot or forgave the snub by Behrman and the Regulars, alleging they stole the 1924 election by stuffing ballot boxes in New Orleans with fraudulent votes.[9]

The feud between Behrman and Huey Long erupted into an all-out war when Democrats gathered at their state convention to select delegates for the Democratic National Convention of 1924. A practice had developed over the years whereby a handful of Democratic leaders, including the governor and the New Orleans mayor, met privately and picked the at-large delegates for the national convention. This group was then rubber-stamped by the delegates at the state convention in Louisiana and sent off to carouse in whatever city had been selected for the national convention.

The pattern for selecting delegates changed abruptly in 1924. In this particular year, it was decided for political reasons that the state's two U.S. senators would be excluded from the at-large slate. When Huey Long heard the news, he used the opportunity to burnish his upstart credentials. "Why should the 'rejects' have these places?" asked Huey. Historian T. Harry Williams, who published a biography of Long in 1969, described the tense atmosphere, the chatter, and the chaos that erupted at the state convention:

Behrman called the meeting to order and was elected permanent chairman. Quickly he announced that, hearing no objection, he would name Sanders as chairman of the resolutions committee. Just as quickly Sanders moved that no resolutions be debated or voted or even read to the convention until they had been passed on by his committee. A stentorian voice from the rear of the hall interrupted the smooth flow of the proceedings: "I object." It came from Huey, who rose from his seat and began to speak. . . . a roar of boos and imprecations shook the building and continued for several minutes. Behrman pounded his gavel on a marble-topped table until he broke the marble. Finally, he quieted the bedlam sufficiently to announce that he was ruling Huey out of order. . . . Huey, on his feet again, demanded a roll-call vote. . . . Behrman ruled against him. . . . A Long supporter shouted: "Don't run the steamroller too fast over us." The calling of the roll on the motion to table consumed twenty-five minutes and was conducted in a continuous uproar. . . . Finally the result was announced—536 votes to table and 180 votes against.[10]

Huey made another unsuccessful attempt to sway the convention, but this time he got to the podium and was the only speaker not from the Behrman-Sanders-Fuqua group to quiet the raucous crowd long enough to get a word in: "He had to stand at the rostrum five minutes before he could gain the attention of the crowd. But when he got it, he held it. He was the only speaker of the evening who commanded absolute silence. Looking directly at Behrman, he denounced the 'bosses and bosslets,' 'the clicksters and ringers' who were 'contaminating' democratic government in the state. . . . His plan would permit rejects like Behrman and Sanders to retain their places, he said, while opening up seats to men who represented the people."[11] Long's resolution was defeated and, notably, the very newspapers that mauled Behrman and the Regulars so badly in 1920, the *Times-Picayune* and the *Item,* delighted in the way Behrman stifled Huey Long. The *Times-Picayune* compared Long to "chaff before the wind," and the *Item* asserted that Long was "finished."[12]

✦   ✦   ✦

By 1925, a large national debt resulted in significant cuts in military spending. After World War I, demobilization closed many naval facilities, and the Algiers Navy Yard hospital was taken over by the Veterans Administration. Ship repair was cut back and eventually eliminated.[13] Therefore, as Behrman's sixth and final municipal campaign approached, the fact that he may have previously imperiled the navy yard held little sway over voters. Moreover, the people of New Orleans, like much of the rest of the country, had generally soured on reform.

Prohibition was perhaps the least popular of the progressive-era reforms.[14] The optics of gang wars and government intrusion into the personal lives and businesses of freedom-loving citizens strengthened opposition to the ban. On June 24, 1921, for example, federal agents stormed the American, National, Standard, Columbia, Union, and Dixie breweries in one massive bust. They seized thousands of cases of beer valued at around $35,000, alleging it contained more than the allowable 0.5 percent alcohol content. The brewery properties themselves were also taken into the custody of the federal government. Members of Louisiana's congressional delegation protested, and the breweries were eventually allowed to resume operations with the payment of tax penalties. Yet, they were soon closed again by the U.S. District Court in New Orleans. This was apparently the first order issued to a brewery to comply with the Volstead Act—the legislation that implemented national Prohibition.[15]

In this environment, Behrman's handling of alcohol and prostitution issues seemed a distant memory. "Papa" had not been one of the sanctimonious reformers trying to save private citizens from the saloon and the brothel. Instead, he had taken the middle road by supporting common-sense regulation of vice. He seemed like the kind of politician a regular guy could enjoy having a beer with. This political landscape helped Behrman win his fifth term as mayor of New Orleans. It wasn't easy, however. Behrman had to overcome significant opposition from a coalition organized principally by Huey Long. And while Huey couldn't stop the Regulars from retaking Gallier Hall, he gained powerful allies such as newspaper publisher Robert Ewing and former Parker campaign manager John Sullivan. The two men would go on to be key figures in Huey's successful 1928 campaign for governor.

When Behrman took office in May of 1925, his physicians warned him to reduce his workload, lose some weight, and give up cigars. Either he ignored their advice or his efforts were too little, too late. He died after less than a year in office. The circumstances of his passing are difficult to describe with twenty-first-century precision. In the fall of 1925, he traveled to Port Arthur, Texas, for a convention related to inland waterways, where he contracted a "cold" that developed into influenza and perhaps ultimately into pneumonia. Behrman was ill throughout the holidays and agreed to stop working long enough for a rest in Bogalusa, a quiet town in northeast Louisiana near the Mississippi border. After two weeks, he returned home, where he stayed until the time of his death on January 12, 1926.

Behrman's death certificate states his cause of death as "chronic myocarditis," a form of heart disease. His personal physician, Dr. J. M. Batchelor, attributed Behrman's death to a severe state of exhaustion acquired in the performance of his job, "chronic appendicitis," and "degeneration of the heart muscles, caused from overwork."[16] Mayor Behrman, he said, "has been doing the work of two men for the last sixteen years, more than any man could expect to and keep his health; I warned him repeatedly against it, but he was so absorbed in city affairs that he continued to overwork."[17]

The *Times-Picayune,* a Behrman antagonist for so many years, speculated that the mayor's death after six months in office was likely due to "overwork."[18] One senses a twinge of guilt in the *Times-Picayune* coverage of his death. The newspaper that had skewered Behrman in 1920 now glowed about how Behrman put "his heart and soul" into his final term as mayor. The newspaper praised Behrman's "attention of the most intensive and detailed nature" for projects such as "the enlarged paving program, the lakefront development, the City Park extension, city beautification, the Mississippi river bridge, a convention and publicity bureau, a new criminal court building, a new and modern parish prison, a municipal auditorium, a modern garbage collection and disposal system, a co-operative anti-mosquito campaign along the entire gulf coast, [and] the improvement and beautification of Canal street."[19]

The *Times-Picayune* called Behrman's goodbye "an outpouring of affection that ranked his funeral above any other that has taken place in the city's colorful history." Noting that his achievements played a significant role in the destiny of New Orleans, the newspaper asserted that "nothing in words could visualize the immensity or the intensity of New Orleans's last farewell to the man who had been its mayor for more than sixteen years and who was just at the beginning of a fifth term as chief executive when death stepped in Tuesday morning."[20] Providing a vivid description of the event, the *Times-Picayune* asserted that the city had experienced nothing like it since the funeral of the president of the Confederacy, Jefferson Davis. Crowds filled Jackson Square, clogged the streets around Gallier Hall, and formed lines all the way across the city to the cemetery where Behrman was laid to rest. Artillery thundered, and the soulful sound of taps filled the air.

The reaction in support of Behrman was nearly universal. Even African American citizens, with their many legitimate grievances against Behrman and the Regulars, heaped praise upon the mayor. Bishop Robert E. Jones of the Methodist Episcopal Church, a leading voice in the African American community, asserted that "almost to a man we were Behrmanites and if that made us Democrats, then we were Democrats." Bishop Jones emphasized that, in spite of their lack of political power, Black citizens knew they could appeal to Behrman "on the basis of righteousness, justice and fair play." He was "trusted," "revered," and even "loved."[21] That is quite a testimony considering Behrman openly bragged of disenfranchising Black voters at the 1898 Constitutional Convention. It speaks to the tremendous strides he made in other areas and how life improved for the public at large during his tenure in office.

Behrman's body lay in state through the night—more than seventeen hours, giving an estimated fifty thousand citizens the opportunity to bid the longtime mayor goodbye. At 9:30 a.m. a priest prayed over Behrman and the casket was closed. Governor Fuqua, former mayor McShane, and a handful of friends and family watched as the casket was draped with an oversized blanket of white roses. In a subtle but sweet break with military regulation, Behrman's grandchildren, Natalie and Joel Bond, presented a white lily that was placed next to an American flag covering the casket. Behrman so adored Natalie and Joel that city business was put on hold when the children showed up at Gallier Hall.

The artillery caisson waiting on St. Charles Street was draped in black, and when Father Cotter was finished, six pallbearers carried the casket out of city hall and placed it carefully in the two-wheeled wagon. The massive crowd was silent as six horses flanked on either side by four soldiers solemnly, and slowly, marched away. The procession was led by a "detachment of motorcycle police." Close behind the caisson trailed nearly one thousand sailors, soldiers, policemen, and firemen, followed by the cars carrying family, friends, and VIPs.

On the way to St. Louis Cathedral, thousands of citizens removed their hats and bowed their heads as Behrman's casket passed by. Many people turned and followed on foot, swelling the waiting cathedral crowd so large that the funeral procession could barely get inside. There was no standing room. Julia, Stanley, and Mary Helen held places of honor next to the altar and the casket. So ended the life of Martin Behrman. With his passing, one period of social and political upheaval drew to a close and another began.[22]

✦ ✦ ✦

Martin Behrman was a consensus builder and reformer who implemented solutions to thorny public health and infrastructure problems. He sought to contain the "scatteration" of prostitution across the city by limiting it to one geographic area in Storyville. He balanced a wave of unpopular alcohol regulation with the need to respect the law and curb alcoholism, and he fought disease through construction of new pumps, canals, and levees.

Some of these ideas worked in the short term but failed in ways that were unforeseeable to Behrman and others. But as chief architect of New Orleans's twentieth-century future, Behrman balanced the old and the new, and he enjoyed more success than failure. The one shameful mark on his career—a stain on his legacy that will never disappear and cannot be explained away—is the disenfranchisement of Louisiana's Black people. The disenfranchisement of Black citizens at the 1898 Constitutional Convention reinforced the pattern of post-Reconstruction civil rights violations that continued into the mid-twentieth century.

Behrman's opponents faced plenty of their own failures. The anti-machine reformers were equally complicit in disenfranchising Black voters. The Parker and McShane administrations were inconsequential and mostly failed to deliver promised reforms. Many anti-machine reformers helped to create Storyville because, like Behrman, they believed that limiting prostitution to a confined area would restrict its growth. Instead, the number of prostitutes and brothels dramatically increased, and the vice district became the most infamous in the United States. Later, they claimed that closing Storyville was going to fix the prostitution problem. In the end, this strategy failed, too. Ultimately, the anti-machine reformers' attacks on Behrman contributed to Huey Long's ascent while doing nothing to stop corruption.

❖ ❖ ❖

No single event led to the rise of Huey Long, but when New Orleans newspapers teamed up with anti-machine reformers to destroy Behrman, they gave Huey a boost. Behrman and the Regulars were the only thing standing between Huey and the governor's mansion. Long employed much of the same anti-machine rhetoric used by John Parker in his own campaign for governor. He adopted Parker's strategy of running against Behrman when Behrman wasn't even a candidate. And when New Orleans's longtime mayor and machine leader died, the last politician with the political skills to go toe-to-toe with Huey was gone. So too was the last barrier between Long and the governor's mansion. Shortly thereafter, the Regular-backed Governor Fuqua passed away and Huey filled the political vacuum in 1928 when he became Louisiana's fortieth governor.

Huey's mastery of self-promotion led to the adoption of a myth behind his rise to power. The false narrative proposes that, after Reconstruction, New Orleans and all of Louisiana were controlled by a conventional oligarchy that maintained power until—like the peasant serfs of Russia suppressed by the Romanov dynasty—the country people of Louisiana followed Huey and dethroned the ruling family. The chosen had ignored the needs of ordinary citizens for too long, and the people would no longer tolerate the elites' corruption and incompetence. Under Huey's leadership, Louisiana left the poverty and neglect of the nineteenth century behind and moved boldly into the prosperous twentieth century "with castles and clothing and food for all."[23] Hollywood adopted the narrative wholesale, and even many scholars found merit in certain elements.[24]

While it is true that a temporary coalition formed to defeat the political arrangement imposed on the state by Reconstruction, the group was not tight-knit. The ephemeral nature of the coalition is proven by its rapid evaporation in the years following the end of Reconstruction. The band broke up, so to speak, well before the rise of Huey Long. This lack of cohesion is further evident in the endless parade of Democratic Party reform factions in New Orleans—with names seemingly too numerous to count. Such enduring divisions demonstrate that no post-Reconstruction oligarchy existed.

Robert Penn Warren summarized the Huey Long myth in the classic *All the King's Men* character Willie Stark: "You are a hick and ain't nobody ever helped a hick but a hick his self. It's up to you. It's up to you and me and God. Nail up Joe Harrison. Nail up McMurphee. And nail up any bastard gets between you and the roads and the bridges and the schools and the food you need. You give me the hammer and I'll do it. I'll nail their hides to the barn door. Nail 'em up!"[25]

Like Huey himself, the fictional Willie Stark is a powerful character. Alan Brinkley notes that "for almost fifty years, the popular image of Long has been in many ways inseparable from Warren's portrayal of Stark."[26] Comparing Long and the fictional Stark, historian Hugh Davis Graham explains one of the earliest myths associated with both men—their mission "to achieve noble ends through sordid means" but ultimately becoming "possessed by the evil and destroyed by it."[27] Graham argues that, although Robert Penn Warren consistently denied Huey Long was the model for Willie Stark, many scholars accepted the parable as fact. This complicates our perception of Huey personally and our understanding of his career in politics.[28]

Graham's explanation of the Willie Stark myth sheds light on a complex historiographical debate—one in which scholars' views have alternated between hate, love, "and now a critical attitude toward Long."[29] Graham, for instance, described the work of Arthur M. Schlesinger Jr., V. O. Key, and Allan Sindler as ranging from "fearful criticism to vituperation," and more importantly, as incomplete. Yet Graham was generally supportive of T. Harry Williams's biography, *Huey Long.* His assessment included the assertion that "it is a tribute to Williams that he left the warts intact, for they were abundant."[30] Other scholars held a different view.

Glenn Conrad, who served as editor of the journal *Louisiana History* for two decades, argued that T. Harry Williams rationalized Long's excesses.[31] Comparing the Williams biography to one released twenty years later by William Ivy Hair, Conrad praised Hair's unapologetic view of Long, asserting that Hair was willing to "call a spade a spade or a dictator a dictator."[32] In spite of this praise, he questioned the need for Hair's book and suggested the better form would have been a scholarly journal article. Conrad's views demonstrate how, over the last fifty years, historians reassessed Huey and rejected much of the old scholarship on the Kingfish. Today, historians generally agree that Huey Long's rise to power is peppered with myth, misinterpretation, and outright fiction. Nevertheless, we continue to evaluate and reevaluate his accomplishments, bombastic rhetoric, and political philosophy. There is also agreement, perhaps not unanimous but a healthy majority, that Huey Long was not a liberal reformer in any sense.

In short, the historical evidence caught up with Huey. His bitter and harsh attacks on enemies, manipulation of the state legislature, and threat of force and violence against New Orleans have become more than historians can tolerate. Jeansonne captured the state of current Long historiography, asserting that "whatever he [Huey Long] may have accomplished in the short run, he accomplished very little in the long run."[33] Jeansonne challenges Long's public policy successes in education, health care, and infrastructure. He argues that Huey discriminated against state universities other than LSU and, furthermore, that teachers' salaries went down during his rule. Huey's "Share-Our-Wealth" program was, according to Jeansonne, "no more an alternative to the New Deal than flubber is an alternative to gravity."[34] Moreover, he asserted, "As a United States Senator, Long never even came close to enacting a law."[35] Of Long's political accomplishments, Jeansonne urges that Long did not "impose liberalism on a reactionary state," but rather, "he impose[d] order upon chaos."[36] Finally, he argues that, contrary to T. Harry Williams's assertion, Huey Long did not overcome a dominant "shadowy elite." Rather, Louisiana was instead "decentralized" and "characterized by fragmentation."[37]

◆   ◆   ◆

Historian Hugh Davis Graham asked the question, "What does it tell us of the weakness and possible strengths of American political thought that [Huey] Long's contemporaries could not agree whether he should be labeled with a leftist term like radical democrat or a rightist term like fascist?"[38] A response to this question could fill the pages of another book, but insofar as it adds context to the Behrman years, let's consider it for a moment.

Political ideology in the United States changed dramatically during Behrman's lifetime, roughly between the Civil War and the Roaring Twenties. It was a time F. A. Hayek described as implementing "a complete change in the direction of our ideas and social order."[39] Thus, when Behrman first entered politics in New Orleans, the movement away from classical liberalism was just beginning.[40] This is not to suggest there had previously been a consensus in American politics—far from it. Rather, until the late nineteenth and early twentieth centuries, political debate in the United States was anchored in the same Hamiltonian and Jeffersonian principles.[41] Both founders emphasized the importance of individual rights and diverged mostly on the question of how best to secure such rights. The individual was paramount.

In contrast, progressivism emphasized the rights of the group over the individual. Progressive leader Herbert Croly, for example, "called for the adoption of Hamiltonian means to achieve Jeffersonian ends."[42] In combining the ideas of the two founders, Croly discarded Hamilton's caution against a pure national democracy and Jefferson's support for limited government because both were tied to classical liberalism and individual rights. Croly sought instead a transcendent "national political community."[43]

Behrman governed during this transformation, and Huey Long rose to power as it neared completion—the crescendo being FDR's New Deal programs. Therein lies the response to Graham's riddle of American political thought. As society grew more complex, public desire for a more active government permitted breaking up monopolies, enacting new labor laws, and banning alcohol, to name just a handful of revolutionary policy changes of the era. In New Orleans, these changes manifested themselves in government control of public health to end yellow fever epidemics, build canals and levees, pave roads, and eliminate the Storyville vice district.

This Behrman-era transformation in American politics rendered the linear left-right spectrum useless. Yet many of us continue to think about politics within its boundaries, even though a simple linear tool cannot measure an oddity like the Kingfish. The better tool is a circular political spectrum, which accounts for similarities between seemingly opposing ideologies by not assuming they will run forever in opposite directions.

Imagine bending a line into a circle. Fascism and socialism meet at the bottom—the point of maximal government coercion and authoritarian power. There stands Huey Long. Behrman is closer to the top, representing consensus, compromise, and triangulation. Consider another example—the points of differentiation between Martin Behrman and Raymond Fosdick.

Fosdick wrote one of the earliest and most influential books on policing and police reform. He was a passionate progressive from New York with an Ivy League education, and the person primarily responsible for the closure of Storyville. In contrast, Behrman was a pragmatic machine politician from New Orleans. He never went to college and fought Fosdick's attempts to close Storyville until he was left with no alternative. The two men could hardly be more different.

Yet, at least rhetorically, Fosdick and Behrman agreed that "you can't enforce a really unpopular law." Their speeches and writings further suggest consensus on this key point: a government that cannot enforce its own laws is subject to a loss of legitimacy, either through unpopular strict enforcement, or a policy of what Behrman described as "unobtrusive nonobservance of the law."[44] On this key point, Behrman isn't "further to left" or "further to right" of Fosdick. Instead, they are similarly situated on the circular ideological spectrum.

This complexity is reflected in twenty-first-century headlines, including progressive calls for police reforms such as elimination of qualified immunity.[45] Conservatives respond with appeals to "back the blue," urging better pay and more resources for police. At the same time, conservatives warn of the dangers of politicizing the FBI and corrupt investigations of former president Donald Trump. Progressives assert the FBI must respond forcefully to uphold the rule of law and preserve democracy.

Putting the merits aside, these arguments appear to contradict themselves. How can conservatives back the blue and oppose the FBI? How can progressives support the FBI and call for defunding the police? Each side of the debate uses these arguments to poke holes in the logic of the other. In fact, these arguments are not inconsistent—at least from the logician's standpoint. Progressive and conservative views on law enforcement reflect the reality that, when it comes to enforcing the law, government often vacillates between heavy-handedness and permissive neglect. The delicate balance is rarely executed with perfection, and policing issues therefore move around the circular spectrum, along with the conservative and progressive ideologies. Sometimes they blend together, and at other times they are diametrically opposed. In this context, the seemingly contradictory idea of a reform-oriented, turn-of-the-century political machine like the Regular Democratic Organization makes a lot more sense. And it was Martin Behrman who made the Regulars' sustained dominance possible. His legacy, though far from perfect, is that he governed by consensus as one of the nation's longest-serving and most accomplished mayors. The evidence of this historical fact lies not only in Behrman's life but in the course of events that followed his death.

✦   ✦   ✦

Huey Long's southern drawl warmed the cold ears of his loyalists during an outdoor rally in New Orleans. Mayor Walmsley is a "Turkey Head," shouted Huey. "You know the turkey head usually goes on the block, and we're fixing to have a little execution here."[46] Since Behrman's death, Huey had created his own political machine and was in complete control of Louisiana. The *New York Times* described Huey as the "de facto dictator" of the state.[47] What little countervailing political power remained could be found in New Orleans with Walmsley and the Regulars. But months before Huey's hostile tirade in New Orleans, the fragile alliance he maintained with Walmsley and the Regulars had fallen apart. Now, Huey wanted his own man in the mayor's parlor—one that he could control.

Mayor Walmsley did not appreciate Huey's turkey metaphor and threatened to "choke those words down Huey Long's cowardly throat."[48] The feud nearly erupted into a shooting war when Huey sent machine-gun-toting National Guardsmen into New Orleans. He claimed the guardsmen were there to clean up vice and corruption. Instead, they busted the locks off the doors of the elections office and took the place over. As Mayor Walmsley and the police arrived, a tense standoff ensued. Huey's puppet governor in Baton Rouge declared martial law in New Orleans, and the city found itself begging for mercy from the state militia and the cruel hand of the Kingfish. An outraged Walmsley took to the radio and lambasted Huey.

The Kingfish responded on the airwaves, alleging that Walmsley gave advance warning to the prostitutes and vice-peddlers, sending word that they should go into hiding.[49] By 1935, Huey had taken complete control of the police and fire departments and squeezed the city by cutting off so many different sources of revenue that it had to lay off thousands of employees. Walmsley resigned, leaving only a remnant of the Regular Democratic Organization—a shell of its former self without the leadership of Martin Behrman. Did those anti-machine reformers and newspaper editors who attacked Behrman so viciously for so many years wish that he were still available for public service in 1935? Most certainly. Could Huey have brought New Orleans to its knees with Behrman in the mayor's office? We'll never know, but it seems unlikely. The historical evidence tells us that, at minimum, it would have been one hell of a fight.

NOTES

INTRODUCTION

1. "Great Crowds Cheer Parker, Ring Breaker," *Times-Picayune,* January 28, 1920, 1.

2. "Great Crowds Cheer Parker, Ring Breaker," 1.

3. "Great Crowds Cheer Parker, Ring Breaker," 1.

4. "Great Crowds Cheer Parker, Ring Breaker," 1.

5. "Great Crowds Cheer Parker, Ring Breaker," 1.

6. "Great Crowds Cheer Parker, Ring Breaker," 1.

7. R. Williams, "Martin Behrman: Mayor and Political Boss of New Orleans, 1904–1926," 2.

8. Reynolds, *Machine Politics in New Orleans,* 220. McShane garnered only four thousand votes and likely helped swing the election to Behrman. See also T. H. Williams, *Huey Long,* 224.

9. T. H. Williams, *Huey Long,* 223.

10. T. H. Williams, *Huey Long,* 223, 224. Williams notes that Ewing, who also published the *Shreveport Times* and two newspapers in Monroe County, sought influence and statewide power. He was "searching for a rising country politician who would like to be advised," according to Williams.

11. T. H. Williams, *Huey Long,* 224.

12. This political alignment was new and temporary. It should not be misconstrued as a perpetuation of the T. Harry Williams "oligarchy" myth as described by Jeansonne and others. See Glen Jeansonne, "Huey Long and the Historians," 124–25.

13. Reynolds, *Machine Politics in New Orleans,* 222.

14. T. H. Williams, *Huey Long,* 225.

15. T. H. Williams, "The Gentleman from Louisiana," 3–4.

16. T. H. Williams, "The Gentleman from Louisiana," 4.

17. T. H. Williams, "The Gentleman from Louisiana," 4.

18. Riordan, *Plunkitt of Tammany Hall,* 3.

19. Golway, *Machine Made,* ix–xii.

20. Colburn and Pozzetta, "Bosses and Machines," 459.

21. McDonald, "The Politics of Urban History versus the History of Urban Politics," 299.

22. Ostrogorski, *Democracy and the Organization of Political Parties,* vol. 2, 93–95.

23. Salter, *Boss Rule,* 4.

24. Salter, *Boss Rule,* 253.

25. Salter, *Boss Rule,* 267.

26. Reynolds, *Machine Politics in New Orleans,* 227.

27. Merton, *Social Theory and Social Structure,* 132.

28. Colburn and Pozzetta, "Bosses and Machines," 453.

29. Huthmacher, "Urban Liberalism and the Age of Reform," 234.

30. McDonald, "The Politics of Urban History versus the History of Urban Politics," 300.

31. McDonald, "The Politics of Urban History versus the History of Urban Politics," 447.

32. R. Williams, "Martin Behrman: Mayor and Political Boss of New Orleans, 1904–1926," 2.

33. R. Williams, "Martin Behrman: Mayor and Political Boss of New Orleans, 1904–1926," 2.

34. "News of Death Shocks Friends in Metropolis," *Times-Picayune,* January 13, 1926.

35. R. Williams, "Martin Behrman: Mayor and Political Boss of New Orleans, 1904–1926," 6.

36. R. Williams, "Martin Behrman and New Orleans Civic Development," 373.

37. Kemp, *Martin Behrman of New Orleans,* xi.

38. Jeansonne, *Huey at 100,* 8–9.

39. Jeansonne, "Huey Long and the Historians," 124–25.

40. "Civic Leaders, Business Men Join in Tribute," *Times-Picayune,* January 13, 1926.

41. Hofstadter, *The Age of Reform,* 177, 290.

42. Bell, *The Radical Right,* 449; Collins, "The Originality Trap," 150–67.

43. Fitzmorris, "Pro Bono Publico," 4.

44. Shumsky, "Tacit Acceptance," 665.

45. Cartoon, *Time-Picayune,* August 27, 1920. This story covered multiple days and several issues of the newspaper.

46. Campbell, "Clinton's Encounter with the Separation of Powers," 157. Jonathan Cohn of the *New Republic* compared Obama's triangulation to Clinton's ("How Obama Triangulates," December 8, 2010, newrepublic.com/article/79758/obama-clinton-triangulation), as did Ben Smith of *Politico* ("So Is It Triangulation?" December 8, 2010, www.politico.com/blogs/ben-smith/2010/12/so-is-it-triangulation-031298).

47. Kemp, *Martin Behrman of New Orleans,* 60.

48. Fitzmorris, "Pro Bono Publico," 4.

49. Haas, *Political Leadership in a Southern City,* 28–29; Long, *The Great Southern Babylon,* 23–24 and 209.

50. Binkley, *American Political Parties,* 317.

51. Binkley, *American Political Parties,* 317.

52. Dethloff, "Huey Long and Populism," 68–69.

53. Dethloff, "Huey Long and Populism," 68–69.

54. Kemp, *Martin Behrman of New Orleans,* 158.

55. Later, *Muller* was criticized by feminists because it "embedded in constitutional law an axiom of female difference. . . . women could be treated as a class in different ways than men." See Woloch, *Muller v. Oregon,* 4–7.

1

PASSAGES
Surviving New Orleans

1. Duffy, "Nineteenth Century Public Health in New York and New Orleans," 325–37.

2. Adler, "Murder, North and South," 297–324; Kurtz, *Organized Crime in Louisiana History,* 355–76.

3. Carrigan, "Mass Communication and Public Health," 5.

4. Carrigan, "Impact of Epidemic Yellow Fever on Life in Louisiana," 5.

5. Pfeifer, "Lynching and Criminal Justice in South Louisiana, 1878–1930," 155–77.

6. Shea and Winschel, *Vicksburg Is the Key,* 12–13.

7. Greenwald and Rothman, "New Orleans Should Acknowledge Its Lead Role in the Slave Trade," *Times-Picayune,* February 19, 2016.

8. Shea and Winschel, *Vicksburg Is the Key,* 12–13.

9. *United States Census 1870.*

10. *Trow's New York City Directory,* vol. 76 (1863): 66.

11. New York Public Library, www.nypl.org/collections/articles-databases/castle-garden-immigration-center-1830-1892.

12. "Aufbruch in die Neue Welt," *Stern,* no. 19, April 5, 2005.

13. "Aufbruch in die Neue Welt."

14. "In the Steerage of a Cunard Steamer," 9–12.

15. Babies six months and less exhibit less distress than children six months to five years. Boys appear to be affected more than girls. See Ambron, Brodzinsky, and Gormly, *Lifespan Human Development,* 133.

16. Ambron, Brodzinsky, and Gormly, *Lifespan Human Development,* 2.

17. Deacon, Lucy, and Coleman, *Martin Behrman Administration Biography,* 62–64.

18. Haas, *Political Leadership in a Southern City,* 3.

19. Merrill, *Germans of Louisiana,* 62–64.

20. "Dixie Brewing Company."

21. Merrill, *Germans of Louisiana,* 170.

22. Kemp, *Martin Behrman of New Orleans,* 3.

23. Ambron, Brodzinsky, and Gormly, *Lifespan Human Development,* 551.

24. Ambron, Brodzinsky, and Gormly, *Lifespan Human Development,* 553.

25. Sengendo and Nambi, *The Psychological Effect of Orphanhood,* 105.

26. "Martin Behrman's Marriage and His First Venture in Politics," *New Orleans Item,* October 22, 1922.

27. Downs and Sherraden, "The Orphan Asylum in the Nineteenth Century," 272–90.

28. "Orphanages: An Historical Overview," 2–3.

29. "Orphanages: An Historical Overview," 2–3.

30. Clement, "Children and Charity," 339.

31. Clement, "Children and Charity," 342.

32. Clement, "Children and Charity," 342.

33. Lang and Luttrell, "Vignettes," 260.

34. "Martin Behrman's Marriage and His First Venture in Politics," *New Orleans Item,* October 22, 1922.

35. Merrill, *Germans of Louisiana,* 87; Federal Census of the United States, State of Louisiana, Parish of Orleans, June 16, 1880, Supervisor District 1, Enumeration District 89, p. 44; Deutsch, "New Orleans Politics—The Greatest Free Show on Earth," 315.

36. In 1870, Algiers was incorporated into the city of New Orleans and became the Fifth District. See Merrill, *Germans of Louisiana,* 87.

37. "Former Mayor Begins Story of His Life, and His Rise to Prominence and Political Power in N.O.," *New Orleans Item,* October 22, 1922.

38. "Behrman Tells of Opening Scenes in the Great Political Convention in 1898," *New Orleans Item,* November 6, 1922. Behrman also predicted that children would one day receive "free pencils and paper, free lunch, [and] free moving pictures of an educational character."

39. Martin Behrman, "Former Mayor Begins Story of His Life, and His Rise to Prominence and Political Power in N.O.," *New Orleans Item,* October 22, 1922.

40. Hennessey, "Race and Violence in Reconstruction New Orleans," 80.

41. Holzman, "Ben Butler in the Civil War," 338; Haas, *Political Leadership in a Southern City,* 4-5. For a timeline and description of the riot, see U.S. Department of the Interior, "The Era of Reconstruction: 1861-1900."

42. Hennessey, "Race and Violence in Reconstruction New Orleans," 78.

43. Hennessey, "Race and Violence in Reconstruction New Orleans," 81-82.

44. Haas, *Political Leadership in a Southern City,* 8-9.

2

THE ARENA
Marriage and Politics

1. Kemp, *Martin Behrman of New Orleans,* 5.

2. Lawton Ancestry website.

3. Sarah Waits, archivist, Archdiocese of New Orleans, in email communication describes New Orleans's "long history of creating 'national' parishes to serve different immigrant communities, so there were Irish, German, Italian, etc. churches built in the neighborhoods with the largest concentration of those immigrants."

4. Waits, email communication. For more on the history of the Catholic Church in the South, see Nolan, "In Search of Southern Parish History," 11-21.

5. Terrence Fitzmorris, email correspondence, October 13, 2022.

6. Thomas, "Mugwump Cartoonists," 218.

7. Charles Nolan, "New Orleans Civic Culture Imbued with Catholicism," *Clarion Herald,* January 25, 2018.

8. Archdiocese of New Orleans, noladceff.org/our-rich-history.

9. Catherine Arnold, "Centennial of Algiers Sparks Memories of Reign by Behrman," *Clarion Herald,* March 12, 1970.

10. Sts. Peter and Paul Church, Marriage vol. 1887–1910, pt. 1, p. 3, act 10.

11. *New Orleans Item,* October 22, 1922.

12. Arnold, "Centennial of Algiers Sparks Memories."

13. Arnold, "Centennial of Algiers Sparks Memories."

14. Jackson, *New Orleans in the Gilded Age,* 2. Historian C. Vann Woodward describes Democrats' immediate post-Reconstruction priorities as getting Black citizens out of politics and erasing all remnants of Northern control. See Woodward, *Origins of the New South,* 107–8.

15. Haas, *Political Leadership in a Southern City,* 9.

16. Fitzmorris, "Pro Bono Publico," 456–59.

17. Jackson, *New Orleans in the Gilded Age,* 22.

18. Dawson, ed., *The Louisiana Governors,* 215.

19. Kemp, *Martin Behrman of New Orleans,* 7.

20. Kemp, *Martin Behrman of New Orleans,* 12, 13.

21. Kemp, *Martin Behrman of New Orleans,* 8.

22. R. Williams, "Martin Behrman: Mayor and Political Boss of New Orleans, 1904–1926," 3.

23. Kendall, *History of New Orleans* 2:1.

24. Garvey and Widmer, *Beautiful Crescent,* 198–99.

25. Baranoff, "Shaped by Risk," 561.

26. Algiers Historical Society, "Algiers History."

27. Algiers Historical Society, "Algiers History."

28. "Algiers Is Near Destroyed," *New Orleans Item,* October 29, 1922.

29. "Algiers Is Near Destroyed."

30. Kendall, *History of New Orleans* 2:219.

31. Kemp, *Martin Behrman of New Orleans,* 29.

32. Haas, *Political Leadership in a Southern City,* 20, 28–29. Hass notes that "Many New Orleans Democrats" attributed the Citizens' League win to "manipulated black votes."

33. Kendall, *History of New Orleans* 2:22.

34. White, *Kingfish,* 30.

35. White, *Kingfish,* 30.

36. Kemp, *Martin Behrman of New Orleans,* 35.

37. Kemp, *Martin Behrman of New Orleans,* 35.

38. Haas, *Political Leadership in a Southern City,* 28–29.

39. Haas, *Political Leadership in a Southern City,* 28–29.

40. Kemp, *Martin Behrman of New Orleans,* 42.

41. Parker and his allies therefore supported "color-blind" disenfranchisement ensnaring Italians and anyone else who was poor, illiterate, and ethnic. Behrman and the Choctaws were focused primarily on disenfranchising Black voters.

42. Haas, *Political Leadership in a Southern City,* 30–31.

43. Kemp, *Martin Behrman of New Orleans,* 39.

44. Haas, *Political Leadership in a Southern City*, 36.

45. Long, *The Great Southern Babylon*, 58–59, 209–10. Long describes a series of laws related to interracial relationships and "social contact between white and 'colored' in schools, bars, restaurants, and public conveyances—in short, wherever the races interacted on the basis of equality," 209.

46. Kemp, *Martin Behrman of New Orleans*, 41.

47. Kemp, *Martin Behrman of New Orleans*, 43.

48. "Behrman Tells of Opening Scenes in the Great Political Convention in 1898," *New Orleans Item*, November 6, 1922.

49. Kemp, *Martin Behrman of New Orleans*, 41.

50. "Behrman Tells of Opening Scenes in the Great Political Convention in 1898," *New Orleans Item*, November 6, 1922.

51. "Behrman Tells of Opening Scenes in the Great Political Convention in 1898."

52. Schafer, *Brothels, Depravity, and Abandoned Women*, 145.

53. Schafer, *Brothels, Depravity, and Abandoned Women*, 144–45.

54. Rose, *Storyville*, 35.

55. Kemp, *Martin Behrman of New Orleans*, 35–37.

56. Rose, *Storyville*, 39. For an excellent discussion of *L'Hote v. New Orleans*, see Long, *The Great Southern Babylon*, 104–49.

57. Rose, *Storyville*, 37. See also Keire, "The Vice Trust," 18.

3

ASCENT

Don't Let Them Make You Do It

1. Catherine Arnold, "Centennial of Algiers Sparks Memories of Reign by Behrman," *Clarion Herald*, March 12, 1970.

2. Lawton Ancestry website.

3. Arnold, "Centennial of Algiers Sparks Memories."

4. Arnold, "Centennial of Algiers Sparks Memories."

5. Kemp, *Martin Behrman of New Orleans*, 59.

6. Kemp, *Martin Behrman of New Orleans*, 74.

7. "Behrman Tells of Campaign in Which He Became Auditor," *New Orleans Item*, November 16, 1922.

8. "Behrman Tells of Campaign in Which He Became Auditor."

9. "Behrman Tells of Campaign in Which He Became Auditor."

10. Kemp, *Martin Behrman of New Orleans*, 75.

11. Replacing party nominating conventions with direct primaries became a basic goal of reformers seeking to loosen the grip of city and state political machines in many states.

12. Kemp, *Martin Behrman of New Orleans*, 78.

13. R. Williams, "Martin Behrman: Mayor and Political Boss of New Orleans, 1904–1926," 99.

14. Kemp, *Martin Behrman of New Orleans*, 79.

15. Kemp, *Martin Behrman of New Orleans,* 80–81.

16. Kemp, *Martin Behrman of New Orleans,* 80–81.

17. R. Williams, "Martin Behrman: Mayor and Political Boss of New Orleans, 1904–1926," 15.

18. Kemp, *Martin Behrman of New Orleans,* 56.

19. R. Williams, "Martin Behrman: Mayor and Political Boss of New Orleans, 1904–1926," 16–17.

20. Reynolds, *Machine Politics in New Orleans,* 108.

21. Reynolds, *Machine Politics in New Orleans,* 20.

22. Hair, *The Kingfish and His Realm,* 12–14.

23. Krist, *Empire of Sin,* 44.

24. Parkerson qtd. in Krist, *Empire of Sin,* 48.

25. Krist, *Empire of Sin,* 48.

26. Kemp, *Martin Behrman of New Orleans,* 10.

27. Krist, *Empire of Sin,* 52.

28. *St. Mary Banner* and *American Law Review* qtd. in Hair, *The Kingfish and His Realm,* 14.

29. Parkerson qtd. in Krist, *Empire of Sin,* 52.

30. Krist, *Empire of Sin,* 53.

31. "Parkerson Adds to Behrman Charges," *Daily Picayune,* October 28, 1904.

32. "Parkerson Adds to Behrman Charges."

33. "Parkerson Adds to Behrman Charges."

34. "Martin Behrman Makes More Reply to Parkerson," *Daily Picayune,* October 27, 1904.

35. "Martin Behrman Makes More Reply to Parkerson."

36. "Martin Behrman Makes More Reply to Parkerson."

37. Kendall, *History of New Orleans* 2:34.

38. "Martin Behrman Makes More Reply to Parkerson."

39. R. Williams, "Martin Behrman: Mayor and Political Boss of New Orleans, 1904–1926," 21.

40. R. Williams, "Martin Behrman: Mayor and Political Boss of New Orleans, 1904–1926," 30.

41. "Behrman Struck in a Barbershop," *Daily Picayune,* October 30, 1904.

42. R. Williams, "Martin Behrman: Mayor and Political Boss of New Orleans, 1904–1926," 31.

43. R. Williams, "Martin Behrman: Mayor and Political Boss of New Orleans, 1904–1926," 32.

44. Kendall, *History of New Orleans* 2:34.

45. R. Williams, "Martin Behrman: Mayor and Political Boss of New Orleans, 1904–1926," 33.

46. Reynolds, *Machine Politics in New Orleans,* 117.

47. Reynolds, *Machine Politics in New Orleans,* 117.

48. John Wilds, "In 1904 We Were Here . . . when a mayor began his record stay in City Hall," *Times-Picayune,* June 5, 1977, 42.

49. Wilds, "In 1904 We Were Here."

50. White, *Kingfish,* 31.

51. R. Williams, "Martin Behrman: Mayor and Political Boss of New Orleans, 1904–1926," 7.

52. R. Williams, "Martin Behrman: Mayor and Political Boss of New Orleans, 1904–1926," 118.

53. Reynolds, *Machine Politics in New Orleans,* 109.

54. Reynolds, *Machine Politics in New Orleans,* 109.

55. Reynolds, *Machine Politics in New Orleans,* 112–13.

56. Reynolds, *Machine Politics in New Orleans,* 115–16.

57. R. Williams, "Martin Behrman: Mayor and Political Boss of New Orleans, 1904–1926," 11.

58. R. Williams, "Martin Behrman: Mayor and Political Boss of New Orleans, 1904–1926," 12.

59. *Presidential Elections, 1789–1996,* 130.

60. Morris, *Theodore Rex,* 539.

61. Kemp, *Martin Behrman of New Orleans,* 178.

62. Kemp, *Martin Behrman of New Orleans,* 180–81.

63. Kendall, *History of New Orleans* 2:35.

64. Kendall, *History of New Orleans* 2:35. See also Kemp, *Martin Behrman of New Orleans,* 194n2, regarding Populist priorities in Louisiana, including direct primaries and election of parish school boards.

65. Kemp, *Martin Behrman of New Orleans,* 183–84.

66. Dawson, ed., *The Louisiana Governors,* 204.

67. Dawson, ed., *The Louisiana Governors,* 204.

68. T. H. Williams, *Huey Long,* 271–72, 238.

4

CIVIC DEVELOPMENT
Fighting the Saffron Scourge

1. Woodward, *Origins of the New South,* 107–8.

2. Woodward, *Origins of the New South,* 107–8.

3. Fitzmorris, "Pro Bono Publico," 3.

4. Duffy, "Nineteenth Century Public Health in New York and New Orleans," 101.

5. Duffy, "Nineteenth Century Public Health in New York and New Orleans," 101. For more on the history of yellow fever in Louisiana, see Carrigan, "Impact of Epidemic Yellow Fever on Life in Louisiana," 5–34.

6. Carrigan, "Impact of Epidemic Yellow Fever on Life in Louisiana," 5–34.

7. Duffy, "Nineteenth Century Public Health in New York and New Orleans," 101, 106.

8. Derr, *Some Kind of Paradise,* 171; Reed, "Recent Research Concerning the Etiology, Propagation, and Prevention of Yellow Fever," 108–12.

9. Founded by the Daughters of Charity (an order established by St. Vincent de Paul), Hotel Dieu was one of the finest hospitals in the South.

10. Kemp, *Martin Behrman of New Orleans,* 132.

11. Kemp, *Martin Behrman of New Orleans,* 132.

12. Kemp, *Martin Behrman of New Orleans,* 131.

13. Carrigan, "Mass Communication and Public Health," 8.

14. Newton C. Blanchard, Governor of Louisiana, to Martin Behrman, Mayor of New Orleans, September 23, 1905.

15. Felix J. Dreyfus, lawyer, to Martin Behrman, Mayor of New Orleans, August 14, 1905.

16. D. H. Chick, nurse, to Martin Behrman, Mayor of New Orleans, September 10, 1905.

17. Kemp, *Martin Behrman of New Orleans,* 132.

18. Kemp, *Martin Behrman of New Orleans,* 132.

19. Carrigan, "Mass Communication and Public Health," 15.

20. Kemp, *Martin Behrman of New Orleans,* 153.

21. Behrman speech, "New Orleans: A History of Three Great Public Utilities."

22. Behrman speech, "New Orleans: A History of Three Great Public Utilities."

23. Behrman speech, "New Orleans: A History of Three Great Public Utilities."

24. Behrman speech, "New Orleans: A History of Three Great Public Utilities."

25. Behrman speech, "New Orleans: A History of Three Great Public Utilities."

26. Behrman speech, "Street Paving Problem."

27. Behrman speech, "The Port of New Orleans."

28. George G. Earl, General Superintendent to Sewerage and Water Board of New Orleans, "The Hurricane of Sept. 29th, 1915, and Subsequent Heavy Rainfalls," October 14, 1915.

29. Earl, "The Hurricane of Sept. 29th, 1915."

30. Behrman speech, "The Port of New Orleans."

31. Behrman speech, "The Port of New Orleans."

32. Behrman speech, "The Port of New Orleans."

33. Behrman speech, "The Port of New Orleans."

34. Behrman speech, "New Orleans: A History of Three Great Public Utilities."

35. Behrman speech, "New Orleans: A History of Three Great Public Utilities."

36. R. Williams, "Martin Behrman: Mayor and Political Boss of New Orleans, 1904–1926," 44.

37. "Inner Harbor Navigation Canal and the Lower Ninth Ward."

38. Dunn, "The Pumps That Built (and Sank) the City of New Orleans."

39. Tim Craig, "It Wasn't Even a Hurricane, but Heavy Rains Flooded New Orleans as Pumps Faltered," *Washington Post,* August 9, 2017.

40. Behrman, "Street Paving Problem."

41. Behrman, "Street Paving Problem."

42. Behrman, "Street Paving Problem."

43. Behrman, Correspondence to major cities across the United States regarding street paving.

44. Behrman, Correspondence to major cities across the United States regarding street paving.

5

TEMPERANCE AND PROHIBITION
A Damnable Outrage Spurs Action

1. See Fitzmorris, "Pro Bono Publico," 9–10.

2. Blocker, *American Temperance Movements,* 96.

3. Fitzmorris, email communication, May 5, 2022.

4. Historian Terrence Fitzmorris notes, "Though several hundred Irish and Germans pledged to temper their use of alcohol, the association faced intense opposition. Most Irish and

Germans saw temperance as an assault on their cultures and Catholic faith. The Irish saw it also as evidence of British meddling in the affairs of America, as was abolition." Email communication, May 5, 2022.

5. Abraham Lincoln Presidential Library and Museum, www.chroniclingillinois.org/items/show/29168.

6. Pelican Publishing Co., *Inside Old Treme,* 22.

7. Merrill, *Germans of Louisiana,* 171.

8. Merrill, *Germans of Louisiana,* 171. Krost was also the first to import bock beer in 1852, and to bring bottled German beer to New Orleans. See *Merrill, Germans of Louisiana,* 167–78, for an excellent discussion of the history of beer in New Orleans.

9. Merrill, *Germans of Louisiana,* 167

10. Merrill, *Germans of Louisiana,* 168.

11. Robertson, *The Great American Beer Book,* 26.

12. Labadie and Wolf-Knapp, *New Orleans Beer,* 26.

13. Robertson, *The Great American Beer Book,* 26.

14. Robertson, *The Great American Beer Book,* 27–28.

15. Robertson, *The Great American Beer Book,* 27–28.

16. Merrill, *Germans of Louisiana,* 168.

17. Stack, "Local and Regional Breweries in America's Brewing Industry," 440.

18. Appel, "Artificial Refrigeration and the Architecture of 19th-Century American Breweries," 26.

19. Pleck, "Feminist Responses to Crimes against Women," 452–53.

20. Pleck, "Feminist Responses to Crimes against Women," 452–53.

21. Pleck, "Feminist Responses to Crimes against Women," 463.

22. Pegram, *Battling Demon Rum,* 68–69.

23. Pegram, *Battling Demon Rum,* 69–71.

24. Pleck, "Feminist Responses to Crimes against Women," 462.

25. Stack, "Local and Regional Breweries in America's Brewing Industry," 440.

26. "Dixie Brewing Company."

27. Tompkins, ed., *American Decades 1900–1909,* 277.

28. Kemp, *Martin Behrman of New Orleans,* 162.

29. Kemp, *Martin Behrman of New Orleans,* 161.

30. Thomann, "Is Beer Drinking Injurious?" 24–25.

31. Thomann, "Is Beer Drinking Injurious?" 24–25.

32. Lamme, "The Brewers and Public Relations History," 455.

33. Reilly, *Jannus: An American Flier,* 67–80. The beer was supposedly so good that Jannus drank it all before arriving in New Orleans and delivered a case of empty bottles to Behrman. Press reports, and there were many, do not indicate that Jannus committed such a faux pas. See "Jannus Congratulated by Mayor Behrman," *Times-Picayune,* December 17, 1912.

34. Landau, *Spectacular Wickedness,* 3–5.

35. "The Night President Teddy Roosevelt Invited Booker T. Washington to Dinner," 24–25.

36. "The Night President Teddy Roosevelt Invited Booker T. Washington to Dinner," 24–25.

37. Scheiner, "President Theodore Roosevelt and the Negro, 1901–1908," 171.

38. Scheiner, "President Theodore Roosevelt and the Negro, 1901–1908," 171.

39. K. Kemp, "Jean and Kate Gordon," 393.

40. Jean Gordon, "Committee of 100 Hears of Saloon Law Violations," *Times-Picayune,* July 1, 1917.

41. Sismondo, *America Walks into a Bar,* 183–91.

42. Rose, *Storyville,* 103–24.

43. Barker, *Buddy Bolden and the Last Days of Storyville,* 26. Barker attributes the quote to Dude Bottley, a composite character he created to synthesize his interviews and research into the early days of jazz in New Orleans. According to the book's editor, Alyn Shipton, "Dude was a way to ground all of Danny's material about jazz history in a single story." See Cleaver, "The Folklore of Danny Barker," 1.

44. Rose, *Storyville,* 162.

45. Jackson, "Prohibition in New Orleans," 261.

46. Lewis, "Cultural Norms and Political Mobilization," 31.

47. Kemp, *Martin Behrman of New Orleans,* 158.

48. Kemp, *Martin Behrman of New Orleans,* 158n35.

49. Kemp, *Martin Behrman of New Orleans,* 158.

50. Kemp, *Martin Behrman of New Orleans,* 159.

51. Jackson, "Prohibition in New Orleans," 262.

52. French Market Improvement Association to Martin Behrman, undated.

53. Kemp, *Martin Behrman of New Orleans,* 166.

54. Kemp, *Martin Behrman of New Orleans,* 166.

55. Kemp, *Martin Behrman of New Orleans,* 166.

56. Kemp, *Martin Behrman of New Orleans,* 162.

57. Public School Alliance to Martin Behrman, November 15, 1906.

58. Public School Alliance to Martin Behrman, November 15, 1906.

59. Public School Alliance to Martin Behrman, November 15, 1906.

60. Jean Gordon, "Committee of 100 Hears of Saloon Law Violations," *Times-Picayune,* July 1, 1917.

61. Long, *The Great Southern Babylon,* 181.

62. Landau, *Spectacular Wickedness,* 165.

63. Landau, *Spectacular Wickedness,* 166.

64. Qtd. in Landau, *Spectacular Wickedness,* 166.

65. Schluter, *The Brewing Industry and the Brewery Workers' Movement in America,* 90–91.

66. Schluter, *The Brewing Industry and the Brewery Workers' Movement in America,* 90–91.

67. Schluter, *The Brewing Industry and the Brewery Workers' Movement in America,* 138.

68. Schluter, *The Brewing Industry and the Brewery Workers' Movement in America,* 204–5, 264.

69. Schluter, *The Brewing Industry and the Brewery Workers' Movement in America,* 136.

70. Stack, "Local and Regional Breweries in America's Brewing Industry," 441, 448.

6

REFORM

The Rising Tide in New Orleans

1. Szymanski, "Beyond Parochialism," 108.

2. *Lower Coast Gazette,* vol. 1 (November 27, 1909).

3. Letter from Kate Gordon to Martin Behrman, June 21, 1908.

4. Gordon to Behrman, June 21, 1908.

5. K. Kemp, "Jean and Kate Gordon," 392.

6. Carrie Chapman Catt, "Crisis in Suffrage Movement, Says Mrs. Catt," *New York Times,* September 3, 1916, ProQuest Historical Newspapers, SM 5.

7. "Brief News and Notes," *Caldwell Watchmen,* Columbia, LA, vol. 30 (August 18, 1916).

8. "A Woman of Many Votes," *New York Times,* June 8, 1902, ProQuest Historical Newspapers: New York Times (1851–2008), SM 12.

9. K. Kemp, "Jean and Kate Gordon," 389–401.

10. "Hidden from History: Unknown New Orleanians"; "Kate and Jean Gordon," *Encyclopedia of Louisiana.*

11. Keire, "The Vice Trust," 9.

12. Rose, *Storyville,* 64.

13. Szymanski, "Beyond Parochialism," 108.

14. Stanonis, "A Woman of Boundless Energy," 11.

15. Stanonis, "A Woman of Boundless Energy," 11.

16. R. Williams, "Martin Behrman: Mayor and Political Boss of New Orleans, 1904–1926," 45.

17. R. Williams, "Martin Behrman: Mayor and Political Boss of New Orleans, 1904–1926," 214.

18. Schott, "The New Orleans Machine and Progressivism," 143.

19. Schott, "The New Orleans Machine and Progressivism," 143.

20. Kemp, *Martin Behrman of New Orleans,* 294–95.

21. Kemp, *Martin Behrman of New Orleans,* 301–2.

22. R. Williams, "Martin Behrman: Mayor and Political Boss of New Orleans, 1904–1926," 35.

23. Historian Robert Webb Williams cites several newspaper stories in his retelling of this episode, including the *Daily Picayune,* August 26 and 27, 1912, and the *New Orleans States,* September 1, 1912.

24. Dempsey, *Introduction to Private Security,* 12. See also Federal Bureau of Investigation, "William J. Burns, August 22, 1921–June 14, 1924."

25. R. Williams, "Martin Behrman: Mayor and Political Boss of New Orleans, 1904–1926," 37.

26. R. Williams, "Martin Behrman: Mayor and Political Boss of New Orleans, 1904–1926," 41.

27. R. Williams, "Martin Behrman: Mayor and Political Boss of New Orleans, 1904–1926," 39–41.

28. Kendall, *History of New Orleans* 2:37.

29. R. Williams, "Martin Behrman: Mayor and Political Boss of New Orleans, 1904–1926," 45.

30. Fitzmorris, "Pro Bono Publico," 124.

31. Kendall, *History of New Orleans* 2:35; Collin, "Theodore Roosevelt's Visit to New Orleans," 7.

32. National Governors Association, "Past Governors."

33. Kemp, *Martin Behrman of New Orleans,* xi.

34. Brown, "The Election and Prohibition," 852. Brown asserted "the prohibition idea presupposes the conviction that the end justifies the means of accomplishing reform."

35. Brown, "The Election and Prohibition," 853.

36. Hofstadter, *The Age of Reform,* 290.

7

STORYVILLE

Mecca of Whores

1. Foster, "Tarnished Angels," 387–97. Foster cites Henriques, *Prostitution in Europe and the Americas,* 254.

2. Foster, "Tarnished Angels," 387–97.

3. Landau, *Spectacular Wickedness,* 21–23.

4. Rose, *Storyville,* 61.

5. Rose, *Storyville,* 61.

6. Sismondo, *America Walks into a Bar,* 176–77.

7. Sismondo, *America Walks into a Bar,* 176–79.

8. John Wilds, "In 1904 We Were Here . . . when a mayor began his record stay in City Hall," *Times-Picayune,* June 5, 1977, 42.

9. City of New Orleans HDLC, "Irish Channel Historic District."

10. City of New Orleans HDLC, "Irish Channel Historic District."

11. City of New Orleans HDLC, "Irish Channel Historic District."

12. Rose, *Storyville,* 42.

13. Barker, *Buddy Bolden and the Last Days of Storyville,* 54. This is a second quote Barker attributes to Dude Bottley, the composite character he created. See Cleaver, "The Folklore of Danny Barker," 1.

14. Rose, *Storyville,* 43.

15. Long, *The Great Southern Babylon,* 69–71.

16. Citizens' correspondence to Martin Behrman, April 8, 1907.

17. Pleck, "Feminist Responses to Crimes against Women," 469–70.

18. Rose, *Storyville,* 47–49.

19. Rose, *Storyville,* 48.

20. Rose, *Storyville,* 98.

21. Rose, *Storyville,* 48.

22. Rose, *Storyville,* 48.

23. Rose, *Storyville,* 80.

24. Rose, *Storyville,* 98.

25. Rose, *Storyville,* 44.

26. Shumsky, "Tacit Acceptance," 665; Keire, "The Vice Trust," 5–41.

27. Wagenaar and Amesberger, "Prostitution Policy beyond Trafficking," 227.

28. Keire, "The Vice Trust," 5–41.

29. Keire, "The Vice Trust," 19–20.

30. Keire, "The Vice Trust," 19.

31. Keire, "The Vice Trust," 19.

8

AMERICAN EXPANSION
The Algiers Navy Yard

1. Erin M. Greenwald and Joshua D. Rothman, "New Orleans Should Acknowledge Its Lead Role in the Slave Trade," *Times-Picayune,* February 19, 2016; Rothman, *Slave Country,* 73–119.

2. Rothman, *Slave Country,* 3–4.

3. Jefferson qtd. in Marler, *The Merchants' Capital,* 19.

4. Jefferson qtd. in Marler, *The Merchants' Capital,* 19.

5. Schneider, *Old Man River,* 180.

6. Schneider, *Old Man River,* 181.

7. Powell, *The Accidental City,* 314.

8. Powell, *The Accidental City,* 317. As a result of the French and Indian War of 1756, also known as the Seven Years' War, the British won Canada from France.

9. U.S. Department of the Interior, National Park Service, National Register of Historic Places Registration Form, NRIS Reference 13000695, U.S. Naval Station Algiers Historic District, 14. September 11, 2013.

10. U.S. Senate, "Report of the Secretary of Navy." December 7, 1852.

11. U.S. Department of the Interior, National Park Service, National Register of Historic Places Registration Form, NRIS Reference 13000695, U.S. Naval Station Algiers Historic District, September 11, 2013, 15.

12. Tompkins, ed., *American Decades, 1878 to 1879,* 203.

13. U.S. Department of the Interior, National Park Service, National Register of Historic Places Registration Form, NRIS Reference 13000695, U.S. Naval Station Algiers Historic District, September 11, 2013, 15.

14. U.S. Department of the Interior, National Park Service, National Register of Historic Places Registration Form, NRIS Reference 13000695, U.S. Naval Station Algiers Historic District, September 11, 2013, 15.

15. Tompkins, ed., *American Decades, 1878 to 1879,* 202.

16. Tompkins, ed., *American Decades, 1878 to 1879,* 203.

17. U.S. Department of the Interior, National Park Service, National Register of Historic Places Registration Form, NRIS Reference 13000695, U.S. Naval Station Algiers Historic District, September 11, 2013, 16.

18. Roosevelt qtd. in Millett, Maslowski, and Feis, *For the Common Defense,* 282. For more

on the state of the U.S. Navy in the early twentieth century and the origins of Roosevelt's plans, see Craig, *Josephus Daniels,* 225–29.

19. Millett, Maslowski, and Feis, *For the Common Defense,* 282.

20. Millett, Maslowski, and Feis, *For the Common Defense,* 284

21. Millett, Maslowski, and Feis, *For the Common Defense,* 284.

22. Millett, Maslowski, and Feis, *For the Common Defense,* 284.

23. McKinley, "Cruise of the Great White Fleet."

24. For more on the Great White Fleet, see Hearn, *The Illustrated Directory of the United States Navy,* 136–37.

25. "The Pensacola Navy-Yard," *Daily Picayune,* October 22, 1901, 4.

26. U.S. Department of the Interior, National Park Service, National Register of Historic Places Registration Form, NRIS Reference 13000695, U.S. Naval Station Algiers Historic District, September 11, 2013, 16.

27. Paul Purpura, "After 110 Years, Naval Support Activity's Algiers Base Is Closed," *Times-Picayune,* September 15, 2011.

28. U.S. Department of the Interior, National Park Service, National Register of Historic Places Registration Form, NRIS Reference 13000695, U.S. Naval Station Algiers Historic District, September 11, 2013, 16–17.

29. Meyer, "Naval Appropriation Bill," 11.

30. U.S. Department of the Interior, National Park Service, National Register of Historic Places Registration Form, NRIS Reference 13000695, U.S. Naval Station Algiers Historic District, September 11, 2013, 15–16.

31. "Navy Yard Administration," *Times-Picayune,* December 25, 1907, 6.

32. Hearn, *The Illustrated Directory of the United States Navy,* 137.

33. Hearn, *The Illustrated Directory of the United States Navy,* 137.

34. "Navy Yard Administration," *Times-Picayune,* December 25, 1907, 6.

35. "Navy Yard Administration," 6.

36. "The Navy Yard Problem," *Times-Picayune,* October 12, 1908, 7.

37. "Navy Yard Economy," *Times-Picayune,* March 7, 1911, 8.

38. "Navy Yard Discrimination," *Times-Picayune,* May 31, 1911, 9.

39. "Navy Yard Discrimination," 9.

40. "News from Pensacola," *Daily Picayune,* August 30, 1911.

41. Paul Wooten, "Navy Yard Here Saves Uncle Sam Much Hard Cash," *Times-Picayune,* April 11, 1915, 1. See also U.S. Department of the Interior, National Park Service, National Register of Historic Places Registration Form, NRIS Reference 13000695, U.S. Naval Station Algiers Historic District, September 11, 2013, 17.

42. "Opened Again at Last," *New Orleans Herald,* January 7, 1915, 4.

43. "City Must Assist Navy Yard Fight," *Daily Picayune,* July 3, 1913, 3.

44. "City Must Assist Navy Yard Fight," 3.

45. National Institutes of Health, National Library of Medicine, "Raymond B. Fosdick (1883–1972): Ardent Advocate of Internationalism," www.ncbi.nlm.nih.gov/pmc/articles/PMC3478029/.

46. "Roosevelt Is to Visit Navy-Yard and Give Ruling," *Daily Picayune,* September 13, 1913, 1.

47. "Roosevelt Is to Visit Navy-Yard and Give Ruling," 1.

48. McChesney to Secretary of the Navy Daniels, June 18, 1914.

49. "Opened Again at Last," *New Orleans Herald,* January 7, 1915, 4.

50. U.S. Department of the Interior, National Park Service, National Register of Historic Places Registration Form, NRIS Reference 13000695, U.S. Naval Station Algiers Historic District, September 11, 2013, 17.

51. U.S. Department of the Interior, National Park Service, National Register of Historic Places Registration Form, NRIS Reference 13000695, U.S. Naval Station Algiers Historic District, September 11, 2013, 17.

52. Reynolds, *Machine Politics in New Orleans,* 196.

53. Kendall, *History of New Orleans* 2:37.

9.
A GATHERING STORM
The Commission on Training Camp Activities

1. Kendall, *History of New Orleans* 2:122.

2. Fosdick, *Chronicle of a Generation,* 123.

3. Fosdick, *Chronicle of a Generation,* 123.

4. Historian Robert M. Collins argues that *The Age of Reform* "engendered an unusually bitter historiographical controversy.... In the eyes of some, Hofstadter had reduced the Populists to a horde of xenophobic, anti-Semitic, delusional cranks." Collins, "The Originality Trap," 150–67.

5. Kendall, *History of New Orleans* 2:10.

6. Kendall, *History of New Orleans* 2:10.

7. Fosdick, *Chronicle of a Generation,* 42.

8. Fosdick, *Chronicle of a Generation,* 42.

9. Cooper, *Woodrow Wilson,* 84.

10. Fosdick, *Chronicle of a Generation,* 59.

11. Fosdick, *Chronicle of a Generation,* 60.

12. Fosdick, *Chronicle of a Generation,* 66–68.

13. Fosdick, *Chronicle of a Generation,* 70.

14. Fosdick, *Chronicle of a Generation,* 70.

15. Fosdick, *Chronicle of a Generation,* 73.

16. Fosdick, *Chronicle of a Generation,* 100.

17. Fosdick, *Chronicle of a Generation,* 101.

18. Stoughton, "Principled Policing," 620.

19. Fosdick, *Chronicle of a Generation,* 125.

20. Fosdick, *Chronicle of a Generation,* 125. The cities Fosdick visited included London, Liverpool, Paris, Lyon, Berlin, Budapest, Rome, Brussels, and Amsterdam.

21. Fosdick, *European Police Systems,* 125.

22. Fosdick, *European Police Systems,* 379–80.

23. Fosdick, *European Police Systems,* 379–80.

24. Fosdick, *European Police Systems,* 379–80.

25. Fosdick, *Chronicle of a Generation,* 125.

26. Katz, "Pancho Villa and the Attack on Columbus, New Mexico," 101; Matthews, "The U.S. Army on the Mexican Border," 60–65.

27. "Henchman of Villa Discusses Chief's Motives for Atrocities," *Albuquerque Morning Journal,* May 27, 1916.

28. Matthews, "The U.S. Army on the Mexican Border," 60–65.

29. Matthews, "The U.S. Army on the Mexican Border," 60–65.

30. Fosdick, *Chronicle of a Generation,* 136.

31. Fosdick, *Chronicle of a Generation,* 137.

32. Fosdick, *Chronicle of a Generation,* 138.

33. Fosdick, "The Commission on Training Camp Activities," 163.

34. Fosdick, *Chronicle of a Generation,* 138.

35. Fosdick, *Chronicle of a Generation,* 138.

36. Fosdick, *Chronicle of a Generation,* 138.

37. Fosdick, *Chronicle of a Generation,* 141.

38. Wilson delivered his war message to Congress on April 2, 1917. Soon thereafter, Congress declared war on Germany.

39. Fosdick, *Chronicle of a Generation,* 142, 143.

40. "President Asks for Declaration of War," *Times-Picayune,* April 3, 1917.

41. Hearn, *The Illustrated Directory of the United States Navy,* 154–55.

42. Knox, "American Naval Participation in World War I."

43. Hearn, *The Illustrated Directory of the United States Navy,* 154–55.

44. Smith, *The Utility of Force,* 66–81.

45. Smith, *The Utility of Force,* 66–81.

46. Starkweather, "U.S. Immigration Online."

47. Davis, "Welfare, Reform and World War I," 525.

48. Davis, "Welfare, Reform and World War I," 525.

49. U.S. Department of the Interior, National Park Service, National Register of Historic Places Registration Form, NRIS Reference 13000695, U.S. Naval Station Algiers Historic District, September 11, 2013, 17.

50. Fosdick, "The Commission on Training Camp Activities," 165–66.

51. Fosdick, *Chronicle of a Generation,* 143.

52. Daniels reply telegram to Camp, July 7, 1917.

53. Fosdick, "The Commission on Training Camp Activities," 166.

54. Fosdick, "The War and Navy Departments Commissions on Training Camp Activities," 139.

55. Fosdick, "The War and Navy Departments Commissions on Training Camp Activities," 139.

56. Fosdick, "The War and Navy Departments Commissions on Training Camp Activities," 139.

57. Fosdick, "The Commission on Training Camp Activities," 165–66.

58. Fosdick, "The Commission on Training Camp Activities," 166.

59. Brandimarte, *Women on the Home Front,* 201.

60. Fosdick, "The Commission on Training Camp Activities," 165.

61. Connelly, *The Response to Prostitution in the Progressive Era,* 143–44.

62. Fosdick, "The Commission on Training Camp Activities," 169.

63. Quoted in Pope, "An Army of Athletes," 435–36.

64. Fosdick, *Chronicle of a Generation,* 144.

65. Fosdick, *Chronicle of a Generation,* 144.

66. United States Department of the Interior, National Register of Historic Places Registration Form, U.S. Naval Station Algiers Historic District, 17.

67. Foster, "Tarnished Angels," 387–97.

68. Kemp, *Martin Behrman of New Orleans,* 308.

69. Kemp, *Martin Behrman of New Orleans,* 315.

70. Kemp, *Martin Behrman of New Orleans,* 315–17.

71. Baker, Letter to Mayors and Sheriffs in Cities and Counties near Training Camps.

72. Baker, Letter to Mayors and Sheriffs.

73. Baker, Letter to Mayors and Sheriffs.

74. Fosdick letter to Josephus Daniels, Library of Congress, Josephus Daniels Papers 1829–1948, box 458, reel 1.

75. Fosdick to Daniels.

76. Craig, *Josephus Daniels,* 243.

77. *Philadelphia Evening News,* year unknown but presumably 1915, approximately six months after the dry order was given on June 1, 1914, Newspaper Clippings—Various, Josephus Daniels Collection, reel 2.

78. *Philadelphia Evening News,* year unknown but presumably 1915.

79. *Philadelphia Evening News,* year unknown but presumably 1915.

80. Craig, *Josephus Daniels,* 245.

81. Watts, Judge Advocate General, U.S. Navy, memorandum to Josephus Daniels, Secretary of the Navy, Washington, DC, May 26, 1917.

82. Watts, memorandum to Daniels, May 26, 1917.

83. Desmarais and McGovern, *The Essential Documents of American History,* Sixty-Fifth Congress, First Session, chap. 15: 76–83.

84. Desmarais and McGovern, *The Essential Documents of American History,* Sixty-Fifth Congress, First Session, chap. 15: 76–83.

85. Desmarais and McGovern, *The Essential Documents of American History,* Sixty-Fifth Congress, First Session, chap. 15: 76–83.

86. Watts, memorandum to Daniels, May 26, 1917.

87. Watts, memorandum to Daniels, May 26, 1917.

88. *Church of the Holy Trinity v. United States,* 143 U.S. 457.

89. Watts, memorandum to Daniels, May 26, 1917.

90. Watts, memorandum to Daniels, May 26, 1917.

91. Josephus Daniels, Secretary, U.S. Navy, letter to Thomas Watt Gregory, U.S. Attorney General, Washington, DC, May 26, 1917.

92. Daniels, letter to Gregory, May 26, 1917.

93. Grant, "World War I: Wilson and Southern Leadership," 46.

94. Thomas Watt Gregory, U.S. Attorney General, letter to Josephus Daniels, Secretary, U.S. Navy, Washington, DC, June 2, 1917.

95. Gregory, letter to Daniels, June 2, 1917.

96. Gregory, letter to Daniels, June 2, 1917.

97. Gregory, letter to Daniels, June 2, 1917.

98. E. L. Guptil, Municipal Court Judge, Portsmouth, New Hampshire, telegram to Josephus Daniels, Secretary of the Navy, Portsmouth, New Hampshire, May 28, 1917.

99. Daniels, reply telegram to Guptil, May 28, 1917.

100. William Sheafe Chase, Chairman, Social Service Committee of the Episcopal Church, telegram to Josephus Daniels, Secretary, United States Navy, Brooklyn, NY, June 9, 1917.

101. Adam Christmann, attorney for saloon keepers, letter to Josephus Daniels, Secretary, United States Navy, Brooklyn, NY, June 6, 1917.

102. W. C. Watts, Judge Advocate General, U.S. Navy, memorandum to the Chief of the Bureau of Navigation, Washington, DC, July 12, 1917.

103. Qtd. in Landau, *Spectacular Wickedness,* 190.

104. Qtd. in Landau, *Spectacular Wickedness,* 190.

105. Raymond Fosdick, Chairman, Navy Department Commission on Training Camp Activities, letter to Josephus Daniels, Secretary, U.S. Navy, Washington, DC, August 29, 1917.

106. Fosdick, letter to Daniels, August 29, 1917.

107. Fosdick, *Chronicle of a Generation,* 157.

108. Fosdick, *Chronicle of a Generation,* 157.

109. Fosdick, *Chronicle of a Generation,* 158.

110. Fosdick, *Chronicle of a Generation,* 171.

10

THE TRICKS AIN'T WALKING
Closing Time in Storyville

1. Josephus Daniels, Secretary, U.S. Navy, memorandum to W. C. Watts, Judge Advocate General, U.S. Navy, Washington, DC, September 4, 1917.

2. Navy Secretary Josephus Daniels, correspondence to Louisiana Governor Ruffin Pleasant, U.S. Library of Congress, Josephus Daniels Collection, reel 2.

3. Navy Secretary Josephus Daniels correspondence to New Orleans Mayor Martin Behrman, U.S. Library of Congress, Josephus Daniels Collection, reel 2.

4. New Orleans Mayor Martin Behrman, correspondence to Navy Secretary Josephus Daniels, U.S. Library of Congress, Josephus Daniels Collection, reel 2.

5. *Statutes of the United States of America,* First Session of the Sixty-Fifth Congress, 1917, Washington, DC: Government Printing Office, 393.

6. Kemp, *Martin Behrman of New Orleans,* 312n15.

7. "Closing of District Is War Measure," *Times-Picayune,* October 2, 1917.

8. Barker, *Buddy Bolden and the Last Days of Storyville,* 54. This is another quote Barker attributes to Dude Bottley, a composite character he created to synthesize his interviews and research into the early days of jazz in New Orleans. See Cleaver, "The Folklore of Danny Barker," 1.

9. Fosdick, *Chronicle of a Generation,* 146.

10. Fosdick, *Chronicle of a Generation,* 147.

11. Letter from Secretary Daniels to Martin Behrman, October 18, 1917.

12. "Navy Yard Here Saves Uncle Sam Much Hard Cash," *Times-Picayune,* April 11, 1915, 1.

13. Anderson, "Making the Camps Safe for the Army," 149.

14. Clarke, "The Promotion of Social Hygiene in War Time," 178–89; Zinsser, "Working with Men outside the Camps," 194–203; Anderson, "Making the Camps Safe for the Army," 149.

15. Rose, *Storyville,* 167.

16. Fosdick, "The Commission on Training Camp Activities," 169.

17. Fosdick, *Chronicle of a Generation,* 47.

18. Fosdick, *Chronicle of a Generation,* 47.

19. Senator Trammell, telegram to Secretary Daniels, May 2, 1918.

20. Reverend R. A. Smith, telegram to Secretary Daniels, May 2, 1918.

21. Secretary Daniels, telegram to Reverend R. A. Smith, May 6, 1918.

22. John Sherwin, letter to Assistant Secretary of the Navy Franklin Roosevelt, May 28, 1918.

23. Raymond Fosdick, letters to Secretary of Navy Josephus Daniels, October 10, 1917, and December 26, 1917.

24. Josephus Daniels, letter to Raymond Fosdick, October 17, 1917.

25. Pastor Henry G. Porter and Pastor William B. Phillips, telegram to Josephus Daniels, March 9, 1918. For more on state senator Edwin E. Grant, see ballotpedia.org/Edwin_Grant_recall,_California_(1914).

26. Edwin E. Grant letter to Josephus Daniels, October 5, 1917.

27. Edwin E. Grant, letter to Josephus Daniels, October 5, 1917.

28. Fosdick, *Chronicle of a Generation,* 147–48.

29. Fosdick, *Chronicle of a Generation,* 147–48.

11

REPERCUSSIONS

The Election of 1920

1. Woytinsky, "Postwar Economic Perspectives," 20–21.

2. Troy, *The Changing Role of the Presidential Candidate,* 142.

3. Beschloss, *The Presidents,* 337.

4. Sabato and Ernst, *Encyclopedia of American Political Parties and Elections,* 340–41.

5. Jackson, "Prohibition in New Orleans," 261; Message from the President of the United States, "List of States Approving the Eighteenth Amendment."

6. Jackson, "Prohibition in New Orleans," 261.

7. Jackson, "Prohibition in New Orleans," xi, 317.

8. "Parker's Election Declared Certain," *Times-Picayune,* January 6, 1920, 3.

9. "Parker Speakers Lambast Ring," *Times-Picayune,* January 7, 1920.

10. "Parker Speakers Lambast Ring."

11. "Ring Rule Exposed: Charles Rosen, New Orleans Lawyer, Tells Shreveport Democrat How Machine Menaces the State," *Times-Picayune,* January 14, 1920.

12. Ring Rule Exposed."

13. "Home Ward Cheers Parker," *Times-Picayune,* January 17, 1920.

14. "Home Ward Cheers Parker."

15. "Enthusiasm Runs Riot for Parker at Big Meeting," *Times-Picayune,* January 15, 1920.

16. "Home Ward Cheers Parker," *Times-Picayune,* January 17, 1920.

17. Walmsley's dual role in law enforcement and politics is an excellent example of policing in an era Seth Stoughton described as the "Political Era." Stoughton, "Principled Policing," 620.

18. "Captain Walmsley Passes Quiet Day: Few Calls for Quick Action by Riot Squad Are Received by Chief," *Times-Picayune,* January 21, 1920, 5.

19. "Captain Walmsley Passes Quiet Day," *Times-Picayune,* January 21, 1920, 5.

20. "Captain Walmsley Passes Quiet Day," 5.

21. Kemp, *Martin Behrman of New Orleans,* 289.

22. "You've Picked the Wrong People to Use Threats On!" *Times-Picayune,* January 2, 1920, 1.

23. "You've Picked the Wrong People to Use Threats On!" 1.

24. "Victory for the Truth," *Times-Picayune,* January 21, 1920, 8.

25. "Great Crowds Cheer Parker, Ring Breaker," *Times-Picayune,* January 28, 1920, 1.

26. "Behrman's Hat Again in Municipal Arena, Is Persistent Rumor," *Times-Picayune,* January 29, 1920.

27. "Behrman's Hat Again in Municipal Arena."

28. "Mayor Asks Fifth Term," *Times-Picayune,* July 18, 1920, 1.

29. "Both Sides Have Complete Ticket for Fall Primary," *Times-Picayune,* July 25, 1920, 1.

30. "Mayor Asks Fifth Term," *Times-Picayune,* July 18, 1920, 1.

31. "His Honor's Error," *Times-Picayune,* July 30, 1920, 8, rpt. from the *New Orleans Daily States,* July 28, 1920.

32. "His Honor's Error." 8.

33. R. Williams, "Martin Behrman: Mayor and Political Boss of New Orleans, 1904–1926," 118.

34. "Behrman's Boasters," *Times-Picayune,* August 17, 1920.

35. "Martin Behrman, Mayor 16 Years, Opens Campaign," *Times-Picayune,* August 6, 1920.

36. "Martin Behrman, Mayor 16 Years, Opens Campaign."

37. "Martin Behrman, Mayor 16 Years, Opens Campaign."

38. "Martin Behrman, Mayor 16 Years, Opens Campaign."

39. "Martin Behrman, Mayor 16 Years, Opens Campaign."

40. "Our Reasons," *Times-Picayune,* August 9, 1920, 1.

41. "Our Reasons," 1.

42. "Behrman Makes Another Hot Attack on Times-Picayune," *Times-Picayune,* August 26, 1920.

43. "Behrman Makes Another Hot Attack."

44. "Behrman Makes Another Hot Attack."

45. "Behrman Makes Another Hot Attack."

46. "Behrman Makes Another Hot Attack."

47. "Behrman Makes Another Hot Attack."

48. "Mayor Howled Down in Shipyard Address," *Times-Picayune,* September 8, 1920.

49. "Women Join O.D.A. to Crush Bossdom," *Times-Picayune,* August 26, 1920.

50. "Women Join O.D.A. to Crush Bossdom."

51. "Women Join O.D.A. to Crush Bossdom."

52. "Women Join O.D.A. to Crush Bossdom."

53. "Suffrage Chiefs Delay Real Work," *Times-Picayune,* May 13, 1920, 4.

54. "Suffrage Chiefs Delay Real Work," 4.

55. "Suffrage Chiefs Delay Real Work," 4. James Wilkerson, a speaker at the rally, thanked Woodrow Wilson and Mayor Behrman, among others, for their support of the Nineteenth Amendment.

56. "Suffrage Chiefs Delay Real Work," 4. This opinion was voiced by Miss Ethel Hutson, who also asserted the right to vote was a "sovereign right."

57. "Ring Women Score Trinity's Rector," *Times-Picayune,* September 8, 1920.

58. "Ring Women Score Trinity's Rector."

59. *Times-Picayune,* September 14, 1920.

60. "Harrison Wins Council Place, Henriques Says," *Times-Picayune,* September 19, 1920.

61. "Ray Wins Council Place on Official Primary Figures," *Times-Picayune,* September 22, 1920.

62. "Ray Wins Council Place on Official Primary Figures."

63. Kemp, *Martin Behrman of New Orleans,* 313.

64. "Martin Behrman Is Vice President of American Bank," *Times-Picayune,* August 4, 1921, 9.

12

PAPA AND THE KINGFISH
Fact versus Fiction

1. "Behrman's Career One of Romances of Modern Politics," *Times-Picayune,* January 12, 1926, 1.

2. Kemp, *Martin Behrman of New Orleans,* 306.

3. Kemp, *Martin Behrman of New Orleans,* 315.

4. Kemp, *Martin Behrman of New Orleans,* 305.

5. T. H. Williams, *Huey Long,* 166–67.

6. Reynolds, *Machine Politics in New Orleans,* 218.

7. Jeansonne, "Huey Long and the Historians," 124–25.

8. T. H. Williams, *Huey Long,* 212.

9. Reynolds, *Machine Politics in New Orleans,* 219n42.

10. T. H. Williams, *Huey Long,* 217–18. While the historiographical consensus on Long has

evolved, at nearly a thousand pages, Williams's biography stands as the most complete, and perhaps most entertaining, account of Huey Long ever written.

11. T. H. Williams, *Huey Long,* 218.

12. T. H. Williams, *Huey Long,* 219.

13. U.S. Department of the Interior, National Park Service, National Register of Historic Places Registration Form, NRIS Reference 13000695, U.S. Naval Station Algiers Historic District, September 11, 2013, 18.

14. Jackson, "Prohibition in New Orleans," 271.

15. Jackson, "Prohibition in New Orleans," 271.

16. "Behrman's Career One of Romances," *Times-Picayune,* January 12, 1926.

17. "Behrman's Career One of Romances."

18. "Behrman's Career One of Romances."

19. "Behrman's Career One of Romances."

20. "City Bowed in Grief as Martin Behrman Is Laid to Rest," *Times-Picayune,* January 14, 1926.

21. "City Bowed in Grief."

22. "Twenty Thousand Pass Mayor's Bier in City Hall while Guard Keeps Vigil," *Times-Picayune,* January 13, 1926.

23. See "Every Man a King," a song cowritten by Huey Long and Castro Carazo.

24. Jeansonne, "Huey Long and the Historians," 120.

25. Warren, *All the King's Men,* 102.

26. Brinkley, "Mass Politics in the Literary and Historical Imaginations," 18.

27. Graham, "The Enigma of Huey Long," 205.

28. Graham, "The Enigma of Huey Long," 205.

29. Jeansonne, "Huey Long and the Historians," 120.

30. Graham, "The Enigma of Huey Long," 208.

31. Conrad, "Huey Long and the Two Louisiana Historians," 127.

32. Conrad, "Huey Long and the Two Louisiana Historians," 138.

33. Jeansonne, "Huey Long and the Historians," 122.

34. Jeansonne, "Huey Long and the Historians," 122-23.

35. Jeansonne, "Huey Long and the Historians," 122-23.

36. Jeansonne, "Huey Long and the Historians," 124-25.

37. Jeansonne, "Huey Long and the Historians," 124-25.

38. Graham, "The Enigma of Huey Long," 210.

39. Hayek, "Resurrecting the Abandoned Road," 59.

40. For a broad discussion of classical liberalism, see Hayek, "Resurrecting the Abandoned Road," 53-65.

41. For a discussion of Jeffersonian politics, see Ingersoll and Mathews, *The Philosophic Roots of Modern Ideology,* 104-6.

42. Nichols, "The Promise of Progressivism," 27.

43. Nichols, "The Promise of Progressivism," 27.

44. Kemp, *Martin Behrman of New Orleans,* 158.

45. See, for example *Jamison v. McClendon,* 476 F. Supp. 3d 386 (S.D. Miss. 2020), reciting and criticizing the history of qualified immunity. On lack of accountability in police violations of constitutional rights, see Stoughton et al., "Policing Suspicion," 36–78.

46. T. H. Williams, *Huey Long,* 193–94; Hair, *The Kingfish and His Realm,* 264.

47. White, *Kingfish,* 171.

48. White, *Kingfish,* 171.

49. T. H. Williams, *Huey Long,* 722–24.

BIBLIOGRAPHY

Archives and Manuscripts

Baker, Newton. Letter to Mayors and Sheriffs in Cities and Counties Near Training Camps. "Documents Regarding the Question of Alcohol and Prostitution in the Neighborhood of Military Camps." Published by the *War Department Commission on Training Camp Activities,* Washington, DC, 9. National Archives.

Behrman, Martin. Correspondence to major cities across the United States regarding street paving. Mayor Martin Behrman Records, Louisiana Division, City Archives, New Orleans Public Library, ser. I (1904–20), carton I, "B" miscellaneous.

———. Correspondence to Navy Secretary Josephus Daniels, U.S. Library of Congress, Josephus Daniels Collection, reel 2.

———. "New Orleans: A History of Three Great Public Utilities, Sewerage, Water and Drainage, and Their Influence upon the Health and Progress of a Big City." *Convention of League of American Municipalities,* September 29, 1914. Historical New Orleans Collection, Williams Research Center, ID no. 69-98-LP.5, rare pamphlets holdings.

———. "The Port of New Orleans: What the City Is Doing and Has Done to Facilitate Foreign and Domestic Commerce." Address by Honorable Margin Behrman, Mayor of New Orleans, Louisiana, at the National Foreign Trade Conference, April 18–20, 1918. Tulane University Special Collections, 10. Louisiana Research Collection, Howard-Tilton Memorial Library, call no. 976.31 (387.1) B421s, Tulane University, New Orleans.

———. "Street Paving Problem." Address by Honorable Margin Behrman, Mayor of New Orleans, Louisiana. *Fourteenth Annual Convention of the League of American Municipalities,* St. Paul, Minnesota, August 23 to 26, 1910. Tulane University Special Collections, 10. Louisiana Research Collection, Howard-Tilton Memorial Library, call no. 976.31 (625.7) B421s, Tulane University, New Orleans.

Blanchard, Newton C., Governor of Louisiana. To Martin Behrman, September 23, 1905. Mayor Martin Behrman Records, Louisiana Division, City Archives. New Orleans Public Library, ser. I (1904–20), carton I, "B" miscellaneous.

Chase, William Sheafe, Chairman, Social Service Committee of the Episcopal Church. Telegram to Josephus Daniels, Secretary, U.S. Navy, Brooklyn, New York, June 9, 1917. ID no. 26509-201:6. Correspondence of the Secretary of the Navy, 1897–1926, Record Group 80, General Records of the Department of the Navy, 1798–1947, National Archives Building, Washington, DC.

Chick, D. H. To Martin Behrman, Mayor of New Orleans, September 10, 1905. Mayor Martin Behrman Records, Louisiana Division, City Archives, New Orleans Public Library, ser. I (1904–20), box 1, "C" miscellaneous.

Christmann, Adam, attorney for saloon keepers. To Josephus Daniels, Secretary, U.S. Navy., Brooklyn, New York, June 6, 1917. ID no. 26509-201:5 LP. Correspondence of the Secretary of the Navy, 1897–1926, Record Group 80, General Records of the Department of the Navy, 1798–1947, National Archives Building, Washington, DC.

Citizens' correspondence to Martin Behrman. April 8, 1907. Mayor Martin Behrman Records, Louisiana Division, City Archives, New Orleans Public Library, ser. I, box 3, petitions.

Daniels, Josephus, Secretary of the Navy. Letter to Martin Behrman, October 18, 1917. Library of Congress, Josephus Daniels Papers 1829–1948, box 458, reel 1, Alcohol and Vice Control, Commission on Training Camp Activities, hdl.loc.gov/loc.mss/eadmss.ms010320.

———. Letter to New Orleans Mayor Martin Behrman. U.S. Library of Congress, Josephus Daniels Collection, reel 2.

———. Letter to Raymond Fosdick, October 17, 1917. U.S. Library of Congress, Josephus Daniels Collection, reel 2.

———. Letter to Thomas Watt Gregory, U.S. Attorney General. Washington, DC, May 26, 1917. ID no. 26509-201:1. Correspondence of the Secretary of the Navy, 1897–1926, Record Group 80, General Records of the Department of the Navy, 1798–1947, National Archives Building, Washington, DC.

———. Letter to Thomas Watt Gregory, U.S. Attorney General. Washington, DC, June 9, 1917. ID no. 26509-201:1, Correspondence of the Secretary of the Navy, 1897–1926, Record Group 80, General Records of the Department of the Navy, 1798–1947, National Archives Building, Washington, DC.

———. Letter to Louisiana Governor Ruffin Pleasant. U.S. Library of Congress, Josephus Daniels Collection, reel 2.

———. Memorandum to W. C. Watts, Judge Advocate General, U.S. Navy. Washington, DC, September 4, 1917, ID no. 26509201:14, Correspondence of the Secretary of the Navy, 1897–1926, Record Group 80, General Records of the Department of the Navy, 1798–1947, National Archives Building, Washington, DC.

———. *Philadelphia Evening News*, [1915]. Newspaper Clippings—Various. U.S. Library of Congress, Josephus Daniels Collection, reel 2.

———. Reply telegram to Walter Camp, July 7, 1917. Library of Congress, Josephus Daniels Papers, reel 2.

———. Reply telegram to E. L. Guptil, Municipal Court Judge, Washington, DC, May 28, 1917. ID no. 26509-201:2. Correspondence of the Secretary of the Navy, 1897–1926, Record Group 80, General Records of the Department of the Navy, 1798–1947, National Archives Building, Washington, DC.

———. Reply telegram to Reverend R.A. Smith, May 6, 1918. U.S. Library of Congress, Josephus Daniels Collection, reel 3.

Dreyfus, Felix, J. lawyer, to Martin Behrman, Mayor of New Orleans, August 14, 1905. Mayor Martin Behrman Records, Louisiana Division, City Archives, New Orleans Public Library, ser. I (1904–20), carton I, "D" miscellaneous.

Fosdick, Raymond. Letter to Josephus Daniels, Secretary, U.S. Navy. Washington, DC, August 29, 1917. ID no. 26509201:14. Correspondence of the Secretary of the Navy, 1897–1926, Record Group 80, General Records of the Department of the Navy, 1798–1947, National Archives Building, Washington, DC.

———. Letter to Secretary of Navy Josephus Daniels, October 10, 1917, and December 26, 1917. U.S. Library of Congress, Josephus Daniels Collection, reel 2.

———. Letter to Josephus Daniels. Library of Congress, Josephus Daniels Papers 1829–1948. box 458, reel 1. Alcohol and Vice Control, Commission on Training Camp Activities, hdl.loc.gov/loc.mss/eadmss.ms010320.

French Market Improvement Association to Martin Behrman, undated. Mayor Martin Behrman Records, Louisiana Division, City Archives, New Orleans Public Library, ser. I (1904–20), box 1.

Gordon, Kate, to Martin Behrman, June 21, 1908. Mayor Martin Behrman Records, ser. II, carton 2, "N" miscellaneous, National American Woman Suffrage Association, City of New Orleans Archives, New Orleans Public Library.

Grant, Edwin E. Letter to Josephus Daniels, October 5, 1917. U.S. Library of Congress, Josephus Daniels Papers, reel 2.

Gregory, Thomas Watt, U.S. Attorney General. Letter to Josephus Daniels, Secretary, U.S. Navy, Washington, DC, June 2, 1917. ID no. 185818-28, Correspondence of the Secretary of the Navy, 1897–1926, Record Group 80, General Records of the Department of the Navy, 1798–1947; National Archives Building, Washington, DC.

Guptil, E. L., Municipal Court Judge, Portsmouth, New Hampshire. Telegram to Josephus Daniels, Secretary of the Navy, Portsmouth, New Hampshire, May 28, 1917. ID no. 26509-201:2. Correspondence of the Secretary of the Navy, 1897–1926,

Record Group 80, General Records of the Department of the Navy, 1798–1947, National Archives Building, Washington, DC.

McChesney, Tiley S. To Secretary of the Navy Josephus Daniels, June 18, 1914. Correspondence of the Secretary of the Navy, 1897–1926, Record Group 80, General Records of the Department of the Navy, 1798–1947. National Archives Building, Washington, DC.

Meyer, Adolph. Naval Appropriation Bill. "Speeches of Adolph Meyer in the House of Representatives," February 19, 23, and 25, 1904, p. 11. Historic New Orleans Collection, Williams Research Center.

Porter, Henry G., Pastor, and William B. Phillips, Pastor. Telegram to Josephus Daniels, March 9, 1918. U.S. Library of Congress, Josephus Daniels Collection, reel 2.

Public School Alliance. To Martin Behrman, November 15, 1906. Mayor Martin Behrman Records, ser. I, box 2. Enclosed undated article, "Raising Saloon Licenses," author, newspaper, and publisher unknown.

Sherwin, John. Letter to Assistant Secretary of the Navy Franklin Roosevelt, May 28, 1918. U.S. Library of Congress, Josephus Daniels Collection, reel 2.

Smith, R. A., Reverend. Telegram to Secretary Daniels, May 2, 1918. U.S. Library of Congress, Josephus Daniels Collection, reel 3.

Sts. Peter and Paul Church. Marriage vol. 1887–1910, pt. 1, p. 3, act 10.

Trammell, Park, U.S. Senator. Telegram to Secretary of the Navy Josephus Daniels, May 2, 1918. U.S. Library of Congress, Josephus Daniels Collection, Reel 3.

U.S. Senate. "Report of the Secretary of Navy." 32nd Congress, 2nd Session, December 7, 1852. Historic New Orleans Collection, Williams Research Center.

Watts, W. C., Judge Advocate General, U.S. Navy. Letter to Josephus Daniels, Secretary, U.S. Navy, Washington, DC, June 2, 1917. ID no. 185818-28, Correspondence of the Secretary of the Navy, 1897–1926, Record Group 80, General Records of the Department of the Navy, 1798–1947, National Archives Building, Washington, DC.

——. Memorandum to the Chief of the Bureau of Navigation, Washington, DC, July 12, 1917. ID no. 26509201:10, Correspondence of the Secretary of the Navy, 1897–1926, Record Group 80, General Records of the Department of the Navy, 1798–1947, National Archives Building, Washington, DC.

——. Memorandum to Josephus Daniels, Secretary of the Navy, Washington, DC, May 26, 1917. ID no. 26509-201:1, Correspondence of the Secretary of the Navy, 1897–1926, Record Group 80, General Records of the Department of the Navy, 1798–1947, National Archives Building, Washington, DC.

Books and Essays

Ambron, Sueann Robinson, David Brodzinsky, and Anne V. Gormly. *Lifespan Human Development*. New York: Holt, Rinehart and Winston, 1986.

Barker, Danny. *Buddy Bolden and the Last Days of Storyville,* ed. Alyn Shipton. Continuum: New York, 2001.

Bell, Daniel. *The Radical Right*. 3rd ed. New Brunswick, NJ: Transaction Publishers, 2002.

Beschloss, Michael. *The Presidents: Every Leader from Washington to Bush*. New York: American Heritage, 2003.

Binkley, Wilfred E. *American Political Parties: Their Natural History*. New York: Alfred Knopf, 1959.

Blocker, Jack S., Jr. *American Temperance Movements: Cycles of Reform*. Boston: G. K. Hall & Co., 1989.

Brinkley, Alan. "Mass Politics in the Literary and Historical Imaginations." In *Huey at 100,* ed. Jeansonne.

Bristow, Nancy K. *Making Men Moral: Social Engineering during the Great War*. New York: New York University Press, 1996.

Carter, Hodding, ed. *Past as Prelude: New Orleans, 1718–1968*. New Orleans: Pelican Publishing, 1968.

Charles River Editors. *The Union's Capture of New Orleans during the Civil War: The Campaign for the Confederacy's Most Important Mississippi River Stronghold*. Unknown city: Charles River Editors, unknown date.

Connelly, Mark Thomas. *The Response to Prostitution in the Progressive Era*. Chapel Hill: University of North Carolina Press, 1980.

Conrad, Glen. "Huey Long and the Two Louisiana Historians." In *Huey at 100,* ed. Jeansonne.

Cooper, John Milton, Jr. *Woodrow Wilson: A Biography*. New York: Vintage, 2011.

Craig, Lee A. *Josephus Daniels: His Life and Times*. Chapel Hill: University of North Carolina Press, 2013.

Dallek, Robert. *The American Style of Foreign Policy*. New York: Alfred A Knopf, 1983.

Dawson, Joseph G., III, ed. *The Louisiana Governors*. Baton Rouge: Louisiana State University Press, 1990.

Deacon, William M., H. P. Lucy, and John P. Coleman. *Martin Behrman Administration Biography, 1904–1916*. New Orleans: John J. Weihing Printing Co., 1917.

Dempsey, John S. *Introduction to Private Security*. Belmont, CA: Wadsworth, 2011.

Derr, Mark. *Some Kind of Paradise*. Gainesville: University Press of Florida, 1998.

Desmarais, Norman P., and James H. McGovern. *The Essential Documents of American History.* New York: Great Neck Publishing, 1997.

Dethloff, Henry C., "Huey Long and Populism." In *Huey at 100,* ed. Jeansonne.

Deutsch, Hermann B. "New Orleans Politics—The Greatest Free Show on Earth." In *Past as Prelude,* ed. Carter.

Drez, Ronald J. *The War of 1812, Conflict and Deception: The British Attempt to Seize New Orleans and Nullify the Louisiana Purchase.* Baton Rouge: Louisiana State University Press, 2014. Electronic version, location 1171.

Foner, Eric. *The Story of American Freedom.* London: Norton, 1998.

Fosdick, Raymond. *Chronicle of a Generation: An Autobiography.* New York: Harper and Brothers, 1958.

——. *European Police Systems.* New York: Bureau of Social Hygiene and the Century Co., 1915.

Garvey, Joan B., and Mary Lou Widmer. *Beautiful Crescent: A History of New Orleans.* Gretna, LA: Pelican Publishing Co., 2014.

Golway, Terry. *Machine Made: Tammany Hall and the Creation of Modern American Politics.* New York: Liveright Publishing Corp., 2014.

Grantham, Dewey W. *Southern Progressivism: The Reconciliation of Progress and Tradition.* Knoxville: University of Tennessee Press, 1983.

Gusfield, Joseph. *Status Politics and the American Temperance Movement.* 2nd ed. Chicago: Board of Trustees of the University of Illinois, 1986.

Haas, Edward F. *Political Leadership in a Southern City.* Ruston, LA: McGinty Publications, 1988.

Hair, William Ivy. *The Kingfish and His Realm: The Life and Times of Huey P. Long.* Baton Rouge: Louisiana State University Press, 1997.

Hayek, F. A. "Resurrecting the Abandoned Road." In *Conservatism in America Since 1930,* ed. Gregory L. Schneider. New York: New York University Press, 2003.

Hearn, Chester G. *The Illustrated Directory of the United States Navy.* St. Paul: Salamander Books, 2003.

Hofstadter, Richard. *The Age of Reform: From Bryan to F.D.R.* New York: Vintage Books, 1955.

Ingersoll, David, and Richard Mathews. *The Philosophic Roots of Modern Ideology.* Upper Saddle River, NJ: Prentice Hall, 2001.

Jackson, Joy. *New Orleans in the Gilded Age.* Baton Rouge: Louisiana State University Press, 1969.

Jeansonne, Glen, ed. *Huey at 100: Centennial Essays on Huey P. Long.* Ruston, LA: McGinty Publications, 1995.

Kemp, John R., ed. *Martin Behrman of New Orleans: Memoirs of a City Boss.* Baton Rouge: Louisiana State University Press, 1977.

Kendall, John Smith. *History of New Orleans. Vol. 2.* Chicago: Lewis Publishing Co., 1922.

Kennedy, David M. *Over There: The First World War and American Society.* New York: Oxford University Press, 2004.

Kraut, John A. *The Origins of Prohibition.* New York: Alfred A. Knopf, 1925.

Krist, Gary. *Empire of Sin.* New York: Crown, 2014.

Labadie, Jeremy, and Argyle Wolf-Knapp. *New Orleans Beer: A Hoppy History of Big Easy Brewing.* Charleston, SC: American Palate, 2014.

Landau, Emily Epstein. *Spectacular Wickedness: Sex, Race, and Memory in Storyville, New Orleans.* Baton Rouge: Louisiana State University Press, 2013.

Link, William A. *The Paradox of Southern Progressivism, 1880–1930.* Chapel Hill: University of North Carolina Press, 1992.

Long, Alecia P. *The Great Southern Babylon: Sex, Race, and Respectability in New Orleans, 1865–1920.* Baton Rouge: Louisiana State University Press, 2004.

Marler, Scott P. *The Merchants' Capital: New Orleans and the Political Economy of the Nineteenth-Century South.* New York: Cambridge University Press, 2013.

Merrill, Ellen C. *Germans of Louisiana.* Gretna, LA: Pelican Publishing, 2005.

Merton, Robert K. *Social Theory and Social Structure.* New York: The Free Press, 1968.

Millett, Allen R., Peter Maslowski, and William B. Feis. *For the Common Defense: A Military History of the United States from 1607 to 2012.* New York: Free Press, 2012.

Morris, Edmond. *Theodore Rex.* New York: Random House, 2002.

Ostrogorski, Moisei. *Democracy and the Organization of Political Parties. Vol. 2.* New York: Routledge, 2017.

Pegram, Thomas R. *Battling Demon Rum: The Struggle for a Dry America, 1800–1833.* Chicago: Ivan R. Dee, 1995.

Pollack, Captain Edwin T., and Lieutenant Paul F. Bloomhardt. *The Hatchet of the United States Ship "George Washington."* Vols. 1–9. Rpt. Charleston, SC: Nabu Press, 2012.

Powell, Lawrence N. *The Accidental City: Improvising New Orleans.* Cambridge, MA: Harvard University Press, 2012.

Presidential Elections, 1789–1996. Washington, DC: *Congressional Quarterly,* 1997.

Reilly, Thomas. *Jannus: An American Flier.* Gainesville: University Press of Florida, 1997.

Reynolds, George M. *Machine Politics in New Orleans, 1897–1926.* New York: Columbia University Press, 1936.

Riordan, William L. *Plunkitt of Tammany Hall: A Series of Very Plain Talks on Very Practical Politics, Delivered by Ex-Senator George Washington Plunkitt, the Tam-*

many Philosopher, from his Rostrum—the New York County Courthouse Bootblack Stand. New York: McClure Phillips, 1905.

Robertson, James D. *The Great American Beer Book.* Ottawa, IL: Caroline House, 1978.

Rose, Al. *Storyville, New Orleans—Being an Authentic Illustrated Account of the Notorious Red Light District.* Tuscaloosa: University of Alabama Press, 1974.

Rothman, Adam. *Slave Country.* Cambridge, MA: Harvard University Press, 2007.

Sabato, Larry J., and Howard R. Ernst. *Encyclopedia of American Political Parties and Elections.* New York: Checkmark Books, 2007.

Salter, J. T. *Boss Rule: Portraits in City Politics.* New York: Whittlesey House, 1935.

Sanders, Elizabeth. *Roots of Reform: Farmers, Workers, and the American State, 1877–1917.* Chicago: University of Chicago Press, 1999.

Schafer, Judith Kelleher. *Brothels, Depravity, and Abandoned Women: Illegal Sex in Antebellum New Orleans.* Baton Rouge: Louisiana State University Press, 2009.

Schlesinger, Arthur M., Jr. *The Almanac of American History.* Greenwich, CT: Barnes & Noble–Brompton Books, 1993.

———. *The Imperial Presidency.* New York: Houghton Mifflin, 1973.

Schluter, Hermann. *The Brewing Industry and the Brewery Workers' Movement in America.* Cincinnati: International Union of the United Brewery Workers of America, 1910.

Schneider, Paul. *Old Man River: The Mississippi River in North American History.* New York: Henry Holt & Co., 2014.

Shea, William L., and Terrence J. Winschel. *Vicksburg Is the Key: The Struggle for the Mississippi River.* Lincoln: University of Nebraska Press, 2003.

Sinclair, Andrew. *Prohibition: The Era of Excess.* Boston: Little, Brown and Co., 1962.

Sismondo, Christine. *America Walks into a Bar.* New York: Oxford University Press, 2011.

Smith, General Rupert. *The Utility of Force: The Art of War in the Modern World.* New York: Alfred A. Knopf, 2007.

Tindall, George Brown. *The Persistent Tradition in New South Politics.* Baton Rouge: Louisiana State University Press, 1975.

Tompkins, Vincent, ed. *American Decades: Development of the Industrial United States—1878 to 1899.* Detroit: Gale Research, 1997.

———. *American Decades, 1900–1909.* Detroit: Gale Research, 1996.

Troy, Gil. *The Changing Role of the Presidential Candidate.* New York: Free Press, 1991.

Van Devander, Charles. *The Big Bosses.* New York: Howell Soskin, 1944.

Warren, Robert Penn. *All the Kings Men.* New York: Harcourt, Brace and Co., 1946.

Wagenaar, Hendrik, Helga Amesberger, and Sietske Altink. "Prostitution Policy beyond Trafficking: Collaborative Governance in Prostitution." In *Designing Prostitution Policy: Intention and Reality in Regulating the Sex Trade,* ed. Wagenaar, Amesberger, and Altink, 227. Bristol, UK: Bristol University Press, 2017.

White, Richard D., Jr. *Kingfish: The Reign of Huey P. Long.* New York: Random House, 2006.

Wiebe, Robert. *The Search for Order, 1877–1920.* New York: Hill and Wang, 1967.

Williams, T. Harry. *Huey Long: A Biography.* New York: Alfred A. Knopf, 1969.

Woloch, Nancy. *Muller v. Oregon, A Brief History with Documents.* Boston: Bedford Books, 1996.

Wood, Gordon. *The Radicalism of the American Revolution.* New York: Alfred A. Knopf, 1992.

Woodward, C. Vann. *Origins of the New South, 1877–1913.* Baton Rouge: Louisiana State University Press, 1951, 1971.

ARTICLES

Adler, Jeffrey S. "Murder, North and South: Violence in Early-Twentieth-Century Chicago and New Orleans." *Journal of Southern History* 74, no. 2 (2008): 297–324.

Anderson, George J. "Making the Camps Safe for the Army." *Annals of the American Academy of Political and Social Science* 79 (September 1918): 143–51.

Appel, Susan K. "Artificial Refrigeration and the Architecture of 19th-Century American Breweries." *Journal of the Society for Industrial Archeology* 16 (1990): 21–38.

Baranoff, Dalit. "Shaped by Risk: The American Fire Insurance Industry, 1790—1920." *Enterprise & Society* 6, no. 4 (2005): 561–70.

Blodgett, Geoffrey. "A New Look at the American Gilded Age." *Historical Reflections* 1, no. 2 (Winter 1974): 235–36.

Brandimarte, Cynthia. "Women on the Home Front: Hostess Houses During World War I." *Winterthur Portfolio* 42, no. 4 (2008), 201–22.

Brinkley, Alan. "Civil Liberties in Times of Crisis." *Bulletin of the American Academy of Arts and Sciences* 59, no. 2 (Winter 2006): 26–29.

Brown, L. Ames. "The Election and Prohibition." *North American Review* 204, no. 733 (December 1916): 850–56.

Campbell, Colin. "Clinton's Encounter with the Separation of Powers: 'United' and 'Divided' Gridlock." *Government and Opposition* 36, no. 2 (2001): 157–83.

Carrigan, Jo Ann. "Impact of Epidemic Yellow Fever on Life in Louisiana." *Louisiana History* 4, no. 1 (1963): 5–34.

———. "Mass Communication and Public Health: The 1905 Campaign against Yellow Fever in New Orleans." *Louisiana History* 29, no. 1 (Winter 1988): 5–20.

Clark, Norman. Review of *Prohibition: The Era of Excess* by Andrew Sinclair. *Pacific Northwest Quarterly* 54, no. 2 (April 1963): 79–80.

Clarke, Walter. "The Promotion of Social Hygiene in War Time." *Annals of the American Academy of Political and Social Science* 79 (September 1918): 178–89.

Cleaver, Molly Reid. "The Folklore of Danny Barker, Five of His Most Memorable Characters." Historic New Orleans Collection, March 10, 2022, www.hnoc.org/publications/first-draft/folklore-danny-barker-five-his-most-memorable-characters.

Clement, Priscilla Ferguson. "Children and Charity: Orphanages in New Orleans, 1817–1914." *Louisiana History* 27, no. 4 (1986): 339.

Colburn, David R., and George E. Pozzetta. "Bosses and Machines: Changing Interpretations in American History." *History Teacher* 9, no. 3 (May 1976): 445–63.

Collin, Richard H. "Theodore Roosevelt's Visit to New Orleans and the Progressive Campaign of 1914." *Louisiana History* 12, no. 1 (Winter 1971): 7.

Collins, Robert M. "The Originality Trap: Richard Hofstadter on Populism." *Journal of American History* 76, no. 1 (June 1989): 150–67.

Davis, Allen F. "Welfare, Reform and World War I." *American Quarterly* 19, no. 3 (Autumn 1967): 516–33.

Downs, Susan Whitelaw, and Michael W. Sherraden. "The Orphan Asylum in the Nineteenth Century." *Social Service Review* 57, no. 2 (1983): 272–90.

Duffy, John. "Nineteenth-Century Public Health in New York and New Orleans: A Comparison." *Louisiana History* 15, no. 4 (1974): 325–37.

Filene, Peter G. "An Obituary for 'The Progressive Movement.'" *American Quarterly* 22, no. 1 (Spring 1970): 20–34.

"Follow-Up Tactics-Anti-Saloon Strategy in the New South." *American Issue* 18 (April 1910).

Fosdick, Raymond. "The Commission on Training Camp Activities." *Proceedings of the Academy of Political Science in the City of New York* 7, no. 4 (February 1918): 163–70.

——. "The War and Navy Departments Commissions on Training Camp Activities." *Annals of the American Academy of Political and Social Science* 79 (September 1918): 130–42.

Foster, Craig. "Tarnished Angels: Prostitution in Storyville, New Orleans, 1900–1910." *Louisiana History* 31, no. 4 (Winter 1990): 387–97.

Gerwitz, Paul. "On 'I Know It When I See It.'" *Yale Law Journal* 105, no. 4 (1996): 1023–47.

Graham, Hugh Davis. "The Enigma of Huey Long: An Essay Review." *Journal of Southern History* 36, no. 2 (1970): 205–11.

Grant, Philip A. "World War I: Wilson and Southern Leadership." *Presidential Studies Quarterly* 6, no. 1–2 (Winter–Spring 1976): 44–49.

Griffith, Joe. "In Pursuit of Pancho Villa 1916–1917 (An Almost Forgotten Episode of Terrorism on American Soil)." *Journal of the Historical Society of the Georgia National Guard* 6, no. 3–4 (Summer–Fall 1997).

Harvey, Paul L. "Southern Baptists and the Social Gospel: White Religious Progressivism in the South, 1900–1925." *Fides et Historia* 27 (Summer–Fall 1995): 59–77.

Hennessey, Melinda Meek. "Race and Violence in Reconstruction New Orleans: The 1868 Riot." *Louisiana History* 20, no. 1 (Winter 1979): 78.

Henriques, Fernando. *Prostitution in Europe and the Americas. Prostitution and Society: A Survey. 3 vols.* New York, 1963–65.

Hines, James R., Jr. "Taxing Consumption and Other Sins." *Journal of Economic Perspectives* 21, no. 1 (Winter 2007): 49–68.

Holzman, Robert S. "Ben Butler in the Civil War." *New England Quarterly* 30, no. 3 (September 1957): 333.

Huntington, Samuel P. "The Marasmus of the ICC: The Commission, the Railroads, and the Public Interest." *Yale Law Journal* 61, no. 4 (April 1952): 467–509.

Huthmacher, J. Joseph. "Urban Liberalism and the Age of Reform." *Mississippi Valley Historical Review* 49, no. 2 (1962): 234.

Ifkovic, John W. Review of *The Whiskey Rebellion Past and Present,* ed. Steven R. Boyd. *Journal of the Early Republic* 6, no. 2 (Summer 1986): 178–79.

"In the Steerage of a Cunard Steamer." *Pall Mall Budget: Being a Weekly Collection of Articles Printed in the Pall Mall Gazette from Day to Day with a Summary of News.* London. Vol. 22 (August 16, 1879): 9–12. GG Archives, www.gjenvick.com (accessed March 21, 2022).

"Inner Harbor Navigation Canal and the Lower Ninth Ward." Midlo Center for New Orleans Studies in the History Department of the University of New Orleans and the Communication Department of Tulane University. neworleanshistorical.org/items/show/289.

Jackson, Joy J. "Keeping Law and Order in New Orleans Under General Butler, 1862." *Louisiana History* 34, no. 1 (Winter 1993): 51.

——. "Prohibition in New Orleans: The Unlikeliest Crusade." *Louisiana History* 19, no. 3 (1978): 261–84.

Jeansonne, Glen. "Huey Long and the Historians." *History Teacher* 27, no. 2 (1994): 124–25.

Katz, Friedrich. "Pancho Villa and the Attack on Columbus, New Mexico." *American Historical Review* 83, no. 1 (1978): 101–30. doi.org/10.2307/1865904.

Keire, Mara L. "The Vice Trust: A Reinterpretation of the White Slavery Scare in the United States, 1907–1917." *Journal of Social History* 35, no. 1 (Autumn 2001): 5–41.

Kemp, Kathryn W. "Jean and Kate Gordon: New Orleans Social Reformers, 1898–1933." *Louisiana History* 24, no. 4 (Autumn 1983): 389–401.

Kirkland, Edward C. Review of *The Age of Reform: From Bryan to F.D.R* by Richard Hofstadter. *American Historical Review* 61, no. 3 (April 1956): 666–68.

Kurtz, Michael L. "Organized Crime in Louisiana History: Myth and Reality." *Louisiana History* 24, no. 4 (1983): 355–76.

Lamme, Margot Opdycke. "The Brewers and Public Relations History, 1909–1919." *Journal of Public Relations Research* 21, no. 4 (October 2009): 455.

Lang, James O., P. S. Luttrell, and George A. Stokes. "Vignettes." *Louisiana History* 1, no. 3 (1960): 260–62.

Lewis, Michael. "Cultural Norms and Political Mobilization: Accounting for Local and State-Level Liquor Laws, 1907–1919." *Journal of Cultural Geography* 24, no. 2 (Spring–Summer 2007): 31–52.

Matthews, Matt M. "The U.S. Army on the Mexican Border: A Historical Perspective." *Long War Series Occasional Paper* 22 (2007).

McDonald, Terrence J. "The Politics of Urban History versus the History of Urban Politics." *History Teacher* 21, no. 3 (1988): 299.

Nichols, David K. "The Promise of Progressivism: Herbert Croly and the Progressive Rejection of Individual Rights." *Publius* 17, no. 2 (Spring 1987): 27–39.

Niebuhr, Reinhold. "A Protest Against a Dilemma's Two Horns." *World Politics* 2, no. 3 (April 1950): 338–44.

"The Night President Teddy Roosevelt Invited Booker T. Washington to Dinner." *Journal of Blacks in Higher Education* 35 (Spring 2002): 24–25.

Nolan, Charles E. "In Search of Southern Parish History: A View from St. Mary's of Natchez." *U.S. Catholic Historian* 14, no. 3 (Summer 1996): 11–21.

——. "New Orleans Civic Culture Imbued with Catholicism." *Clarion Herald,* January 25, 2018.

"Orphanages: An Historical Overview; The Role of Orphanages in Child Welfare Policy." Family and Children's Services Division, Minnesota Department of Human Services, March 1995.

Pegram, Thomas. "Temperance Politics and Regional Political Culture: The Anti-Saloon League in Maryland and the South, 1907–1915." *Journal of Southern History* 63 (February 1997), 57–90.

Pfeifer, Michael J. "Lynching and Criminal Justice in South Louisiana, 1878–1930." *Louisiana History* 40, no. 2 (1999): 155–77.

Pleck, Elizabeth. "Feminist Responses to "Crimes against Women, 1868–1896." *Signs* 8, no. 3 (Spring 1983): 451–70.

Pope, Steven W. "An Army of Athletes: Playing Fields, Battlefields, and the American Military Sporting Experience, 1880–1920." *Journal of Military History* 59, no. 3 (July 1995): 435–56.

Reed, Walter. "Recent Research Concerning the Etiology, Propagation, and Prevention of Yellow Fever by the United States Army Commission." *Journal of Hygiene* 2, no. 2 (April 1902): 161–85.

Rodgers, Daniel T. "In Search of Progressivism." *Reviews in American History* 10, no. 4 (December 1982): 113–32.

Rozeboom, L. E. Review of *The Yellow Fever Mosquito: It's Life History, Bionomics and Structure* by Rickard Christophers. *Quarterly Review of Biology* 35, no. 3 (September 1960): 237.

Sanchez, Tonya Marie. "The Feminine Side of Bootlegging." *Louisiana History* 41, no. 4 (Autumn 2000): 403–33.

Scheiner, Seth M. "President Theodore Roosevelt and the Negro, 1901–1908." *Journal of Negro History* 47, no. 3 (July 1962): 169–82.

Schott, Matthew J. "The New Orleans Machine and Progressivism." *Louisiana History* 24, no. 2 (Spring 1983): 141–53.

Sengendo, James, and Janet Nambi. "The Psychological Effect of Orphanhood: A Study of Orphans in Rakai District." *Health Transition Review*, supplement to vol. 7 (1997): 105.

Shumsky, Neil Larry. "Tacit Acceptance: Respectable Americans and Segregated Prostitution, 1870–1910." *Journal of Social History* 19, no. 4 (Summer 1986): 665–79.

Stack, Martin. "Local and Regional Breweries in America's Brewing Industry." *Business History Review* 74, no. 3 (Autumn 2000): 435–63.

Stanonis, Anthony. "'A Woman of Boundless Energy': Elizabeth Werlein and Her Times." *Louisiana History* 46, no. 1 (Winter 2005): 5–26.

Stoughton, W. Seth. "Principled Policing: Warrior Cops and Guardian Officers." 51 *Wake Forest L. Rev.* 611 (2016): 611.

Stoughton, W. Seth, Kyle McLean, Justin Nix, and Geoffrey Alpert. "Policing Suspicion: Qualified Immunity and 'Clearly Established' Standards of Proof." *Journal of Criminal Law and Criminology* 112, no. 1 (2022): 36–78.

Surdam, David G. "Union Military Superiority and New Orleans Economic Value to the Confederacy." *Louisiana History* 38 no. 4 (Autumn, 1997): 389–408.

Szymanski, Ann-Marie. "Beyond Parochialism: Southern Progressivism, Prohibition, and State-Building." *Journal of Southern History* 69, no. 1 (February 2003): 107–36.

Thomann, G. "Is Beer Drinking Injurious?" *Science* 9, no. 206 (January 1887): 24–25.

Thomas, Samuel J. "Mugwump Cartoonists, the Papacy, and Tammany Hall in America's Gilded Age." *Religion and American Culture* 14, no. 2 (Summer 2004): 213–50.

Williams, Robert W., Jr. "Martin Behrman and New Orleans Civic Development." *Louisiana History* 2, no. 4 (1961): 373–400.

Williams, T. Harry. "The Gentleman from Louisiana: Demagogue or Democrat." *Journal of Southern History* 26, no. 1 (1960): 3–4. doi.org/10.2307/2954345.

Woytinsky, W. S. "Postwar Economic Perspectives: Experience after World War I." *Social Security Bulletin* 8, no. 12 (December 1945): 20–21.

Zink, Harold. Review of *Machine Politics in New Orleans, 1897–1926* by George M. Reynolds. *American Sociological Review* 2, no. 4 (August 1937): 581.

Zinsser, William H. "Working with Men outside the Camps." *Annals of the American Academy of Political and Social Science* 79 (September 1918): 194–203.

Theses, Dissertations, and Reports

City of New Orleans HDLC. "Irish Channel Historic District." Prepared by Dominique M. Hawkins of Preservation Design Partnership, LLC, in Philadelphia, and Catherine E. Barrier. May 2011.

Earl, George G., General Superintendent to Sewerage and Water Board of New Orleans. "The Hurricane of Sept. 29th, 1915, and Subsequent Heavy Rainfalls." October 14, 1915.

Fitzmorris, Terrence, "Pro Bono Publico: New Orleans Politics and Municipal Reform in the Progressive Era, 1912–1926." 2 vols. *LSU Historical Dissertations and Theses,* 1989.

Message from the President of the United States. "List of States Approving the Eighteenth Amendment." U.S. Congressional serial set, issue 7670, Senate Documents, vol. 14, Sixty-Sixth Congress, Second Session, document no. 169.

Statutes of the United States of America. First Session of the Sixty-Fifth Congress, 1917. Washington, DC, Government Printing Office.

United States Census 1870. www.familysearch.org, household ID 460, line no. 15, affiliate name: The U.S. National Archives and Records Administration (NARA), affiliate publication no. M593, GS film no. 000552020, digital folder no. 004269437, image no. 00619.

U.S. Department of the Interior, National Park Service, National Historic Landmarks Program. "The Era of Reconstruction: 1861–1900." www.nps.gov/subjects/nationalhistoriclandmarks/upload/Reconstruction.pdf (accessed February 12, 2023).

U.S. Department of the Interior, National Park Service, National Register of Historic Places Registration Form. NRIS Reference 13000695, US Naval Station Algiers Historic District, September 11, 2013. www.nps.gov/nr/feature/places/pdfs/13000695.pdf.

Williams, Robert Webb. "Martin Behrman: Mayor and Political Boss of New Orleans, 1904–1926." MA thesis, Tulane University, 1952.

Websites, Blogs, and Electronic Communications

Algiers Historical Society. "Algiers History." www.algiershistoricalsociety.org/algiers-history.html (accessed February 13, 2023).

Carnegie, Andrew. "The Gospel of Wealth." www.carnegie.org/fileadmin/Media/Publications/PDF/THE_GOSPEL_OF_WEALTH_01.pdf.

"Dixie Brewing Company." Tulane University Media NOLA Project. medianola.org/discover/place/115/Dixie-Brewing-Company (accessed March 8, 2015).

Dunn, Katherine Jolliff. "The Pumps That Built (and Sank) the City of New Orleans." Historic New Orleans Collection, August 3, 2020. www.hnoc.org/publications/first-draft/pumps-built-and-sank-city-new-orleans.

Federal Bureau of Investigation. "William J. Burns, August 22, 1921–June 14, 1924." www.fbi.gov/history/directors/william-j-burns (accessed February 19, 2023).

Fitzmorris, Terrence. Miscellaneous email communications, May 11, 2022–October 31, 2022.

"Hidden from History: Unknown New Orleanians." New Orleans Public Library. nutrias.org/exhibits/hidden/hidden_contents.htm (accessed July 11, 2012).

Hollandsworth, James G., Jr. "Union Soldiers on Ship Island During the Civil War." Mississippi Historical Society. mshistorynow.mdah.state.ms.us.

"Kate and Jean Gordon." *Encyclopedia of Louisiana.* www.knowla.org/entry.php?rec=811 (accessed July 11, 2012).

Kinley, Michael. "Cruise of the Great White Fleet." Naval History Heritage Command. www.history.navy.mil/research/library/online-reading-room/title-list-alphabetically/c/cruise-great-white-fleet-mckinley.html (accessed May 18, 2015).

Knox, Dudley. "American Naval Participation in World War I." Naval History and Heritage Command. www.history.navy.mil/research/library/online-reading-room/title-list-alphabetically/a/american-naval-participation-in-the-great-war-with-special-reference-to-the-european-theater-of-operations.html.

Lawton Ancestry website. www.lawtonancestry.com/lawton-behrman-collins/.

McKinley, Mike. "Cruise of the Great White Fleet." *Naval History and Heritage Command,* April 1, 2015. www.history.navy.mil/research/library/online-reading-room/title-list-alphabetically/c/cruise-great-white-fleet-mckinley.html.

National Governors Association. "Past Governors." www.nga.org/cms/home/governors/past-governors-bios/page_louisiana/c012-content/main-content-list/title_parker_john.html (accessed July 21, 2015).

Pelican Publishing Co. "1790s: Inside Old Treme." pelicanpub.com/content/ 9781589805644_R-01.pdf.

Starkweather, Sarah. "U.S. Immigration Online." A project of the University of Washington–Bothell. library.uwb.edu/static/USimmigration/1917_immigration_act. html.

Street Law and the Supreme Court Historical Society. www.streetlaw.org/en/landmark/cases/plessy_v_ferguson (accessed April 6, 2015).

Trow's New York City Directory. Vol. 76. New York: John F. Trow, 1863. archive.org/ details/trowsnewyorkcity1863trow/page/n1/mode/2up.

Waits, Sarah, Archivist, Archdiocese of New Orleans. Various email communications.

Warren, Robert Penn. *All the King's Men.* Screenplay. East Carolina University Digital Collection. digital.lib.ecu.edu/215.

Wilson, Woodrow. Executive Orders. The American Presidency Project of the University of California. www.presidency.ucsb.edu/index.php.

——. "War Message to the United States Congress." April 2, 1917. wwi.lib.byu.edu/ index.php/Wilson%27s_War_Message_to_Congress.

INDEX

Printed in the USA
CPSIA information can be obtained
at www.ICGtesting.com
LVHW091051071023
760462LV00027B/202/J